"Dr. Jaffe cuts through the mythology that engulfs addiction and presents us with scientifically backed ideas to help resolve this growing problem. This book is an absolute must-read for anyone who is struggling or trying to help someone and wants real solutions that are not based on hand-me-down wisdom."

—Andy Ramage, author of *The 28 Day Alcohol-Free Challenge*

"Jaffe combines great storytelling, including the powerful story of his own journey, with a deep appreciation of the scientific literature on addiction and change. We can feel his pain, his courage, his discoveries, his self-acceptance, and his growth. Then he goes beyond the personal, to articulate an approach to change fully in accord with both common sense and science. His approach will be welcomed by anyone looking for something to replace the dominant one-size-fits-all US approach."

—A. Tom Horvath, PhD, ABPP, president, Practical Recovery Psychology Group, La Jolla, CA; author of *Sex, Drugs, Gambling & Chocolate: A Workbook for Overcoming Addictions*

"No one has confronted America's abstinence myth like Adi Jaffe. He has done so in his own life, leaving a meth addiction behind in favor of a fully lived family life and career. He has done it in his practice, escorting people personally from excess to moderation. And he has done so politically, confronting America's abstinence fixation forthrightly and righteously. This book is his testament to all of those journeys."

—Stanton Peele, author of *Love and Addiction, The Meaning of Addiction*, and more

# UNHOOKED

ALSO BY ADI JAFFE, PHD:

*The Abstinence Myth: A New Approach for Overcoming
Addiction Without Shame, Judgment, or Rules*

# UN
# HOOKED

FREE YOURSELF
FROM ADDICTION
FOREVER

# Adi Jaffe, PhD

balance

NEW YORK BOSTON

Balance
Hachette Book Group
1290 Avenue of the Americas
New York, NY 10104
GCP-Balance.com
@GCPBalance

First Edition: January 2025

Balance is an imprint of Grand Central Publishing. The Balance name and logo are registered trademarks of Hachette Book Group, Inc.

The publisher is not responsible for websites (or their content) that are not owned by the publisher.

The Hachette Speakers Bureau provides a wide range of authors for speaking events. To find out more, go to hachettespeakersbureau.com or email HachetteSpeakers@hbgusa.com.

Balance books may be purchased in bulk for business, educational, or promotional use. For information, please contact your local bookseller or Hachette Book Group Special Markets Department at special.markets@hbgusa.com.

Print book interior design by Sheryl Kober.

Library of Congress Control Number: 2024945769

ISBNs: 978-0-306-83346-5 (hardcover), 978-0-306-83348-9 (ebook)

Printed in the United States of America

LSC-C

Printing 2, 2025

*This book is dedicated to all the incredible people I've had the honor of working with and all the ones I haven't yet met. You are the ones who make the work worth it. Your stories inspire, motivate, and propel me forward. I hope you find what you need in these pages.*

# CONTENTS

# AUTHOR'S NOTE

I've worked with thousands of people over the past fifteen years; their challenges and victories continue to motivate and inform my work. I share stories throughout *Unhooked*; some of these are composites, most have names and identifying details altered for privacy.

The ultimate decisions regarding medical care should always be made with your doctor. I want to underscore that this is of particular importance. One additional important note: If you have been struggling with heavy alcohol use, or taking high doses of anxiolytics, such as benzodiazepines, for years, suddenly stopping can be harmful and even result in death. If you use these substances heavily and on a daily or near-daily basis, you must consult with a physician before stopping.

# INTRODUCTION

There was a noise.

Usually, there wasn't much that could overcome the deadening effect of the drugs on my sleep. But on this particular morning, a constant buzzing was breaking through. I wasn't fully awake, but the noise had pulled me back to consciousness. I didn't want to be awake.

Then, there was pain.

Since the accident, it sometimes seemed as if physical pain was the primary motivating factor in my life. It got me drugs, after all. This latest cycle had started with the Vicodin prescribed by my doctor. A thousand whole milligrams every four hours. That left me feeling deeply groggy and numb. Life took on a hazy, foggy sort of quality. I wanted something to counter that sensation. I didn't like being so out of it. Plus, the Vicodin didn't really mask the slow, intense throbbing of my broken, useless leg.

Now, there was light too.

It was pouring through the blinds, directly onto my still-closed eyes. My large bedroom window, which took up more than half of the wall next to my bed, faced east. Not great for someone who wants to sleep in and avoid reality. The noise was still there, growing ever louder, maybe closer? Without even opening my eyes, I knew that something was wrong. Even in this hazy dream state, I knew I should recognize this noise. I couldn't place it, but I'd definitely heard it before. I tried to open my eyes but the light flooded my vision and, for a moment, I couldn't make anything out. The only thing I could see were shadows, hazy shapes floating around me. I needed to focus, but even such a simple task proved much more difficult than I'd expected. The sound was starting to clarify and come into focus. I suddenly realized that the "noise" was actually a series of loud voices. There were people. They seemed to be repeating a phrase, over and over.

They were screaming at *me*.

Now, I knew that something was seriously wrong. I felt my heart beating furiously in my chest, and I struggled to sit upright. I had to get up. The words were coming together now, and I felt a wave of panic wash over me. I finally knew what they were saying.

They were screaming my name.

Suddenly, I heard the sound of glass shatter and I could make out people running into the room, swarming around me. This was no dream. It wasn't even a nightmare. I was awake.

As I sat up in my bed, all I could focus on was the loaded shotgun pointed directly at my face.

### A REALITY CHECK: WE'RE ALL HOOKED ON SOMETHING.

It's true.

Even when we don't want to admit it.

Despite its prevalence and wide repercussions, we tend to think of addiction as something that happens to other people. In reality, we're *all* either addicted to something or close to someone who is. Nicotine, caffeine, alcohol, food, video games, work, heroin, social media, porn, television, cocaine, gambling, cannabis, pain pills, shopping, or methamphetamine—you can likely find yourself, and many people you know, somewhere on the list.

Today, after decades of effort and admonition, addiction is still destroying the fabric of society. Over 100 million people in the United States struggle with substance problems—28 million struggle with alcohol, 57 million with nicotine, and 24 million with drugs, including prescription pills.[1] Add to those the growing number (21 million and climbing) estimated to compulsively use technology, porn, and online gaming[2] and the 40 million or so showing signs of food addiction,[3] and it's clear—we're more hooked as a nation than ever before. With as many as 165 million Americans struggling with an addiction to something and approximately 200,000 dying every year from drug- and alcohol-related deaths,[4] the damage is devastating. Over 40 percent of Americans are related to a person who's overdosed on opiates,[5] and 50 percent of those considered obese in the US struggle with food addiction that leads to heart attacks, strokes, and lives made shorter by decades.[6] Finally, as many as 85 percent of those incarcerated either struggle with addiction or are serving time for drug-related offenses.[7] Broken marriages, destroyed businesses, shattered homes, and a massive impact on our health and criminal justice system make up the reality we've grown used to. And it all costs the US economy between $800 billion[8] and $2 trillion to deal with every year.[9]

So, while many people think the addiction problem looks like this:

EVERYONE IN THE WORLD

PEOPLE WHO STRUGGLE WITH ADDICTION

THE REST OF THE WORLD, NORMAL & DISCONNECTED FROM ADDICTIONS

It actually looks much more like this:

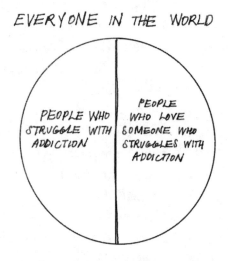

The idea that the world is separated into addicts and "normal people" is not only false, but causes shame, isolation, and hopelessness. Labeling people as addicts, telling them they suffer from an intractable disease, and declaring them powerless in the face of their condition has not worked. Indeed, the only way we even get away with this is by ignoring the actual prevalence of addiction struggles. How can people be "abnormal" if they belong to a group that makes up 50 percent of our society? It turns out that the all-or-nothing methods we employ for addiction are the *reason* behind the obscenely high failure rates we've come to expect.[10]

Scores of organizations and thousands of experts have tried fixing the addiction issue for decades. From complex brain research to severe criminal penalties and prohibition efforts, we've spared no expenses. And yet, we've hardly made a dent in the problem. More and more people are dying every year, societal costs are higher than ever, and rates of addiction have not budged.

What are we missing?

The problem is in our fundamentally flawed approach to defining and understanding addiction. Our mistaken assumptions about what addiction *is* keep preventing us from addressing it and transforming its impact. We're focused on the wrong pieces of the puzzle, so no one has managed to get a clear picture.

And I used to be in that camp myself.

Over the past thirty years, I've learned a lot through my personal experiences, my classroom education, and my research and teaching. That knowledge has guided the work I've done helping thousands of suffering clients. In the process, I have developed an incredibly intimate understanding of this problem. That moment in my bedroom, waking up to a SWAT team on a Saturday morning, was not the end of the road for my addiction. It was the consequence of years of destructive, compulsive-addictive behavior. But it was also a critical part of my journey to understanding the process of recovering from addiction. There were many other crucial junctures along the way, some of which you'll hear about in this book. I am going to break down for you what I learned, step by step, so that anyone who wants to get unhooked can do so. I am passionate about this work for many different reasons, but the first is certainly my own unexceptional, and yet startling story. It started well before I had that shotgun pointed at my head.

## PHASE 1: THE DOWNWARD SPIRAL

I was fourteen years old when my family moved to the United States. In many ways, the move was an adventure. I mean, who wouldn't want to "go to America" for a few years? I craved seeing those streets paved with gold, full of movie stars, and free of the conflict and war that regularly ravaged my country. It sounded great!

Unfortunately, my parents chose to move us to Skokie, Illinois. The town was made "famous" by a late '70s neo-Nazi march and a single line about a barbershop quartet in the movie *The Usual Suspects*. We didn't have gold streets and there were no movie stars to gawk at. It was colder in the winter than anything I'd ever experienced and we lived right off Elm Street, which I was pretty sure meant Freddy Krueger was

going to murder me in my sleep. (I hadn't yet realized that *every* neighborhood in the US had its own Elm Street.)

What I also hadn't realized was the impact that leaving the intimacy of my neighborhood—and the comfort of the only home I'd
ever known—would have on me. All my friends, all that was familiar
to me, disappeared in a moment. My language, the air I was used to
breathing…it was all gone. I wasn't prepared for that. And I was walking, shaky and angst-ridden, into the first year of high school.

For a kid like me, trying to fit in became incredibly important.
Still, no matter what I did, I felt as if I was on the outside looking in.
I joined sports teams, and that helped a bit. I got to know some of the
other students through football, then soccer, then tennis and swim-
ming. I was good enough to fit in there, but it didn't seem to translate
to our times outside practice. I tried to make friends with the other
Israeli kids, but I always felt that they were in on some joke that I didn't
get. While this feeling of angst had definitely started with my friends
back home, I became engulfed by anxiety and fear in Chicago.

Until that fateful trip to an Israeli sleepaway camp.

I'll never forget it. An Israeli youth group I was part of organized
the trip. As we boarded the plane for New Jersey, I was filled with
excitement and possibility. I practically wriggled in the fake leather
seats throughout the entire six-hour flight. When we finally got there,
our group met up with at least a hundred other kids—from San Fran-
cisco, New York, New Jersey, Los Angeles, and Miami. It was like an
Israeli transplant conference located in a cold and snowy New Jersey
log cabin camp. I was freezing, but I also felt more at home than I had
in months. Leaving the awkwardness of my Skokie high school behind
was an incredible relief. We spent our first day getting to know one
another, playing games, making fools of ourselves, and having fun as
kids should. When the first night came, my life changed.

About thirty or forty of us ended up in one of the bigger cabins.
We weren't supposed to all join together—boys and girls were to be
separate—but try to tell that to a bunch of high school kids. At some

point in the night, while I was deep in conversation with some new friends, a boy tapped me on the shoulder and handed me a *massive* plastic bottle. It was a jug of vodka.

I'd seen vodka before, but I'd never really tried it. My mom would drink some occasionally in her screwdrivers, but my dad didn't drink at all. I'd had a few sips of wine at some Jewish holiday events, but nothing more. Still, packed into this room of boys and girls I liked hanging out with, it was clear what they expected me to do.

"Yalla, take a drink and pass it on," the boy told me.

I froze for a split second, trying to figure out my next move.

A moment later, I grabbed the jug from his hand.

There was exactly a 0 percent chance that, on this night, finally feeling good and comfortable among these kids, I would say no to that drink.

I wasn't about to feel like an outsider again. So, I took a big mouthful and swallowed. Then, I took another.

I can still remember the burn of that vodka on the way down. It tasted horrible and almost made me throw up. But I knew I had to hold it in. So, I steadied myself, put a smile on, raised the jug, and passed it on to someone else. I had passed the test.

Approximately fifteen minutes after that moment, the best feeling I had never known existed took over my body. It was like a warm blanket on a cold night. All my anxiety, my fears of not fitting in, and my constant worry about what others thought of me simply vanished.

I felt GOOD!

For the rest of that night, I talked, danced, and sang with my new friends. By the end of the night, I had even fooled around with one of the girls, which, for a fourteen-year-old boy, felt momentous. By any way I could measure it, that night was one of the best nights of my life. And we still had another night there.

By the time we took the bus back to the Newark airport for the flight home, I was plugged in. I had friends; I was dancing in the aisles (sober) and singing at the top of my lungs. I had arrived. Who knew a few sips of a clear liquid from a jug could make that happen? It was clear to me that I had found the answer to all my problems...

Needless to say, alcohol (and then drugs) became a very regular part of my life. I started getting invited to weekend parties with all those kids I hadn't quite belonged with before. I liked being included, and drinking was a secret pass.

Over the next eleven years, I used alcohol, cannabis, MDMA, cocaine, ketamine, meth, and every other drug imaginable, in what I now refer to as the "embedded lived experience" phase of my life. I traded my cushy upper-middle-class upbringing for a seven-year tour through the gutters of LA. I embraced the role of the classic "drug addict" (a term we'll tear down and do away with in this book), using anything at any time to lose myself. I seemed to care for no one and nothing, myself included. And I suffered the consequences, including four arrests, capped off by that full *NCIS*-style Beverly Hills PD SWAT team arrest you read about earlier. By the time four officers picked me up and carried me off to LA County Jail—leg shattered from a motorcycle accident, gun at my side, broken meth pipe on the table, and a suitcase full of money and drugs in my closet—I had left a trail of wreckage too long and devastating to overcome by almost anyone's reckoning.

I weighed 124 pounds, had alienated everyone important in my life, and was heading straight into the abyss. It was time to end my "lived experience" phase.

## PHASE 2: CLAWING MY WAY BACK

Unfortunately, addiction wasn't quite done with me. I began using again and was caught with drugs in rehab after three months. They promptly kicked me out. As he escorted me out, my counselor told me that I could come back in if I could maintain thirty days of sobriety. He said it with a straight face too. If I knew how to do that, I wouldn't have much use for that rehab, I thought to myself. I had been using and selling drugs for so long that I had forgotten how to live a "normal" life or play by the rules. Maybe I'd never known how to do it all in the first place. Fortunately, by the time I checked into my second rehab, the pieces started coming together. Facing fifteen years in prison, I managed to stay sober and complete the program.

The time of my sentencing, about a year later, was an incredibly tense moment for my family. Even with my newly discovered sobriety and clean-cut image, we had no idea how things would go. I had to plead guilty to nine separate felonies. The judge could have sentenced me to over twenty years in prison and no one (except my father in the courtroom) would have batted an eyelash. My life hung in the balance, and I wouldn't have thought it unjust if it went the wrong way. As it turned out, things worked out well for me. I received a single year in jail with a seven-year suspended sentence. This meant that after jail, if I screwed up again, I'd spend a very long time behind bars.

Like the sword of Damocles, that suspended sentence hung over my head, an ever-present reminder that my freedom could be taken away in an instant.

I got the message.

Still, I knew *nothing* of how to live a normal life. I hadn't done it since the age of fourteen. I knew normal people had jobs, so I started there. I spent a year unsuccessfully searching for work. I couldn't get a job at the local grocery, the mall, or even at the pizza shop as a delivery boy. I got within hours of securing a job at the Genius Bar of the first Apple Store in Santa Monica, but once they reached the background check stage, I received the same response I'd been getting everywhere—complete radio silence. It turns out no one wants to hire a nine-time convicted felon. Unsure what to do, I decided to go down the only path that seemed available to me—school. I barely completed my bachelor's degree at UCLA and graduated on a technicality. But I was out of options. So, I decided graduate school was the answer. My father, who had wanted nothing more than for me to follow in his footsteps as a doctor, had no faith in my abilities. We wondered out loud whether I'd even be allowed to practice medicine if I made it through school. After all, I couldn't even get a job delivering pizza, and it was unlikely that a medical board would let me practice. So, we decided on a graduate degree in psychology.

Although it was a purely rational decision born of necessity, it proved to be a wise choice. The third phase of my transformation began.

## PHASE 3: REDEMPTION

My path through school looked very different this time. After everything I'd been through, I was more committed and driven than ever before. I became the student who organized the study groups instead of ignoring them. I stayed after every class to talk to the professors and made it to all the office hours instead of never showing up to class. I started working on papers weeks in advance, instead of forgetting all about them until after they were due. And there were a lot of papers. Somehow, the lazy, rebellious, smart but incompetent version of me was replaced by that annoying "apple for the teacher" student I'd made fun of my whole life. It was my first true indication that *real* change is possible when the right conditions align. This new version of me became a star student, 4.0 GPA and all. It also got me through two master's degrees and a PhD from UCLA, the top psychology graduate program in the country. It was wild.

I was more motivated than ever before and had greater follow-through than anyone could have predicted. No one—not my parents, not my sister, not my professors from a past life or my friends—would have believed I'd find this version of myself hidden under all the pain and waste that my life had become. My drive was focused on two issues:

1. Making sure I stayed the hell out of prison, and
2. Figuring out how I'd become a meth user and dealer after such a promising and privileged start.

Still, even with this determination and direction, I rose slowly. The pit I had dug for myself was deep, and it was going to take time to get out. Along the way, a deep desire to help others who were going down similar dead-end roads called out to me. I knew, for the first time ever, that I had a true purpose. Over the years, I've put every ounce of motivation I had into this purpose. It started with studying late and learning how to write and communicate the research I was seeing on my All About Addiction blog. It continued with experimenting on myself and then testing theory after theory with those who eventually came to seek help in my treatment center, online programs, and lectures.

For many of us who realize we're "hooked," there is an origin story like mine. But that was merely the beginning of my journey. Here's the thing: most people who read, or tell, stories like this one believe, mistakenly, that we've gotten "hooked" on alcohol, pills, porn, gambling, work, video games, or food. That's even how we identify the problem in the first place—"alcoholism," "porn addiction," and so on. It's a clear indication that we believe the substance, or behavior, is the problem. But these things are not what hooked me at all, or what hooked any of the people I have worked with. Everyone who tried to help me twenty years ago wanted to convince me that there was something inherently wrong with me. They told me that I had some mysterious disease causing these disastrous results. But they were all wrong as well. In reality, that sip of alcohol was the first medicine I took to relieve the pain inflicted by invisible emotional "hooks" embedded in me. Those hooks were my real issue, not the self-medication using alcohol and drugs. Unfortunately, when you focus on the wrong part of a problem, the solutions you come up with are unlikely to help in any real way. The tools you use and the methods you employ are aimed at the wrong target, resulting in either more damage or simply no change. And that's why the mainstream treatment of addictive habits and compulsions has been so unsuccessful. Because it doesn't address the core issue . . . it doesn't unhook the hooks.

As Seymour Chwast once said, "If you're digging a hole in the wrong place, making it deeper doesn't help anything."

I've had the good fortune of studying addiction for the past thirty-two years, starting as an active participant. This book is the result of those thirty years of research: from addiction to academia, and now, to helping others find their own way out. Here, we'll journey from the minuscule (neurochemistry) to the monumental (societal and existential factors) to map the real reasons we get addicted in the first place. Then, we'll use that foundation to address addiction in a new way that finally works.

This book will introduce you to the Unhooked Method, a simple system to identify the hooks that are keeping you anchored while helping you find a way out of the negative habits you've picked up along the way to protect yourself. The method relies on a new behavioral model I've developed over ten years of working with clients. It consists of two main components:

1. The SPARO stages of behavior (Stimulus–Perception–Activation–Response–Outcome)
2. The EAT transformation cycle (Explore–Accept–Transform)

Together, these two elements will allow you to break down *any* behavior you're struggling with, understand its origin and purpose, and alter it forever.

In this book, I share a number of stories and experiences drawn from my professional work with clients, focusing particularly on the interactions and transformations I've witnessed among the individuals I've had the privilege to help. To honor the trust they placed in me and to adhere to the ethical standards of confidentiality, I have made careful adjustments to the identifying details within these narratives.

Please note that while the names, locations, and other specific identifiers have been altered to protect the privacy of the individuals involved, the essence and integrity of their stories remain unchanged.

These accounts are true reflections of real clients: their challenges, triumphs, and the profound insights they have provided.

The core of each story is deeply rooted in actual events and experiences. These alterations do not detract from the truthfulness of the overarching narrative; rather, they serve to safeguard the anonymity and dignity of the people whose lives have informed these pages.

My intention in sharing these stories is to offer readers a genuine glimpse into the transformative power of the work we do. It is my hope that the insights and learnings drawn from these true reflections will resonate with you, offering guidance, inspiration, or a deeper understanding of the human experience.

Thank you for joining me on this journey.

PART 1

# DISCOVERING YOUR HOOKS

# CHAPTER 1

# We Change When It Hurts

Aliyah sat on the cold bathroom floor. The tile felt comforting beneath her, solid. She'd felt lost for such a long time, disconnected from her life, as if looking at someone else playing out a script. The meth had that effect on her, allowing her enough distance inside, so that she didn't have to feel much. But every once in a while, in quiet moments like this one, she remembered. All alone in the thin light of morning, the hard tile pressing against her skin, she thought of Bailey. Her little baby, now her teenage daughter. But Aliyah didn't know what Bailey was up to anymore, not since that night with the police. The night she lost her girl forever.

It was a night of broken dishes, holes punched in the walls, screaming voices, and neighbors knocking on doors. She knew why Bailey had called the cops. She had been through this craziness with her mother so many times before. Now, she was finally old enough to do something about it. So, she did. She picked up the phone and made the call.

When the cop cars showed up outside, sirens blaring, Aliyah barricaded herself with the girls inside the apartment. The cops called her name on their megaphones and told her they were surrounding the building. She looked at her girls' faces. They were terrified. Aliyah had always wanted to protect those little girls and keep them safe. That's why she went to rehab all those times, trying to beat this meth addiction. That's why she kept going to the meetings even when they didn't help. She was searching for a way out, anything that might work.

But she never found one, and now Bailey was gone forever. She was living with another family, and her sisters were probably close behind. Soon, Aliyah would be completely alone in the world, facing the failures of her life. After the horror of her childhood, to know she was visiting the same pain on her own little girls was unbearable. *Hurt people hurt people.* She'd heard that in some meeting once, and it was true. But things didn't have to go on like this.

That's what the gun was for.

Sitting there, on the cold tile of the bathroom floor, Aliyah knew what to do. She would put the gun in her mouth, close her eyes, squeeze the trigger, and everything would be gone. All the pain would disappear. Her girls and her sister would be free of her. They could go on with their lives. Yes, they would be shocked and, yes, they might be sad for a little while, but then it would all be over. *She* would be over and they could move on.

So, in the morning light, with the sun rising above the trees, she put the gun in her mouth. Tears formed in her eyes as she thought of her girls. She tasted the metal, and it was strangely comforting to know everything would soon be done. This was the one good thing she could do for everyone else.

She closed her eyes, the tears now flowing down her cheeks, salty in her mouth. She felt a deep pressure in her chest. She could barely breathe. She let out a little gasp and squeezed the trigger.

Nothing happened.

The gun was jammed.

Fuck.

*This can't be happening*, she thought. She got dressed in a hurry, ran downstairs, and grabbed the keys to her sister's truck. She started the truck and took a hard left out of the driveway toward the freeway. She kept her seatbelt off, headed for the on-ramp, and started going as fast as she could. All she needed was a bridge to drive off, or a wall to hit head-on. At that moment, her mind blank with panic, she heard a man's voice reaching out from the radio. It seemed he was talking directly to her.

As if in a dream, Aliyah slowed the car and pulled over to the side of the freeway. She couldn't focus on anything but the voice. When the man finished speaking, she picked up the phone and called her sister. "Lynne," Aliyah said, "I think I found something that may work."

## THE PAINFUL "REALITIES" OF ADDICTION

Addiction is a scourge that never seems to go away. No matter how many trillions of dollars we throw at it, what corner of the planet we visit, or what season or century, addiction is always there. When we expand our definition to include technology, sex, food, exercise, work, and other compulsive behaviors, no one is safe. Every family, every organization, and every community is dealing with addiction in one way or another.[1]

Addiction is everywhere.

For as long as we've been trying to stop it, and no matter how we measure its impact, addiction's devastation has only grown in magnitude.[2] By any metric, we have failed miserably at addressing this issue.

Something must change. We need a new model for understanding addiction and its role in our lives, if we are to ever stop the pain it inflicts.

To understand what isn't working and what needs to change, we must understand the road we've traveled to get here. Aliyah's story is all too common in the addiction world. It isn't only the thoughts of suicide and childhood trauma that are familiar. Most of all, it's the hopelessness and shame.

Hopelessness and shame are common to so many who suffer with this condition. There is an ever-present sense that, no matter what, they will always be struggling, sick, and causing pain to themselves and others. Whether you're addicted to alcohol, heroin, porn, gambling, money, work, or sugar, that sense of shame is always there. And it's usually hiding.

I know it from my own life, and I've seen it in the thousands of people I've worked with over the years. The reasons are different, and the stories vary, but those feelings are always lurking in the background. Indeed, shame is integral to the condition of addiction itself. While getting my PhD at one of the top institutions in the world, I was taught that addiction is all about brain activity and genetics. I started out taking solace in the research and its conclusiveness. It felt good to know that my struggles were natural outcomes of my brain chemistry and genetic blueprint—not my mistakes. But over the years, I realized that the picture of addiction my schooling painted was far from complete. I have since learned that much of the shame and stigma common to addiction is a consequence of our perception of the condition. We create the pain of those touched by addiction, through the way we talk, think, and judge them. They, in turn, buy into the sense of hopelessness and shame we project upon them. And their borrowed beliefs make them feel powerless to change, and less likely to succeed.

It's a codependent perspective.

Ironically, even as I was learning about addiction as a brain disease, my own advisers were giving me mixed messages. They were recommending that I tell no one about my past. They believed it would change people's perception of, and trust in, me. Knowingly, or not, they were teaching a biological addiction model, while supporting a more moral view.

As in so much of life, the way we perceive things affects every single aspect of the world around us. Perspective affects what we pay attention to and what we dismiss. It impacts the details we pick up and the ones we ignore. It tells us whose opinions to respect and whose we should reject out of hand. You can see this playing out with a simple glance at our political reality. People on opposing sides of the political spectrum rely on their side's information to interpret the events of the day. This leaves them with alternate realities—and responses—as a result. Everyone believes they are "right" not because reality is black and white, but because their biased information makes it look so. Sadly, research has shown us that this effect becomes more entrenched the more sophisticated and opinionated we are. And when it comes to addiction, the perspectives we've taken on can damage the very people we're trying to help.

But our perspective hasn't always been the same. It's evolved over time. Each stage has built on the past and pushed us to rethink the way we see the problem.

I can summarize the four stages of our perspective on mental health in the following way:

In the first stage, which I'll call the Dark Ages, we believed all mental health issues were signs of possession by evil spirits or moonbeam energy (*luna*, Latin for "moon," is the basis for the term *lunacy*). Those who struggled were cast out or given religious and often cruel interventions.[3] During the second stage, we realized that the brain had something to do with mental health. So, we cut it up, zapped it with electricity, and tried to smack it back to normal, like an old rabbit-ears TV set.[4] If we could only hit it the right way, we thought, we could fix a brain forever, returning the person to "normal." In the third stage, we began incorporating talk therapy.[5] Still, many of the available resources were heavily influenced by religion and morality. The idea sprang up of addiction as a disease that caused an allergy-like reaction to alcohol and other mind-altering drugs. Even as new discoveries in psychology advanced mental health, evolving addiction care proved difficult.

## THE CURRENT SAD STATE OF AFFAIRS

As I've explained, the story we tell about addiction is wrong. We've become satisfied with very simple answers to explain a very complex condition.

One of those simple answers comes down to the release of a neurotransmitter, dopamine, in the brain. Dopamine is a chemical "reward signal" that makes us feel motivated. When the brain releases a dopamine surge, it interprets whatever is happening at that moment as rewarding. And so, we seek that dopamine brain-buzz, whether we get it from a piece of chocolate, an eagerly anticipated text, a raise at work, a goal scored, or a line of cocaine. Dopamine release has an impact on brain areas related to motivation, movement, learning, and more. We seek out those dopamine hits, often without being aware of it, by re-creating the behaviors that prompted its release.

Throughout evolution, our brain has used the release of dopamine in certain areas to tell us what's good and novel (more dopamine) and what is not good, or no longer novel (less or no dopamine). In that way, these dopamine bursts teach our brain how we should behave to get a desired

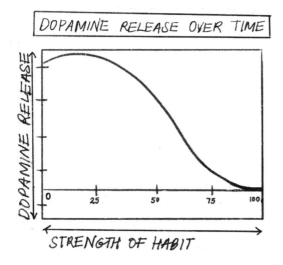

DOPAMINE RELEASE OVER TIME

DOPAMINE RELEASE

0    25    50    75    100

STRENGTH OF HABIT

result. But this only holds for actions that are new. The more this learning occurs, the less conscious effort required for generating the behavior. Once we've repeated a behavior enough for it to become habitual, dopamine release slows down or stops altogether.

Because habits don't require more dopamine to be repeated, they function on near-autopilot. Habits are all about brain efficiency. Our brain *wants* to engage in habits and rituals—automatic practices that require little effort. This is what the brain is built to do. It's economical and saves energy and resources. That said, addiction is no simple matter of cause and effect or stimulus-reward. It's the continuation of habitual behavior that no longer serves us, in the face of mounting repercussions. The question of why we repeat these habits demands a layered answer, but we've been satisfied to see the answer in this basic dopamine-learning story.

This causal, dopamine-first explanation aligns with our definition of addiction as a biological "brain disease." But there are two major problems with that simplistic disease model of addiction:

1. It leads us to seek a solution in the world of biology, where physical diseases are treated or cured. If dopamine release causes addiction, all we need to do is stop taking drugs or block dopamine and we'll break the cycle forever, right? *Wrong*—because, in truth, addiction isn't purely biological. It lives in everything that makes us who we are: the physical machine we inhabit;[6] the psychological experiences we've

been through;[7] the people, cultures, and places that surround us;[8] and the connection (or lack thereof) to something bigger than ourselves.[9] All these factors and circumstances play a role in the complex system that creates dopamine release, along with other important biological systems.[10]

2. It reinforces the false notion of "addicts" as a special, separate group of people. It ignores the fact that *most of us* experience getting addicted to something, and that dopamine drives the same reward mechanisms in us all. This false separation allows us to ignore the real causes, which permits the problem to spread, obscured.[11]

Indeed, the world is getting better at tapping into new sources of engagement and pleasure every day. In the process, we are all becoming more controlled by the quick dopamine hits released in our brain. Unless we intervene, the future is clear: an increasingly dysfunctional relationship with rewards that allows more and more people to be controlled and manipulated.[12]

It's happening all around us in technology, advertising, marketing media, and pharmaceuticals. Our reward systems are being hacked by obsessions that bring about questionable, if any, benefit. And it's only getting worse. From heroin to porn, TikTok, Candy Crush, and texting, our minds are being hijacked. The result is emptiness, desperation, and an ever-growing dissatisfaction with our lives and ourselves.

We are currently entering the fourth stage. Practitioners from different areas, including biology, psychology, spirituality, and other disciplines, are trying to bridge our knowledge into a *unified theory* of mental health and addiction. In the process, we've realized that essentially all mental health struggles, including compulsive habits, lie along a continuum of severity and are not an all-or-nothing, black-or-white, experience.

Still, today's prevailing perspective is that addiction is a chronic, progressive, biological disorder that people are born with or develop over time. The National Institute on Drug Abuse (NIDA),[13] the US government's primary body studying addictions, states that "Addiction is defined as a chronic, relapsing disorder characterized by compulsive drug seeking and use despite adverse consequences. It is considered a brain disorder, because it involves functional changes to brain circuits involved in reward, stress, and self-control. Those changes may last a long time after a person has stopped taking drugs."

The common understanding is that once you have "addiction," you can never get rid of it. That it forever changes your basic functioning in such a profound way it excludes you from being "normal"—if you ever were. "Can't turn a pickle back into a cucumber" is a popular Alcoholics Anonymous saying that tries to convey this view. We're told that "alcoholics" and "addicts" care more about alcohol or drugs than anything else. That they cannot be trusted to tell the truth, as they'll do and say anything to satisfy their cravings. Given this state, the only way to bring this chronic disease into *remission* (note: not *cure*) is to immediately stop any consumption of alcohol/drug/technology/food/sex. Anything short of complete abstinence means the disease will continue to progress and eventually lead to death.

Sound familiar?

Well, it's not true.

To be clear, it's not that this disease concept of addiction doesn't fit *anyone* who struggles with addiction. But it doesn't fit the vast majority of scenarios. And, importantly, no one has ever been able to figure out when it applies and when it doesn't, which makes the concept practically useless.

Some people diagnosed with an addiction recover with no help. In fact, research has shown us that the odds of spontaneous remission—leaving one's alcohol addiction behind on one's own—are much greater than the odds of beating it by going to treatment. Yes, you read that right; as many as 75 percent of those who struggle with alcohol at one point will stop struggling with it later in life—without professional help.[14] Often this happens because of a life-changing event or major motivational change. But only 10 to 15 percent of people who go to rehab stay sober after one year, and less than 10 percent make it to the five-year mark.[15]

Even when it comes to heroin, assumed to be one of the most addictive drugs of all time, we've been surprised. A famous study conducted after the Vietnam War revealed our assumptions are often wrong.

A large number of American soldiers began using heroin while on duty in the South Pacific. As many as 15 percent of the soldiers had developed an addiction to heroin! The drugs were cheap, plentiful, and widely used, and they made the terror of the war more bearable. Terrified of what would happen when these soldiers returned home, the US government wanted to avoid bringing in tens of thousands of "heroin addicts." This fear actually became part of the drive behind then President Nixon's "all-out offensive" on drugs that became known as the "War on Drugs."

Surprisingly, less than 5 percent of returning soldiers used heroin in the year after coming back. And within three years, only 12 percent relapsed. Given the usual relapse rates, which hover at around 60 percent after one month and 90 percent within one year, the numbers were shocking.[16]

Obviously, there is something very wrong with the way we understand, see, and approach addiction. How else could 75 percent of people addicted to alcohol recover on their own from a condition we see as chronic? And how could 90 percent of people addicted to heroin recover with no help, while our rehabs allow only 5 to 15 percent to get better? We can keep blaming the people who are struggling, or we can take a long, hard look in the mirror and realize we've messed up.

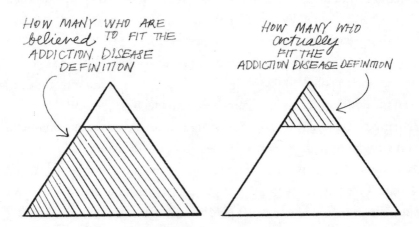

HOW MANY WHO ARE *believed* TO FIT THE ADDICTION DISEASE DEFINITION

HOW MANY WHO *actually* FIT THE ADDICTION DISEASE DEFINITION

To address the inaccuracy and inadequacy of the disease concept of addiction, we need a next step in the evolution of our understanding. To put it simply—*addiction isn't one thing.*

Addiction is certainly not a disease (though some people who struggle with addiction may also have comorbidities that are). Instead, addiction is a syndrome—a collection of symptoms that tend to show up together, even if caused by very different things. The syndrome presents as compulsive habits that produce negative outcomes in many areas of life, typically over a long period of time.

---

### Syndrome Versus Disease

A **syndrome** is a collection of indications and symptoms that appear together but don't have a clear cause, course, or treatment path. This can mean that two different people with the same "syndrome" may have gotten there through completely different causes. A syndrome may include symptoms from various areas of your body, such as problems with movement, cognitive deficits, and changes in behavior.

**Examples of syndromes:**[17]
- Irritable bowel syndrome
- Carpal tunnel syndrome
- Toxic shock syndrome
- Chronic fatigue syndrome
- Substance use disorder

A **disease** is a disorder that affects how your body functions and is more likely to have a known cause, a distinct course, and established treatments. A disease is likely to affect one area or organ system in particular. This means that multiple people diagnosed with the same disease are assumed to have the same problem with the same organ or bodily system, regardless of other factors that are different among them.

---

**Examples of diseases:**

- Diabetes
- Parkinson's disease
- Strep throat
- Influenza (flu)
- Non-Hodgkin's lymphoma
- Hepatitis B

Aliyah's syndrome showed up as the compulsive use of meth (and every other drug she could get her hands on). It resulted in serious criminal justice problems, health issues, social isolation, and poverty. This compulsive drug use left her alone and severely traumatized. It was obvious to everyone around her that Aliyah's life wasn't working out. It was also obvious that, if left on this path, she would most likely die. Since so much of her trouble came after her drug use became habitual, it makes sense that we'd want to put an end to her use. But it's this focus on the presenting problem that has caused much of our failure in both combatting and curing addiction.

So, I propose a new way forward, one that doesn't focus on the presenting problem of the behavior. Because the alcohol use, drugs, porn, overeating, work obsessions, and social media compulsions are not the actual problems at all. *They are simply the compulsive and habitual behaviors formed in response to the real issues—the hidden, embedded emotional hooks formed over many years.* We use habitual "bad" behaviors to avoid the painful jolts that our hooks create in us, because those hooks continue to cause pain, irritation, anxiety, and discomfort whenever they are reactivated and tugged on. The problem is that no one parades around with a list of their hooks on their forehead for you to examine. In fact, people do everything they can to hide the hooks from themselves and from everyone else. You'd be amazed at how many clients I have seen over the years who are either unaware of their primary hooks or so guarded about their pain as to avoid talking about them altogether. And this is after paying good money to find relief. But the true path to happiness always runs through those hooks. Our bad habits are simply what many of us have turned to in our natural inclination to find what we *truly* crave: connection, joy, worth, and meaning in our lives.

The new, alternative understanding of addiction overturns the old cause-and-effect model by first addressing the hooks themselves. Trauma, relationship problems, biological dysregulation, early exposure to drug use, work stress, family dysfunction, sexual confusion, gender dysphoria, perfectionism, insomnia, anxiety, depression, financial struggles, low self-esteem, boredom, and lack of purpose are all common hooks that can result in addiction to negative behaviors.

How many of those hooks ring true as potentially underlying your struggles?

The Unhooked Method allows anyone to first uncover and then dig deep into the core issues that hook people, enabling sufferers to understand why they developed such destructive behaviors in response. That leads to an understanding and acceptance of the consequences of the problematic behaviors. This knowledge unhooks the present pain from past pain, discomfort, and hurt. Finally, once unhooked, the presenting problem—the compulsive behavior itself—can be replaced with more advantageous behaviors that promote wellness and positive functioning. Using the Unhooked Method, you won't be labeled or told you're powerless (you're not). Instead, you will be empowered.

The Unhooked Method gives you a step-by-step recipe for deconstructing and changing any bad habits that have taken over your life and replacing them with good ones. You'll learn how to make sure the forces driving bad habits are minimized while those supporting growth are reinforced. And you'll be guided in the creation of a personalized path out of addiction.

This is the same method that allowed me to go from a hopeless drug dealer, addicted to his own supply and headed straight to prison for the rest of his life, to a blissful husband and father of three who is recognized as a worldwide expert in his field. It wasn't magic, and there's nothing special about me—it took time, deliberate effort, and a method that does its job.

For the past thirty-two years of my life, I have realized the mistakes of the old model of addiction and have methodically studied the true origins of the issues that I (and millions of others) have struggled with. And, in doing so, I have been able to get myself and thousands of others unhooked. It's unlikely, and very rare, that you are truly unable to put these addictive habits behind you. You simply must redirect your efforts, get real about the hidden hooks that have been keeping you trapped, and go about systematically dismantling them.

To better understand this, we have to go back to . . . the end.

## EVERYONE STARTS AT THE END

Whenever someone comes to see me, it's because their life is falling apart. It isn't that they weren't aware of problems at an earlier point. In fact, on average, people have struggled with the painful realities of addiction for eighteen years by the time they seek help.[18] Think of that—eighteen years of suffering before being called to do something about the pain. That's the way it was with Aliyah after that fateful moment. Seconds away from ending her life, she found and then joined my online program, all those years ago.

People take action when the pain of staying the same is greater than the pain of change.

Aliyah came to me because she hated her life. That might be an obvious statement after the story shared earlier, but it's important to note. Regardless of her specific story, Aliyah didn't come to me because she wanted to stop using drugs. She came to me because she was ready to end her life, and something I said made her think that, if we connected, she wouldn't want to end her life anymore.

We make so many assumptions about what it is that leads someone like Aliyah to end up addicted, involved in crime, and unable to care for her daughters. Our assumptions all rely on this end point, her current circumstances, as the source of information. The thing is that when things go wrong, the outcome, or current life circumstance, can seem to make absolutely no sense. It can seem abnormal, crazy, nonsensical, ridiculous. But that's often simply because we don't understand the path. We don't have the context.

Having worked with thousands of people, I can tell you this: To understand someone's outcome, you have to understand their path. You *have to* pay attention to the road they've traveled. You *have to* know what happened to them.

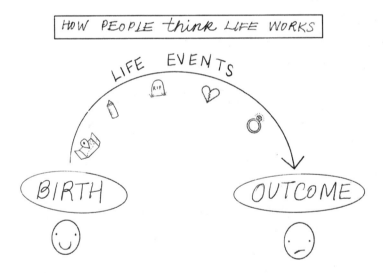

If you've struggled yourself, as I have, you know that we can make the same mistake in judging ourselves. You look at where you are and assume there's something seriously wrong with you. But as you look deeper, it all makes so much more sense.

I've sat in rooms and private jets with multibillionaires who start drinking and using pills the moment they wake up. I've traveled with celebrity musicians who can't make it onstage without using an amount of drugs that would leave most people on the floor for hours. I've spent hours speaking with men and women who've gone to jail or prison more times than most of the people reading this chapter have gone on vacations. I promise you this—if you judge a person by the version of their life you see in this moment, without giving consideration to the path they've been on, you're missing the whole picture. But if you stop and pay attention, you get access to an entirely different world.

To understand someone's journey, you must start with the conditions, and context, at play as their lives unfolded. Then, you always have a clear view of exactly why the path led them to the end result you see in front of you. This has never failed me. It is crucial work if you're hoping to ever be able to help someone change. It gives you actual insight into who they are, what they've been through, and what kept them struggling for years. And that insight is what you'll need to provide the right help.

For many who struggle, this is the first time someone else has actually taken the time to understand their journey. Taking away the notion that addiction is a disease of inevitability and recognizing it as a person's current end point gives you an advantage. It allows you to recognize another very simple, yet empowering, fact—that this end point can also be the start of a whole new future.

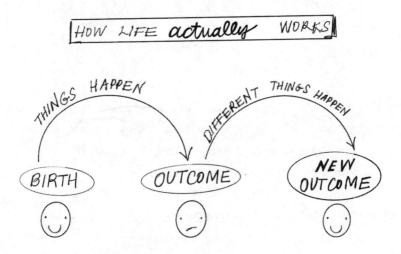

## ALIYAH'S WAY OUT OF DESPAIR

Aliyah grew up in an emotionally, psychologically, and sexually abusive environment, made even more difficult by her parents' own struggles with addiction. By the time she made it to elementary school, she had already learned the painful lessons of sexual assault, abandonment, and drugs. Like so many "addicts," she'd been taught early on that she didn't deserve care and attention, that her feelings didn't count, that she would not be trusted or listened to, and that she had little worth as a human being.

Aliyah's thirty-year struggle with drugs, alcohol, and sexual mistreatment led to terrible relationships, failed jobs, and an endless string of disappointments to herself and everyone around her. Most of the people in her life saw only this version of Aliyah. And it all made perfect sense—she was an "addict," an "alcoholic," and a loser mom who couldn't get her life together because she had the disease of addiction. She had the genes, she had the personality, and she had the track record. If that gun had not jammed, there certainly would have been some sad people, but few who would have been surprised. And that heartbreaking fact points to the real problem—our approach to treating addiction leaves sufferers and loved ones without hope for healing.

According to the third-stage perspective on addiction, Aliyah was living out life as expected. She belonged in the "addict" box and everything she did seemed to prove it. She appeared to care more about herself and her drugs than even her children. If there was ever a progressive disease, Aliyah had it, and it seemed inevitable that her suffering would continue until her death.

So, that fateful morning when she made the call to Lynne about finding another way, nobody had much hope. But about six months later, Aliyah defied all expectations and achieved sobriety for the first time in twenty-five years. Within a year, she began reestablishing a relationship with her daughters. Within a few years, she had the honor of walking Bailey, the daughter she thought she'd lost forever, down the aisle. Today, when people hear about Aliyah's long journey and her amazing triumph, their jaw drops in disbelief. But that's how Aliyah likes it. She wants to keep proving—to the world, to her family, and to herself—that what seems impossible is anything but.

She's become what we call a hero. And she did it by realizing that the end was just the beginning. When I first met Aliyah, it turned out that, if we wanted to end her addiction forever, we'd have to go nearly all the way back to the start of her life. We don't always have to go back that far, but starting at the end is always our opening to explore the beginning of the struggle, so let's go there next ourselves.

# CHAPTER 2

# Getting Back to the Hook

There she was again, standing by the side of the bus. It was a beautiful, sunny day, and Linda's hair was pulled up above her head, in a ponytail. Well, sort of. She was actually holding her own hair above her head in a ponytail, trying to avoid getting any of the vomit she was expelling onto herself. The poor grass. Before every big meet, Linda stood right here and threw up all over it. It must be sick and tired of her by now. Everyone must be sick and tired of her...

Linda couldn't understand why this kept happening to her, but she also had no way of stopping it. Every week, she would find herself vomiting. Whether because of a big student government assembly, or because of a damned volleyball game. Either in the girls' bathroom on the second floor or right here on the grass, next to the bus. The most embarrassing part of it all was that even the bus driver knew this was going to happen. And so the bus waited, sitting right there with all the other girls staring and laughing at her expense.

"DID LINDA THROW UP YET?"

"CAN WE GO ALREADY?" was all she could hear from the bus between heaving and trying to catch her breath. She hated that this was the kind of attention she was getting nowadays... the weird girl who had a screw loose.

Linda was used to a difficult life. There was always trouble at home. Mom and Dad were fighting all the time, getting drunk and screaming obnoxiously loudly at all hours. She didn't exactly grow up in the *Leave It to Beaver* universe. No, Linda was certain that, for the rest of her eternity, she would be standing at the bottom of the world staring up at everyone. Just as she did when she was throwing up.

Except one day, as she was heaving right there on the grass, her friend Emily walked up to her. No one usually walked up to Linda while she was doing that. She was glad to have Emily there. She'd known Emily since before elementary school. They'd been best friends once, years ago, but now they just sort of knew each other. Emily hadn't come over to her house in years...

"Hey," Emily said. "Here, take a little bit of this, it might help." Linda turned around and looked at Emily, who was holding a small joint in her hand, hiding it from the view of everyone on the bus. Linda had never smoked weed. She knew all about it, though.

"This could help what?" she asked Emily.

"All your throwing up, idiot! It can help!"

A few moments passed as Linda absorbed what Emily said.

"Do you want it or not?!" Emily asked, curtly.

Linda looked at her again. She wasn't sure about smoking weed, what with all the warnings and horror stories. But she absolutely knew she hated all this vomiting, and if there was even a small chance that this could help, she thought, *What the hell?!* She grabbed the joint and took a single drag... then another. She coughed a little, then some more, then gave the joint back to Emily. She turned back around, ready to start throwing up again—but weirdly, within seconds, it seemed... the nausea stopped. Linda was confused for a moment. She couldn't believe that it had worked so fast!

If Linda had *any* doubts about weed, she let them all go in that instant. This stuff was a miracle cure! Why had no one told her about this before?!

She stood upright, straightened out her volleyball skirt, and looked at Emily with a smile, saying "Thank you" under her breath. She had a feeling she and Emily were going to be good friends again. For the first time in years, Linda felt hope. It felt good. She'd found the answer to her prayers.

Linda never vomited on that grass, or in the girls' bathroom, again. She also didn't stop smoking weed every day for over twenty years.

## THE START IS OFTEN LOST IN THE OUTCOME

It took Linda nearly three months of working with me to remember that origin story. Like everyone else, she came to me because she couldn't stop her addiction. She'd actually been able to quit all the other stuff—the alcohol, the pills, the occasional party powder. But the weed, she couldn't let go of. And it had been driving her crazy. She'd tried everything she could think of, and then found me online. She figured, "*What the heck? Let's give this a try too.*"

The story Linda came in with was that every time she tried to stop smoking weed, she'd have a terrible time sleeping and painful GI issues. So, she would always go right back to smoking it, because it would allow her to sleep and keep food down without running to the bathroom constantly. But smoking made it impossible to hold a job in the field she wanted to work in. Linda was passionate about working with kids. Being a teacher and shaping young lives through playing, educating, and structuring their days was what she loved. Because the education system required her to get drug tested, cannabis made that impossible. Weed also clouded her judgment a bit and it made her a little lazier. Still, it was better than any alternative she'd found to date. So, the weed stayed.

No matter how hard she tried, Linda couldn't figure out why weed had such a hold on her. She chalked it up to a medical issue with her gastrointestinal system, and let it go. However, addiction being a syndrome, the end point rarely tells us anything useful about the actual origin of the problem.

And so it was with Linda. We had to go back to the origin, not the end point, of her situation to discover the answers to stopping her compulsive weed-smoking habit. I explore how someone's use began because it gives me great insight into what was happening in their life at the time. I get to uncover why starting to use made sense back then. Again, while the behavior might not seem logical to us now, it always does when we go back to when it started.

When it came to unearthing Linda's original stimulus, it took some digging. It happened so long ago, and didn't feel relevant to her current struggles. The nausea in high school didn't even make it on her radar. But her original stimulus as a starting point to her trouble made all the sense in the world:

1. A girl vomits regularly for years, in an embarrassing, shameful way.
2. A friend gives her a simple cure—a substance that stops the problem in seconds.
3. The girl continues taking the medicine.

Linda felt immediate relief when she remembered the originating event. With this memory brought back, she could finally make sense of why she had even started smoking over twenty-five years ago. The GI issues had been there all along, and the weed corrected them. But there was still a big question left: *Why* was Linda throwing up so much in high school? Was there something wrong with her digestive system, or was it bigger than that? We had to dig a little deeper.

As it turned out, Linda had *massive* performance and social anxiety. She loved the thrill of playing and was committed to the practices and the work it took to get really good. She was lauded and celebrated for her wins and performances. She had no problem with the effort it took to succeed, but the reality was, she *hated* playing in front of people. And there were often as many as a hundred or more spectators at the games. She could feel them judge her every move and believed that they could tell when she screwed up, royally. She beat herself up every time she messed up a pass or ran too slowly and didn't get to a ball.

Being in the spotlight was *not* her favorite pastime. Not on the court and not in the auditorium with those student government assemblies. Again, Linda loved being part of her school's student government. She loved the meetings and feeling so involved. But she absolutely hated getting out there in front of people. She would get *so* anxious and scared by the possibility of looking like a fool that she got sick before every game and every student assembly. All she could focus on before these events were endless ways she would end that day being the laughingstock of all her friends.

So, you see, it wasn't her GI tract that was compromised at all. It was Linda's self-confidence, her perfectionism, and her lack of assurance in her abilities. She relied on always looking perfect for everyone else, and that was making her so anxious, she'd throw up.

It was this abject fear of being judged that made Linda vomit for all those years. And when she smoked weed for the first time, its anxiety-reducing and antinausea effects solved it *all* for her, in an instant.[1]

Cannabis *did* provide exactly the medicine Linda needed for what ailed her. But it wasn't "addiction." It was a deep anxiety issue that brought on a near–panic attack every time she had to perform publicly. *This* was her hook—her fear of public failure. *This* was the stimulus triggering her smoking pot. *Not* throwing up.

When you hear Linda's story, it all makes sense. Once introduced to cannabis, she never needed to work on her social fears again. She simply fenced off that fear with the effects of the weed she smoked daily, adding a little extra whenever a big performance came up. This way, even though the hook itself was still embedded in her, she could ignore the pain and suffering it created.

You'd be surprised how often social anxiety and fear of public ridicule play a part in the start, and maintenance, of addictive behavior. In fact, social phobia is the most commonly observed phobia among those who struggle with drug addictions. Generalized anxiety and panic disorders are the most common conditions found along with substance use disorders in national surveys.[2] Those conditions certainly played a major role for me (remember the sleepaway camp story?) as they have for hundreds of those I've worked with.

Too many people are well practiced in hiding their daily pain from others.

The social anxiety that I see in so many of my clients is far from the *only* hook, but it's a common one. Here are some others:

- Erosion of trust after deep trauma
- Physical pain
- Self-judgment due to deeply religious/cultish upbringing
- Attachment issues related to early abandonment or absence of love
- Deep and ongoing relationship struggles
- Rejection or fear of rejection
- Environmental exposure to violence
- Self-doubt and self-esteem issues
- Perfectionism
- Lack of purpose or loss of a belief in any meaning
- Deep isolation

Unfortunately, many of these circumstances are relegated to "co-occurring" disorders instead of being recognized for what they are—the true origin struggles that triggered the addictive behavior in the first place.

*Saying that a person suffers from alcohol use disorder with co-occurring post-traumatic stress disorder (PTSD), depression, and generalized anxiety is a bit like saying that you drive a gas tank with an engine and a metal body connected to four wheels, instead of calling it a car.*

The addiction is a wholesale package—a syndrome.

If we're addicted to anything, it's the quick relief from the physical and emotional pain that these deep and painful hooks create.[3] Because when the hooks get tugged on, we feel an urgent need for pain relief and spring into action. In attempting to get reprieve, we find ourselves relying on "elixirs," chemical and compulsive behaviors we *know* will block the pain. Often, the need for those elixirs becomes habitual because the tug of the hooks is persistent, and *the medicines work!*

For a while.

Eventually, as we've discussed, we develop a tolerance to these medicines, which ultimately results in the medicine not working as well. Over time, we take more medicine, trying to get more relief, with diminishing results. So, we go on and on, experiencing the deep, private, and nearly subconscious pain, responding with well-practiced, but shallow, "cures" to mask it. The pain never truly goes away because these habits never rid us of the hooks themselves.

As noted, trauma is a common cause of such pain. The *Oxford Dictionary* defines trauma as a "deeply distressing or disturbing experience," *or* the "emotional shock following a stressful event, or a physical injury." For centuries, we only thought about trauma as an experience, completely ignoring its impact on much longer-term behavior and functioning. But we now know that we don't easily leave our traumas behind. Experiencing traumatic events creates long-term changes in the ways our brain and our body function. It also changes, in deeply meaningful and basic ways, how we relate to others.

As Bessel van der Kolk says, trauma is "not the story of something that happened back then, but the current imprint of that pain, horror, and fear living inside."[4] Trauma changes who you are and how you see and interact with the world. For individuals who experienced sexual molestation by a family member, for instance, the entire social fabric of close kinship, trust, and safety is disturbed. And who could blame them? How do you rationalize and move on from such a betrayal but by adopting a worldview that looks suspiciously at anyone who offers close and intimate relationships, when even your own family members can't be trusted?

Or what about children who grow up around severe and violent addiction, where inconsistent daily experiences, aggression, violence, and abandonment are commonplace? How are they to grow up expecting anything but disappointment, inconsistency, and upheaval in their lives?

Sure, we all want to move past traumas we've experienced. We want those close to us to move past theirs. But the resultant changes in brain areas related to survival and basic functioning mean that even seemingly irrelevant activation of traumatic experiences can set off entire cascades of hormonal and neurochemical effects that bring about fear, aggression, anxiety, and other intense emotional and physical reactions. Because these responses happen seemingly out of nowhere (there's no flashing sign that calls out, "Your childhood trauma is being activated"), it leaves those who struggle feeling confused, broken, and afraid.[5]

To make matters more confusing, as Dr. van der Kolk identified, whereas some people respond to PTSD triggering by experiencing high levels of anxiety and stress activation (a fight-or-flight response), others find themselves shut down and nearly incapable of responding at all (a freeze response).[6] The difference lies in your experience, your genetic makeup, and your early exposure to bonding with caretakers. This complexity can make it harder to predict the response for both the person experiencing the trigger and those who observe it secondhand.

And so, even as we live out this constant stimulus-outcome chain, this seemingly automatic and inescapable reality of pain and relief, many of us forget about the trigger because we don't *want* to remember it. Much of the addiction industry has developed ignoring those early needs, focusing instead on the resultant outcome. The drunken stupors, the late-night screaming matches, the packets of white powder, the street-bought pills, or the hours of porn binging are much easier to focus on than the childhood trauma, the broken marriage, the crippling self-loathing, or the engulfing sense of existential dread that many of those who struggle with addiction experience.

By focusing on the seemingly irrational end-behavior, we get to point at those who struggle and say, *It's them there is something wrong with—not me.* And thus the "normal" vs. the "addict" characterization is born, with a nearly complete disregard for any of the reasons that the addictive behavior developed in the first place, or for the person who experienced it all. It's easier to hide behind a mask of normality than to admit that many of us are closer to struggle than we'd care to admit.

When I walked into my first-ever treatment center, scared and out of sorts after the SWAT arrest and a week in jail, I was ushered into a group meeting that was in progress while they searched my bags. As I sat there, in relative shock and confusion about where my life had taken me, the group leader turned to me and asked, "Why are you here?" Thinking for a moment, I gave the first answer that came to mind: "I was arrested for drugs and needed to get help." "No," came back the quick reply. "Why are you here?" he repeated. I searched my mind and responded with my second, hopefully more honest and candid, attempt: "Because my lawyer told me I'm obviously addicted to meth and need help to stay out of prison." "No," came his voice again. I was confused. What did this guy want from me? What was he trying to get me to say? "Because I am addicted to meth and couldn't quit on my own?" I tried again. This was definitely closer to a personal truth—I'd tried to stop using meth over seven times on my own and lasted fourteen days only once. "NO!" he said again, more abruptly and bluntly. "You're here because you're an addict," he told me. He made the statement so simply, without hesitation and after never otherwise speaking with me for even a single minute. Still, I got the message. "I'm here because I'm an addict," came back my reply. He gave me the secret password to getting out of that spotlight, and I took it and ran.

In twelve-step meetings, addiction specialists' offices, and lavish treatment centers everywhere, those who struggle with addiction are often told to turn their attention *away* from their early experiences and recognize a simple fact—that they are addicts, and they were likely born that way. This upside-down, inside-out, completely backward reasoning supposes that the life circumstances of those who struggle with addiction are simply by-products of the addiction they were born with, and *not* the actual causes of their destructive chain of behavior.

It's maddening.

But I get it.

Given the collateral damage and the compulsive, habitlike nature of the addiction syndrome, it's understandable why people attack the end symptoms (the presenting problems) as one would for any habit: Stop drinking and you won't get into barroom brawls. Stop overeating and you won't be so fat. But focusing on the end behavior does nothing to relieve the much more important underlying struggles. How do you ignore that the drinking is often used to mitigate anxiety and pain caused by early trauma? Or that binge eating, and the resultant weight gain, have been tied to early sexual assault and rape?[7]

Sure, much of the drinking people engage in fails to improve these conditions! And, of course, eating an entire gallon of ice cream or watching porn for hours doesn't actually solve anything. But these behaviors also help with the momentary problems people are seeking to solve—the pain of the hooks that are being tugged on. And telling someone who is full of shame, trauma, fear, and self-loathing that they are indeed a broken human, damaged from the start and unlikely to change, removes any semblance of agency and hope one might have had. This leaves many who struggle even more vulnerable to pain. They give up on repairing that endless pit of self-hate they've grown up with, because they "really are broken forever."

It's a bit like walking up to someone using a crutch and kicking it from under them, saying, "You'll walk better if you don't use that thing!" We wouldn't do that because we are adept at understanding physical pain. But we are inept at dealing with emotional pain. This despite the fact that both physical and emotional pain are actually processed in the same part of the brain—the anterior cingulate.[8] This is why we say that breaking up "hurts," and that our heart is "broken." It also explains why opioids, useful for relieving physical pain, are often used for emotional relief by those addicted to them.[9]

Exactly the opposite kind of help is needed. Instead of mere habit changes and interventions, addiction help requires the parallel work of recognizing, and then addressing, the hooks that brought about the problem in the first place. Only when we acknowledge and resolve the most important and painful hooks can we create lasting change in the habitual behaviors developed to mitigate the pain the hooks cause. Otherwise, stopping the addictive behaviors merely exposes the raw nerve endings and creates a nearly impossible reality for a person to live through. And hence begins the seemingly endless cycle of quit and relapse attempts that most of those who have found themselves addicted engage in.

I often remind people that experiences are fixed into our consciousness and memory if they are powerful or repeated.[10] A single intense experience can change our consciousness forever—imagine watching a loved one die in front of you, being involved in a serious car wreck, or being sexually assaulted in your home. But hooks don't have to be that dramatic to cause long-term impact, if they occur over and over again. Many of my clients grew up in an environment in which they were repeatedly exposed to the mental health struggles of others, were told they were worthless, felt unloved or unwanted, or had to observe low-grade abuse and neglect for years. That sort of repetition can alter one's reality forever as well. Comparing, or even competing, when it comes to the severity of trauma isn't useful to becoming unhooked. There is no specific trauma "threshold" that you have to cross to be eligible. All that truly matters is the impact the experience left.

When I work with someone, I look for very intense or often repeated behaviors, states, and situations. This combination of intensity and repetition obviously leaves an even deeper and more difficult to mend wound. Think of Linda's heaving publicly for years as people watched and made fun of her. The substantial physical discomfort, combined with the emotional angst of being ridiculed, left quite a mark.

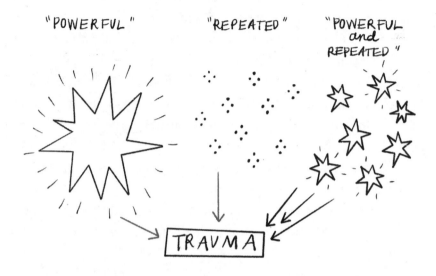

Hooks originate from biological (medical conditions, injuries, genetics), psychological (beliefs, trauma, attachments), environmental (physical and social factors related to country, culture, neighborhood, home environment), and spiritual (purpose, belonging, importance, religion) factors.[11] Hooks vary in their level of intensity, depth of embedding, and in the amount of pain they cause. Some hooks have been present since birth or immediately thereafter (such as perinatal asphyxia, when the newborn's brain and organs do not receive enough oxygen—a condition associated with later mental health dysfunction).[12] Other hooks became embedded during early development, from birth to the age of seven or so. This is when a person forms much of their experience of love, worth, and perspective on themselves and the world.[13] Yet other hooks are not embedded until later in life, in adolescence or even middle age and beyond—such as accidents, bad breakups, tragic deaths, abandonment, divorces, and the like.

I am often personally saddened and affected by the level of suffering experienced by many of my clients. When we sit together, exploring their past and sharing stories, the result is often tears on both sides. When I look at the thousands of individuals I have worked with over the years, one thing is clear: not a single one of them walks in without at least a few hooks embedded deep inside their psyche, tugging, pulling, and causing discomfort and pain. The addictive behavior they've come to me about, even if abhorrent to those around them, is predictably a great medicine when it comes to relieving the pull and making them feel unhooked, even if only for a few hours.

But without true resolution of the impact of these hooks, there is no real long-term recovery. This is why you can find individuals who have been sober for decades but are as miserable as ever. It's also why you'll find that as many as 40 to 60 percent relapse within a single month of spending substantial time and money on promised help in formal addiction treatment.[14] It's why most individuals who struggle with addiction (about 95 percent, by most recent assessments[15]) aren't even willing to try their hand at getting help in the first place. Because telling someone who is in pain that the route to their salvation is getting rid of their pain medicine forever, along with any future medicine they may consider taking—without offering any real and tangible relief to the pain—is about as attractive as giving someone the option to crawl, with bare knees, across a field of broken glass.

No one wants to do it.

I stopped wondering why we've been failing at addiction since my early research on these "treatment barriers." It's why I left academia to help on the ground. Because the system we've created for helping those who struggle is so broken, we may as well throw it out. It helps very few, may even cause more harm than good for many, is detested by most, and is too expensive and unapproachable for the vast majority who need it. But here we are, years later, stuck with many of the same practices that have been failing for decades.

## Common Barriers to Seeking Help

Only 7.5 percent of people with addiction issues get professional help for the problem. With approximately forty million Americans meeting criteria for addiction, less than three million get professional help every year. While at UCLA, I conducted a study, following participants for a full six months after they began looking for help.[16]

Over eighteen months, we were able to recruit forty participants who were actively looking for treatment. We asked our participants,

1. Are you interested in treatment?
2. Did you actively look for it?
3. Did you find suitable treatment?
4. Did you enter treatment?
5. If so, where?
6. If not, why?

The results were telling and startling. We identified four primary barriers to entering treatment:

**Cost**—People couldn't afford to go to treatment, because much of treatment is expensive and many have burned bridges for employment and support.

**Logistics**—They also struggled to find the time and space in their lives. Leaving life and obligations for thirty, sixty, or ninty days or even for ten to fifteen hours per week is generally a massive disruption to family, work, and more for most people.

**Shame**—People didn't want to tell others they were struggling. They wanted to handle the problem alone, and only report on it when they've beaten it. They also felt judged whenever they did mention it to others.

**Abstinence**—While everyone in our study knew they needed help, more than 60 percent said they liked using too much to stop completely.

While cost and logistics were difficult to tackle, I focused on reducing shame, using my "F*ck Shame" motto. I wanted to make sure that people who wanted help but weren't ready to quit had options.

Is it any wonder Linda chose cannabis instead of the deep sense of terror and the embarrassment that followed her as she threw up over and over again? What would you do if someone gave you an answer to the most pressing problem you can imagine? How much would it matter that certain adults in your life told you the solution could be dangerous? As a child, would you be able to see past the relief, and the fact that many of your friends use it?

It's easy to judge a mother sitting on the floor of her bathroom, contemplating a bullet to her head because of the consequences her addictive behavior brought. But is it any wonder Aliyah turned to using anything she could get her hands on to escape the gnawing pain and incredible doubt about her own self-worth, after experiencing continuous childhood sexual abuse, totally disregarded by her family? How would you react if you had to wake up every morning with the memories of those experiences etched into your consciousness?

I have sat in rooms and listened to thousands of stories from people who have struggled with addiction for decades. One thing that has become crystal clear to me is that the path from early childhood to addiction is rarely, if ever, a clean and direct one. We need to start the recovery process by identifying and addressing the hooks that triggered the destructive behavior. This is the first step in what needs to be a one-two punch for treating addiction. We'll discuss the second step, replacing destructive behavior with productive habits, in later chapters. Without this one-two punch, those struggling with addictions will likely find themselves on the all-too-familiar carousel of despair.

It's important that we don't focus only on the beginning and the end, however. If we're going to change behaviors, it's crucial that we turn our attention to the choices people make. Because without the choice, there would be no addiction.

# CHAPTER 3

# Addiction as a Hook Response

Jaylen is a *large* and menacing character. At 6 foot 4 and over 300 pounds, you can't tell from afar whether he is a linebacker, a bodyguard, or a guy who's about to simply walk over you without noticing. That's one of the things that initially attracted Bella to Jaylen—his deep, strong, and protective masculinity. Ironically, though, Jaylen is also the kindest, most gentle, and humble person you could ever meet. You may even call him timid once you know him (though maybe not directly to his face). And his gentle nature and ease also come with an unexpected feature—Jaylen doesn't like conflict.

So, for years, every time Jaylen and his wife fought, he went to porn. Actually, every time he felt uncomfortable in any way, he went to porn. Sure, there was the beer, too, and eventually things got out of hand and made the porn look tame. But for decades, every time Jaylen felt out of sorts, or uncomfortable, or embarrassed or unloved, porn was there to make things better. Jaylen knew that if he chose porn, there would be at least a few moments of relief. And, sometimes, that was enough.

This pattern of seeking a quick source of comfort started long before Jaylen met Bella. Growing up in a one-parent household (his father passed when he was six) with an older sibling, Jaylen was exposed to porn at a relatively young age. He was only ten when his brother first shared the videos with him. He wasn't really sure what to think of the writhing bodies and loud noises when he first viewed them, but his brother thought it was amusing and important, so Jaylen went along with it. When he got a little older, the videos took on a different meaning. He really liked the way they made him feel, and while he was socially anxious with others, he felt very comfortable in the fantasy world of porn.

The only problem was that this constant reliance on porn created some major divisions in his relationships. Porn didn't ask for much, so it was easier, more reliable, and less confrontational than having to address and work on his relationships. And Jaylen *hated* confrontation.

So, porn it was. But as Jaylen continued relying on the lurid videos to help him avoid, numb out, and ignore aspects of his life, the discomfort mounted. The once-satisfactory vanilla videos weren't doing it anymore. Like a drinker needing to double those drinks to get the same effects, Jaylen's videos got more explicit. Eventually, the videos themselves weren't going to do it anymore. He needed more. And this is where the line got crossed in the relationship with his beautiful wife. There he was, this gentle giant who hates conflict, consistently breaking his commitment to the single person he loved more than anyone in the world. It made no sense to him. And it made absolutely no sense to Bella when she found out about it all one Saturday afternoon.

The years of relief Jaylen found by his habit of escaping into sex and porn wound a spring that unleashed its destructive energy on his life in an instant. The moment his wife discovered his habits, that energy got within inches of destroying everything the two of them had together. As far as Bella was concerned, there was hardly a chance of their staying together. That's why he began looking for professional help. He was skeptical when he first met me, but it was my program or a $50,000, thirty-day inpatient program, so he figured he'd give my work a try.

## THE CLEAR CONNECTION

In the previous chapters, we discussed the destructive outcomes that bring people to realize they must change. It's hard to deny that, right before the outcome itself, people make choices that lead to those results. And so, shouldn't we expect that stopping what they're doing would help them to stop experiencing the outcomes they profess to hate so much? If Aliyah chose not to use meth (or any other drug), wouldn't her life improve? If Linda could just get herself to stop smoking cannabis, she'd be able to keep her teaching jobs and move forward in life. If Jaylen would choose not to use porn, or step out of his marriage, wouldn't the whole chain of destructive events break and allow everyone to live happily ever after? Right?

Unfortunately, behavioral choice is not that simple.

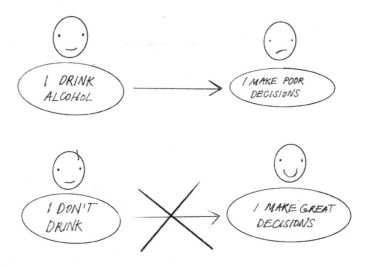

## ADDICTION AS A BEHAVIOR CHAIN

The stimulus → response → reward chain is the basis for a school of thought called behaviorism. It became increasingly popular in the 1940s and '50s thanks to B. F. Skinner, a renowned Harvard professor

and researcher who was known primarily for his pigeon and rat experiments. In his experiments, Skinner taught rats to press levers, and

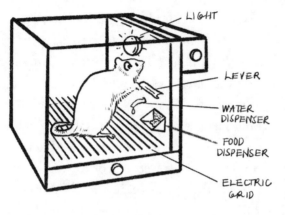

pigeons to play table
tennis and guide mis-
siles. He manipulated
behavior using playful
and involved devices,
such as his Skinner box
(see image).

Skinner's assertion
was straightforward: the
only aspects of behav-
ior we should concern

ourselves with are the visible ones; how you feel about something
doesn't matter. Skinner didn't care about what he couldn't measure,
only about observable actions.

Behaviorism, and the idea that all behavior is observable and
guided only by observable forces, was *very* popular because of its direct
measurement and impressive results at teaching animals to perform
incredible feats. But it never quite made it into the therapeutic world
at large. The reason is that behaviorism ignores, by design, everything
that we understand about what it means to be human. It ignores our
thoughts, our feelings, our beliefs, our culture, and our environment. It
ignores the origin of our learning, the individual variability among us,
and the meaning of past experiences.[1]

Nevertheless, it is easy to see that the behaviorist model created much of the method that makes up our standard treatment for
addiction:

1. If you can stop the behavior, then all the negative outcomes
   will stop occurring.
2. What is happening inside the brain doesn't really matter.
   What matters is how you behave.

3. The past only matters insomuch as it either rewarded or punished your behavior. If a behavior is rewarded, it will be repeated.
4. If we stop rewarding the using behavior, or even punish for engaging in it, the use should stop.

One of the extreme examples of this approach to addiction treatment is something known as aversion therapy. This therapeutic approach pairs drinking alcohol with disulfiram, a chemical that induces vomiting. This pairing creates a punishment for drinking, and therefore reduces its desirability. It makes sense that vomiting every time you drink during treatment would greatly reduce your future desire to drink *if* the rewarding aspects of drinking are the only factors that motivate future drinking. Unfortunately, this approach hasn't proved very effective. In fact, it would sometimes even produce the opposite of the desired results—an increased reliance on drinking. This is likely because the addiction either transfers onto another "elixir" or the need for relief eventually overrides the punishment.[2]

Certainly, aversion therapy is an extreme example. But other more subtle forms of behaviorism are at the core of the methods we've been using with the vast majority of people struggling with addiction. I know of therapists who have told a patient that they will only see them if the patient commits to abstinence and doesn't use during treatment. Some therapists won't see patients unless they have achieved thirty days of continuous abstinence. This is so common, it may not even sound odd to you. Of course, it is better if a patient isn't actively using or drinking while getting treatment. But, for just one second, imagine if we changed the scenario to a different setting.

Picture a well-trained therapist sitting in their office, conducting an intake interview with a potential new patient who is seeking help for her long-standing depression. The patient has been struggling for ten years, and had even contemplated suicide only a few months back. She's truly serious about getting help and is hoping that this time, she can finally leave behind her years of suffering, to find herself free of the pain and sorrow.

After the assessment, the therapist tells this motivated patient that she is ready and willing to work with her. The only rule is that the patient commit to not feel depressed, think about suicide, or have a depressive episode while they work together.

It sounds absurd, doesn't it? The inability to control one's depression is precisely the reason for the treatment. But this is the reality for many who seek help for addiction—the proverbial cart being placed long before the horse is even out of the barn.

This is why the action → reaction approach to fixing addiction breaks down and produces no results. Because, as discussed earlier, the patient's *true* problem isn't really the behavior at all. But it is exactly this chain, the stimulus → response → reward behavioral chain, that is at the core of nearly all treatment for addiction. Patients are encouraged to recognize their triggers and avoid them, refraining from the behavior at all costs. "Don't drink no matter what" is the common refrain. They are assured that, should they do this, the outcome will be positive.

Except it isn't. Because the model is broken. If nothing else, it completely ignores the nuances of how we actually choose our behavior.

## HOW THE BRAIN CHOOSES WHAT ACTIONS TO PERFORM

To perform any action, the motor cortex, the part of the brain responsible for movement, has to get activated. To have a drink, you must activate the muscles that move your hand and arms to open a bottle, pour some liquid into a glass, and then bring the glass to your mouth, open the mouth, and begin drinking.

How does the brain do that? How does the brain choose those specific actions over all others? Well, that's where learning comes in. And without understanding how learning to perform a specific behavior develops, it's difficult to understand how to change that behavior.

Fortunately for me, my focus on behavioral neuroscience during my studies at UCLA taught me a good deal about this chain of events. Let's break it all down.

As mentioned in the story about Linda's first time smoking weed, or Jaylen's initial exposure to porn, the initial introduction to any behavior is usually unexpected and novel. Brand-new behaviors involve entirely new experiences that have no precedent or practice. When Linda first took a drag off that joint, or when Jaylen saw the video his brother showed him, the actions didn't feel easy, natural, or routine. So, why did they keep going?

Certainly, some actions feel good, and others don't. But what does "feeling good" really mean? Well, the answer to that is multifaceted and depends on more factors than you might imagine. First, there is the biological result of the behavior—in Linda's case, the relief of nausea was certainly a reward. In neuroscience, that kind of reward is called "negative reinforcement," because the reward involves the *removal* of an unwanted *negative* experience (the nausea). This is different than positive reinforcement, where a person experiences a feeling of pleasure, euphoria, or other positive effects. There is a great deal of research showing that much of the initiation of addictive behavior has to do with negative reinforcement, rather than positive reinforcement.[3]

This makes a lot of sense, given the discussion we've had up until now in this book. Many people who become addicted are reducing the pain of past negative experiences with their chosen medicine. *But this goes against the idea that people become addicted because they "like the way it feels." Instead, it suggests people use drugs because the drugs remove other feelings that they hate.*

What's important to recognize here is that behavioral choice—the process the brain utilizes to select what to do out of all the available choices it has—depends on a few different factors: previous learning, context, ability, and motivation.

Let's break each of these down:

**Previous learning.** If you've experienced something before and it has led to beneficial experiences, you are more likely to repeat it. This includes removing unwanted feelings. If, however, the behavior led to negative experiences, you're less likely to repeat it. Here's the thing— your individual experience can be positive or negative, whereas other people may experience the exact same behavior in a different way. One very clear example of this with alcohol has to do with genetics. There is a genetic variant in a gene called alcohol dehydrogenase (ALDH2, or ALDH2,2). ALDH provides a genetic blueprint for an enzyme that breaks down alcohol into nontoxic chemicals. People with two copies of the ALDH2,2 variant have an aldehyde dehydrogenase enzyme form that is only 8 percent as effective as the fully active version. This means that they are *much* slower converting alcohol to nontoxic forms. When people with this much less efficient form of ALDH2 drink, they can become very ill. Obviously, if someone with this genetic mutation is given alcohol, their experience (of getting very ill and nauseous and possibly throwing up) will be very different than the experience I had at the age of fourteen in that sleepaway camp. No matter how socially anxious they are, the chances of their developing a habit of drinking alcohol to alleviate anxiety are very low. In fact, individuals with this type of genetic variation are extremely unlikely to drink alcohol at all.[4]

In this way, the subjective experience *your* previous learning provides may be wildly different than that of someone else. The same can be said of many previous variations in initial experience. If you've experienced substantial trauma that has led to ongoing trust issues, an initial exposure to cannabis may make it less difficult to connect with others. But it could also trigger severe panic attacks. The sedating effects of alcohol may be rewarding for one person, but tiresome for another. It's your experience that makes a difference.

That variation matters.

And your experience of a behavior as rewarding or not doesn't depend only on you. Your learning also has to do with other factors that exist *during* these initial behaviors.

That's where context comes in:

**Context.** Your learning is *not* only connected to the behavior itself. In fact, *everything* that is part of your environment when the behavior first occurs becomes part of the context for the behavior itself. Were you alone or with other people? At home or away from home? Inside or outside? Was it daytime or night? How was your body feeling? What were you thinking about? Was there a smell, any specific sounds, or other sensory aspects that set that moment as unique? Each and every one of these aspects of the experience actually becomes part of the learning you're involved in. Research has shown us that learning is *very* context dependent.

For instance, did you know that Hasidic Jews, who smoke like chimneys, have no problem stopping themselves from smoking for twenty-four hours *every week*?! "Why is that?" you may ask. It's because between Friday and Saturday evening, a period known as Shabbat in Judaism, they are not allowed, by creed of their religious laws, to light a match or a lighter, or by extension, a cigarette, cigar, or pipe. That's apparently all it takes to kick a wicked nicotine addiction—a decree from God.

This is why some people have no problem refraining from drinking outside the home but can polish off a bottle between dinner and bedtime. It's why you may not be thinking about drinking at work, but the *moment* you get off, it seems to take over your mind. It's why you find yourself, seemingly out of nowhere, wanting to dive headfirst into your addiction when you go back home to your mother's for Thanksgiving. Context matters *way* more than we give it credit for!

In fact, as your body learns to connect specific environments with your using, you begin preparing yourself (both biologically and psychologically) for the use as you approach the prelearned context. And even small deviations in environments matter. One of my clients, James, was the president of a small liberal arts college, struggling with heavy drinking following a stressful period at work. It was affecting his health, and his marriage was on the rocks because of it. And so, as he told me, he could feel his desire for a drink begin building up as soon as he turned off the main road and onto the street that led to his residential community. However, the desire didn't build fully until he turned onto his street and got a full view of his own home. It was only then that the final decision regarding the likelihood of getting drunk became clear. If the house was empty, with no other cars in the driveway, he knew he'd drink as soon as he got in. But if his wife's car was in the driveway, he knew he'd have to hold off…

That is the power of context.

**Ability.** Obviously, it's impossible to do things we can't do. But this specific variant is one that confuses many of us, because of the mistaken way we think about addiction. If you have no physical access to your chosen drug or behavior, you will stop your use. In a real way, this is the reasoning behind residential and hospital-based addiction treatment. It is also part of the rationale behind jailing those who use illegal drugs. The thought is that by limiting your ability to physically interact with the drug or behavior, your use will subside and then die off. But residential treatment and jails don't permanently impact your *ability*. Instead, they only temporarily limit access, with the ability itself remaining fully intact. This is part of the reason that so many people leave rehab, or jail, and immediately return to using, often within hours. Their ability to use has not changed, and the other forces driving their desire to use have often not been addressed. And so, as soon as they are able to use again, they automatically do what they can to reduce their internal pain.

Interfering with ability is one of the least likely methods to help in addiction long term. In fact, the only way to take advantage of ability when it comes to helping those who struggle with addiction is to *increase* their ability to engage in alternative behaviors.

**Motivation.** This one is a bit complicated. There is an entire body of literature dedicated to what motivation is and what increases or decreases it. However, motivation is connected to both previous experience (reward, or lack thereof), the environment, your ability, *and* the interaction between the behavior and your goals. You are motivated to do things that you know how to do, and that you believe will help you reach your goals, given your circumstances. But people give far too much value to motivation on its own, ignoring many of the factors discussed earlier. We assume that motivation alone results in action. But here's the truth— even if you are *incredibly* motivated to do something (e.g., stop using), you may be in an environment that makes it difficult (e.g., being around others who are actively using). And if you don't have the ability to do it, because you haven't developed active coping skills, it's likely *nothing will change*. What you need is *enough* motivation to act, some experience with the behavior, and a context that supports it, and voilà!

Think of someone going to a happy hour with friends. Even if they don't really want to drink, being there with other people who are drinking plus having easy access to the alcohol can end up with them finding themselves drinking.

Has that ever happened to you?

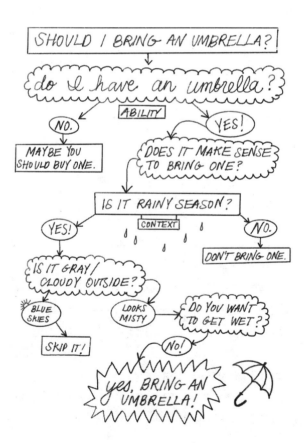

In the end, here's the reality: we perform behaviors supported by a strong enough confluence of all four of these factors—experience, context, ability, and motivation. Each of these factors has a balance of Promoters (that make the behavior more likely) and Inhibitors (that make the behavior less likely). The actual behavior produced depends on whether the Promoters or Inhibitors win out. Later in the book, I'll introduce you to a way to factor all these things together, through something I call the P/I Ratio.

## THE TROUBLE FOR ANYONE WITH AN ADDICTION

How are you supposed to gain control over a behavior that has become central to your experience of life, when no one is willing to acknowledge that your engagement in it is related to unresolved needs?

How do you avoid the outcomes that behavior produces when you're surrounded by endless triggers that set the cycle in motion? A thought, a street corner, a feeling in your stomach, a name, a picture, or a thousand other triggers can launch an entire chain of events that seems to lead you right back to the outcome you abhor.

And how are you to have a scrap of hope when you are told, repeatedly, that you will always struggle with this specific disease caused by your genes, your history, your very existence?

The answer? You don't.

You don't hold on to hope, you don't manage to avoid the outcome, and you don't gain control or manage to avoid the triggers. At least, the vast majority of people don't.

The state of the "addict"—as we've horribly come to talk about people who suffer in this way—reminds me of the fate of the trained elephants in the touristy jungles of Thailand. When my wife, Sophie, came back from a vacation there, she told me tales of long elephant journeys through lush and wet jungles. I wondered a bit about how someone could get an elephant, the largest mammal on land, to simply bow down to tourists and carry them for days. I knew that this practice has existed along trade routes for thousands of years, so I decided to research it a bit more.

I was shocked to discover that the process was incredibly simple, oddly disturbing, and familiar, given my focus on addiction. When a new elephant is born, it is quickly separated from its mother and tied up in chains or rope. After months of spending time tied in this way, trying to move and finding itself unable to, the elephant gives up, recognizing its predicament and inability to escape. From that point on, it is trained in the customs needed for it to serve as a docile service animal. At the end of the day, it is either tied back down with rope or contained within a fenced-in area, or both. Although an adult elephant could easily break through the restraints and the fences, its learning has taught it that there is no use in trying. The elephant has learned that it is powerless, which has made it stop trying to exert its power.

Such is the spirit of nearly every one of the thousands of people I've encountered in my work. Strong spirits, who have endured terrible pain, all while being told they have no power. Eventually, believing this, they give up, broken.[5]

If we are serious about fixing this problem, we have to empower those who struggle, rather than break their spirit. And while a small minority do feel inspired by the current systems of addiction treatment, most feel disempowered, shamed, and beaten.

## WE NEED A NEW SYSTEM

This oversimplified model suggests that, without a stimulus, there is no response and that, without a reward, a response will go away. And yet, this is obviously not the case when it comes to addiction. People's triggers for their addictive behaviors can come from anywhere, including their own thoughts, feelings, and memories. And, even when alcohol, drugs, porn, or gambling create troubling consequences in everyday life, many struggle with stopping.

$$\boxed{STIMULUS} \longrightarrow \boxed{RESPONSE} \longrightarrow \boxed{REWARD}$$

That's because the behaviorist approach ignores so much. It ignores the *original cause* of the behavior, the individual variability in response, and the differences in historical experiences that direct and modify consequences and rewards. And so, while a behaviorist model does an adequate job of *describing* behavior in general, it does little to actually help one create change. And that's all I really care about.

Obviously, we need a more nuanced model.

We can think of the behaviorist model as a starting point. It does a nice job of summarizing *what* is happening. But it does a crummy job of explaining *why* it happens. It's a bit like looking at your phone and saying that when you push a button (the stimulus), the phone makes a sound (the response) and a voice comes on the speaker (the outcome). Sure, that works generally to describe the process of you making a call, but it lacks *all* the nuances of the process: which number and what voice are all that truly matters. Calling your mom because you miss her and wanted to ask for her advice is different than ordering a pizza, even if the steps are the same and both are rewarded.

Behaviorists despise meaning and context, thinking them irrelevant to human behavior. But meaning and context are *actually the most important* parts of being human.

In the phone call example, the part that was so badly missing from the behaviorist approach was the goal (talking to your mother) and the potential ways to achieve that end. Certain outcomes, such as hearing her voice on the answering machine, don't satisfy the goal. Again, when it comes to addiction, we continue making the mistake of thinking that the goal is to use the drug. *But the goal is really to reduce the pain caused by the hooks.* None of the older behaviorist models gets at this difference. This is why none of them is particularly useful for resolving addictive behavior, though they may be useful for getting you to run more in the morning or stop snoozing your alarm.

In the next chapter, I will introduce the SPARO behavioral model, which more appropriately gets at the complexity of our behavior by expanding on the traditional stimulus-response-reward model.

# PART II

# A SYSTEM THAT LETS ANYONE UNHOOK

# CHAPTER 4

# Introducing SPARO and EAT

F riedrich Nietzsche once said that "To live is to suffer, to survive is to find some meaning in the suffering." There is little doubt that most of us imbue our suffering with meaning. We connect it to our worth, our beliefs about what is possible in life, and the communities we feel connected to. Unfortunately, this often results in our value being anchored in our pain, the hooks keeping us stuck. Too few consciously use the pain like compost, to grow. But the rotten waste in our lives can produce fertile soil we can use to grow stronger.

Many people go about their lives barely noticing the pull of their hooks and manage the discomfort with little challenge. But that's not how it was for Aliyah. Not since childhood.

Aliyah couldn't remember whether it started when she was in first grade, but she was certain that life wasn't normal after that. That was when the whole thing with her cousin happened. "The thing" was the name Aliyah gave the experience that produced her biggest hook— mistrust in others due to her cousin's repeated sexual abuse. When she first tried to tell her family about her cousin's behavior, they didn't believe her. It wasn't even just that they didn't believe her. They actually blamed her and called her a liar, saying she was trying to cause a problem in the family. They punished Aliyah for speaking the truth because the truth was too uncomfortable for everyone to bear. Whenever the abuse recurred and was once again brought up, and denied, Aliyah's primary hook took hold of her, dragging her down.

Aliyah couldn't shake that feeling of complete invalidation, no matter how hard she tried. Her family's betrayal and mistrust became yet another hook that constantly tugged, pulled, and pained her. It reminded her that, even when she was severely hurt and needing help, those close to her were more likely to turn away than reach out. When our support network breaks down, it becomes endlessly more difficult to recover from trauma. As Dr. Bessel van der Kolk pointed out in his seminal book *The Body Keeps the Score*, when our adaptive responses to stressful events, such as rape, are blocked, our body continues to send distress signals long after we experience the trauma.[1] The adaptive response to abuse is to be taken care of. Aliyah couldn't have that, so the impact of her trauma lingered for years.

Throughout our time working together, Aliyah always understood that being sexually abused by her cousin at such a young age affected her well-being. But no matter how hard she tried to acknowledge this fact, her grasp on it didn't change the gnawing feeling she'd have every time she met someone new. It was hard to trust anyone. This was especially debilitating when it came to men who showed any romantic interest in her. It was as if every fiber of her being was screaming "DANGER, DANGER!" even when the men were genuine and simply wanted to connect. And that was all Aliyah really wanted, herself.

In addition to being sexually abused by her cousin and witnessing her parents' violence, Aliyah was coerced by her mother to participate in sex exchanges for drugs. Later, she was put into a witness protection program after testifying about the murder of a close friend. It wouldn't be an exaggeration to say that, if you could visualize Aliyah's body embedded with hooks, you'd have a difficult time counting them all. They'd been embedded so deeply, and for so long, that she simply took them for granted. It's hard to imagine that Aliyah barely remembered all of the horrors inflicted on her.

Not all the clients I've worked with have experienced the magnitude and severity of Aliyah's hooks. But the commonality is that this is what happens to people forced to undergo relentless trauma. They repress their memories as a form of defense. And whether you remember them or not, these events leave an indelible mark. Even if you're not conscious of it.

It was in the midst of all this pulling and tugging and deeply felt pain that Aliyah was also trying to raise five girls. She didn't want her past to dictate how she showed up as a mother, and yet, she didn't seem to be able to avoid it. So, is it any wonder that she turned to drugs and alcohol when she could find no other means of relief?

The same holds for Linda. Her experiences of growing up, of extreme perfectionism and acute social anxiety, made it hard for her to feel comfortable in front of others. Her anxiety was obvious to anyone who paid attention and cared. But there weren't many of those people around. And the fact that no one recognized Linda's symptoms for what they were made her anxiety intolerable. The only option she saw for dealing with these tremendous waves of panic was cannabis. *That* became her support system.

And then there is Jaylen. He didn't want to escape into porn; he wanted to connect and feel loved and cared for. His inability to connect with women started with the neglect and conflict he'd experienced with his single mother. Starved for connection and affection, he sought any available source of relief from his fear that intimacy and love were unreachable fantasies. Not knowing how to pursue and handle true intimacy, he kept going back to the closest thing he knew. It's why millions of Americans use porn daily—to escape their inability to connect in more fulfilling ways.

Aliyah, Linda, and Jaylen's individual experiences, like those of thousands of others I've worked with, are very different. Acknowledging the end results (the compulsive behaviors) of these painful ordeals is the start. But *then* returning to the very beginning—the onset of the habitual behaviors—gets one to dive deep, full of curiosity, revealing personal experiences that have been unacknowledged, or misunderstood. This method pulls out hidden meaning and beliefs, allowing us to study the impact of the compulsive behavior on body, mind, spirit. That process enables us to find ways to unwind the negative impact of the current behaviors to create real and lasting change.

## STRINGING IT ALL TOGETHER

My wife, Sophie, and I moved into our dream home in August 2019, mere months before the arrival of the COVID-19 shutdowns. Our family of five had outgrown our little townhouse and we needed a backyard. We were elated when we found a house we could afford, which is not a small feat in Los Angeles. The move itself happened very quickly. Once the movers loaded up the house with our boxes, Sophie and her friends went to work. They took over the living room, organizing and placing everything, thoughtfully, in its place. Recognizing that organization was never my strong suit, they sent me downstairs to help unpack the large number of boxes in the garage.

Everything was going well until I reached into a Christmas decorations box. I was greeted with a large mess of tangled-up Christmas lights. I wasn't sure exactly how many lights were there, but the box held more than a few. No matter how hard I tugged and pulled, the large green ball of wires didn't budge. In fact, my tugging simply seemed to make things worse. After ten minutes, I was ready to give up. How expensive could a ball of Christmas lights be, anyway? But just then, something caught my eye. It was a two-inch wire that ended in a stubby plug—something I could actually use to solve this puzzle. It wasn't easy, but I was able to pull that plug through a loop it was stuck in, and then another. After a few more tries, that two-inch piece of wire grew to at least five times its size. Not wanting to lose momentum, I continued releasing more and more of the wire. Within fifteen minutes, I had the first strands of Christmas lights untangled. With my new skill, I was able to more quickly untangle the other seven Christmas light bundles. Completing the task I had been ready to give up on took me a total of thirty minutes of focused effort.

While Sophie wasn't quite as impressed as I'd hoped, I realized something profound as I was relaying the story to her. My work with people who struggle is not all that different than the Christmas lights project I had just completed.

When people first come to me, they look like a tangled mess. An impossible puzzle. They've been tugged on, pulled at, and messed with, but it's only made things worse. When I examine their entire knotted-up life—from the end to the beginning—I can typically identify a single loose end, almost too small to seem meaningful. Then, if I take my time and honor that little start, freeing it gradually, I see before me a shining, bright, and beautiful human—just like those sparkling lights.

As I've built this system, I have taken part in incredibly emotional and empowering sessions. People have been able to more quickly connect to their underlying struggles, given this judgment-free approach. Connecting the dots provided them with deep insight that is freeing and illuminating. The shifts that followed were sometimes quick and sometimes drawn out. But they were nearly always transformational. In the process, I've had to learn to flesh out ways to measure success differently and more realistically. I've had to leave behind the black/white, success/failure, abstinence/addiction language so common in the addiction treatment world.

This chapter will introduce you to the Unhooked Method, a road map by which anyone can chart their own path out of any addiction or unhealthy and compulsive habits. I will start by introducing the major components of the system in sequence:

1. The SPARO behavioral model (Stimulus–Perception–Activation–Response–Outcome)
2. The EAT principles (Explore–Accept–Transform)

After you read the overview of each of the components, we'll begin working through the method in the same way as I do with my clients. In this way, you will use the following chapters as a sort of "choose your own adventure" book, allowing you to focus your efforts on the areas that are most relevant to you right now.

## SPARO

In the previous chapters, I discussed the reasons that the behaviorist model of Stimulus → Response → Reward is insufficient when it comes to explaining complex human behavior. If someone passes by and yells "Hey, idiot!" at you, seemingly out of nowhere, their choice words are not the only factor that dictates your response toward them. Instead, how you will respond is also based on your understanding of what took place. If you see the person as an inconsiderate a**hole, you're likely to respond differently than if you consider them a dear friend who is simply poking fun. This is a central tenet of cognitive behavioral therapy (CBT). The power of an Activating event comes from your Beliefs about the event, which lead to Consequences—ABC. It is our processing of events that gives them meaning and makes us act.

Obviously, this thinking stands in sharp contrast to the behaviorist approach.

The CBT model recognizes the power of our internal feelings and thoughts in motivating action. Still, I consider beliefs to be a big black box that needs to be further broken down. That's the origin of the SPARO model:

Under the SPARO model, the Stimulus (activating event or trigger) creates a cascade of internal processes—Perception, Activation, and Response selection. These processes, in turn, lead to an Outcome. The model incorporates learning about our internal processes and breaks down "beliefs" into Perception and the early stages of Response. Finally, it incorporates trauma-based work by considering the emotional and physiological Activation associated with our experience. The idea that traumatic experiences change not only our thinking but also our body's natural responses has been sorely missing from behavioral change literature.

We all want simplicity, but we also want effectiveness, and this model breaks down the behavioral process in a way that better allows us to understand where we can intervene to create change. For example, in the earlier scenario about a passerby yelling out "Hey, idiot!" (the Stimulus), we can imagine one perceiving this as a slight by a rude stranger with the outcome now potentially being an aggressive Response and an escalation of the situation.

But this is very different if the perception is of a friend trying to be funny; this time, you may experience being delighted (Activation), either choosing to smile, yell out "Hey, Jessie!" or shoot back a witty comeback of your own (Response). When you choose to shoot back a reply, there is almost no probability of a negative escalation. Same exact stimulus, completely distinct perceptions, and the process and outcomes couldn't be more different. Such is the power of our internal processing.

Once you fully understand this model, you have four different stages in which to intervene to change the future outcomes (at the Stimulus, the Perception, the Activation, or at the Response itself). I will detail these options in later chapters.

Processing the outcomes of our behavior requires a systematic approach, and that's where EAT comes in.

### THE EAT PRINCIPLES

We don't need to understand the SPARO behavioral model to continue living. As I mentioned earlier, most people never think that deeply about their own behavior. But, if you ever encounter problems with the way you experience life (and you have, if you're reading this book), you become very interested in figuring out "What the hell is wrong?" And that's where the SPARO model helps—it allows you to understand your behavior much more deeply. It helps explain the factors that are driving your actions and leading to the outcomes you're experiencing. But people can get overwhelmed at the need to analyze their life in this much detail. Have you ever stayed up at night, thinking about moments in your life over and over? At times, this level of analysis can lead us to feel consumed by the need to carefully dissect every interaction, every incident, and every meaningful event or relationship. This sort of *analysis paralysis* can leave us even more confused, ashamed, and beaten down than simply escaping.

This is why I feel it is important to provide a systematic method for using SPARO to learn and change. Hence, the EAT principles:

- **Explore**—After a negative outcome, most of us want to escape, retreat, or ignore the consequences. We want to take action to reduce the pain, embarrassment, or discomfort we're feeling. But this is a mistake. Moments of failure offer the best learning opportunities. Those feelings are there to give you information. Pain lets you know your body needs attention; ignore it or numb it, and chances are, it will get worse. The same goes for our feelings. When something didn't turn out as intended, it provides us with the perfect opportunity to reflect and adjust. Ignore the lesson, and it will return again, continuing to worsen until we're ready. Most of us end up struggling with addiction because we tried to escape pain, and it didn't work. We don't typically become ready to do something about it until the outcomes become so painful they bring us to our knees. Joseph Campbell once said that "the cave you fear to enter holds the treasure you seek."[2] If you're ready to truly explore the reason behind the failures you're experiencing, you'll discover an incredible path to change. And for most, simply understanding our failures makes us feel better.

- Accept—Unfortunately, while awareness often reduces anxieties it does not, by itself, lead to change. Once my clients discover the reasons for their downward spiral, most want to jump into action immediately. But I believe that to be premature. Before we can go about changing what needs to be addressed, we have to come to terms with and accept what's already been. We can't undo the past, nor can we shut the door on our previous consequences. Accepting ourselves, our misdeeds, our experiences, and even the actions of others as the stepping stones that brought us to this moment is the only way to truly detach from the suffering they bring. We can understand, through exploration, that our trauma led to troubling coping behavior. But if we try to cut away the parts of ourselves that were hurt, we'll have to deal with them again in the future. Acceptance is about coming to terms with everything that brought us to this moment, and understanding that this moment is the beginning of everything we are going to create in the future. Without acceptance, we are working from a false reality. Acceptance allows you to face the truth, without judgment, and gain a sense of peace. It's a necessary component of all long-term change.
- Transform—Once you've come to understand what brought you here and have accepted it as the only real truth, you're ready to transform. It's ironic that, in order to change, you first have to accept what you are. But so it is. The reason transformation sounds so troublesome to us is because many of us have tried it before, but without a true

understanding of what needed to change. And often, we tried to fix the wrong thing. It's a little like having your car make a noise while driving and then changing the oil, because it's what you know how to do. If you'd taken it to a mechanic, they may have told you the car needed a new timing belt or spark plug. But you didn't explore what was really wrong, you just fixed what you knew how to. So, it didn't work, and the noise continued and even got worse. But it's not the oil's fault. Transformation can be an exciting and evolutionary time; it is about changing how you behave, how you think, and how you react. You can create massive change quickly in this stage, because you've prepared yourself for it.

The EAT principles provide you with a step-by-step process to follow when exploring a specific outcome as you work through the SPARO model. Following this process, you can better understand experiences, grasp and acknowledge their impact, and then alter them for the future. I have found that it's important to do these in sequence, recognizing that they build on one another and evolve every time you work through them, continuing perpetually in the journey toward a better and more fulfilling life.

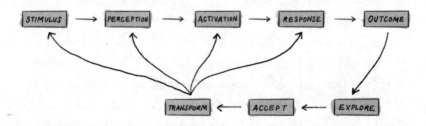

Overall, the EAT principles allow you to understand yourself, come to terms with your current situation, and identify tools to move beyond it. They help you get unstuck, let you know when you're ready to move on, and provide you with guardrails to hold on to.

## OWNING OUR TRUTH: THE IMPORTANCE OF
## HONEST SELF-EXPRESSION

During a recent interview, I was asked, "What would be the single most important thing you would tell anyone who is currently struggling with addiction?" For me, the answer was immediately clear: "We have to stop lying."

Sure, we lie about our actions and our behavior. But many of us who struggle with addictions and bad habits lie about so much more. We lie about aspects of our personality, for fear of being rejected. We lie and hide past experiences from the world, for fear of being judged. We even lie to ourselves, doing everything we can to conceal and keep quiet anything that makes us uncomfortable or awkward.

Aliyah lied about her history of sexual abuse and hid it from everyone she knew, thinking it made her dirty and damaged. Linda hid her social anxiety because she believed others would think less of her. It drove her to overwhelming stress and anxiety, unable to function without vomiting. Jaylen hid his insecurity surrounding women and his need for validation in sports and heavy weights. But he escaped to porn and massage parlor jaunts that nearly destroyed his life. I hid my social anxiety in alcohol, then cannabis, and eventually meth and the money and guns from drug dealing. False security, ego, and bravado were our cloaks. Until they failed us all.

We have to stop hiding in lies.

As we step into the process of change, one thing is more important than any other. We have to deal with *whatever* is true for us in the moment. There will be pain, there will be friction and disagreements, there will be loss. But if we accept these and learn to become present and experience them fully, there will also be joy, connection, intimacy, and fulfillment. The seeming juxtaposition is simply an embodiment of reality—these opposing reactions are echoes of one another. When we feel joy receiving an "A" on an exam, it's because of the hard work we put into studying. When we lose someone close to us, our sadness is a mirror of the intimacy and connection our relationship brought. In trying to erase the experience of the former, we detach ourselves from the latter as well. Pain reflects Joy.

Too many of us live either in regret of the past or anxiety about the future. We dissociate from our current state, unsatisfied with what it is delivering. Instead of living in the present, we transmute ourselves to other times as a form of escape. This all happens subconsciously, of course, but for many it happens constantly. The discomfort of the present moment isn't to be avoided—it is to be embraced and understood. Only then can we move forward.

Let us be clear—*all we can ever do is our best*—and this single fact is true in all moments:

- When you've scored the winning point in a volleyball game, you're doing your best. But you're also doing your best as you're throwing up while you wait for a bus.
- When you finally achieve your first six months of sobriety, you're doing your best. But you're also doing your best when you take another hit because the shame of your early sexual abuse experience has made you unable to get close to anyone.
- When you're graduating from a PhD program, you're doing your best. But you're also doing your best when you're struggling with your identity and decide that selling drugs is a good way to support your music career.

The problem is that, for the clients I deal with, what they believe is "their best" and what they're truly capable of are not the same. Their beliefs about themselves are distorted by their experience. And so their best is subdued, their potential muted, and their hopes crushed. Defeated, alone, hopeless, and desperate, they seek help, hardly believing it will come.

The hardest aspect of my work is making a person feel safe enough to share their truth after a lifetime of training in lying to fit in and avoid being cast out. I have to shake them, jar them, and help them believe.

How do you trust a helper's promise of redemption, when everyone you've known for decades has called you unredeemable? How do you believe that those who are in your corner right now won't abandon you when the going gets tough after it feels like *everyone* in your life has left you? How do you hope for something better when, time and time again, you've been disappointed?

These aren't simple questions, and the answers aren't always obvious. And so, I have found one common thread among nearly everyone who's made it to the other side—a perplexing ability to suspend disbelief for *just* long enough to find a shred of hope to hold on to in trying to make things different. The ability to believe that there is something else out there, without clear evidence of its existence, isn't always easy. But when you find it, you need to squeeze every little bit of it out. You must look, *anywhere you can*, for inspiration, hope, and support from others that may become part of your path to deliverance. I've found that path myself, relying on help from others and then walking forward. I have since been doing everything I can to help pave it farther for those who come behind me.

That's what the Unhooked Method is about.

In the following chapters, I break down each of the elements of the SPARO behavioral model. I will explain the way in which each feeds into compulsive-addictive behavior and behavioral change, in general. After explaining the significance of each phase and its importance in the overall behavioral chain, I will break down the EAT process within that phase. In this way, you'll be able to work along with the book and gain insight into your own behavior, starting now.

## CHAPTER 5

# Let's Start at the End...The Outcome

$\boxed{\textit{STIMULUS}} \longrightarrow \boxed{\textit{PERCEPTION}} \longrightarrow \boxed{\textit{ACTIVATION}} \longrightarrow \boxed{\textit{RESPONSE}} \longrightarrow \boxed{\textit{OUTCOME}}$

I began the book by making this point—people always come to me seeking help after life has gone terribly wrong. They lost a job, woke up in jail having been arrested for a third DUI, got threatened with the end of their marriage, or fell twenty feet off a retaining wall (all actual experiences of clients I've worked with). There is often an urgency to the initial search, focused on resolving the disaster at hand. This is not a bad thing, per se. But it does mean that many clients aren't actually looking to stop drinking or using, or to truly change their behavior. They want to change the outcome. The consequences.

But they *are* very motivated to change.

And that's a good enough start for me.

It's the very tip of that Christmas light.

This is why we will start our SPARO discussion where my clients typically begin their journey, at the end. This is very different than starting out by focusing on the behavior ("Response" in the SPARO model) that caused the outcome. Unfortunately, that behavior is where *most* treatment will urge you to focus your effort. "Just stop drinking," they'll say. But that approach hasn't worked for decades. Starting at the end point that is making you want to change in the first place makes more sense, because we're focusing on what *you* want to change, instead of on what *they* (and maybe you, too, before reading this) think you need to change.

It's a question of motivation.

Being motivated to engage in the change process is monumentally important when it comes to compulsive behaviors and habits. Changing behavior is difficult as it is, but when the behavior is entrenched and has been serving a protective role for decades, it is that much more difficult to transform. Clients are more likely to change for the long term if they are internally (sometimes called intrinsically) motivated. Internal motivation to change would entail engaging in the process for personal satisfaction and growth, and not for some specific consequences or rewards, which would be defined as external motivation. Research has shown us that *both* internal and external motivation sources can help initiate behavioral change. But high internal motivation predicts better persistence, performance, and improved psychological well-being.[1]

And you're looking for long-term change.

In one study, individuals at risk for coronary artery disease (CAD) participated in a three-year lifestyle-change program to reduce their risk of health problems and death. The external motivation to take part in the study was the referral from the doctor. But that referral alone didn't predict success. The findings showed that *both* the patient's and the doctor's orientation toward an internal ability to change predicted improved diet, more exercise, and less smoking by the end of the program. Those higher in internal motivation were also more likely to complete the program. The findings showed that our own perception of our ability to change mattered, and so did the beliefs of others involved in our care![2] This is known as a Growth Mindset, and we'll discuss it at length later in the book.

In my own story, when my back was against the wall, the outcome I wanted to change was the prospect of ending up in prison for fifteen to twenty years. My attorney made things very clear: "If you don't get help for your drug use, the judge is going to throw the book at you. You're going to do a lot of time," he told me. There it was. My external motivation—prison time as punishment if I *didn't* go to treatment. I didn't have a lot of internal motivation to quit drugs or become a better person. Not yet, anyway. But staying out of prison was motivation enough for me.

I don't believe people have to want to change their use, not initially. I've seen hundreds of individuals who simply wanted to get out of trouble or get their loved ones off their back. They got some actual help, learned some tools, and were forever transformed. The change can be nearly instantaneous, or it can take months. Still, for long-term success, we're going to have to find a way to move that motivation from the outside, in.

And so, when someone comes to me with an outcome they're trying to change, I look for only one thing—what is driving *their* desire to take action now? Is it that they want to keep their marriage alive? Are they looking to save their job? Did they embarrass themselves and are looking to save face? Did a serious accident make them want to be sure they stick around long enough to see their grandchildren grow up?

I don't care what it is. I have to discover what motivates *them*. Because with that in hand, we can actually set about working on transformation. One of the most common mistakes we make in the addiction field is to think we need to tell people how important it is for them to change. But telling someone they need to change is almost always guaranteed to only do one thing—create resistance.

One of the quickest ways to find that motivating factor is to allow a person to share their own story of how they ended up here. To do this, I do my best to let a person tell me everything *they* see as leading up to them entering my office (or Zoom room). Some start at their childhood; others identify a distinct moment at which their life took a turn—a death, a divorce, having children, losing a home, and so on.

You'd be amazed at how many of my clients report that each of their previous attempts at help started with a very simple assertion: you're here because you're an alcoholic/addict. Everything else that was part of their story was therefore a *result* of their condition, rather than the *cause* of it. In this way, most addiction helpers believe that the addiction "disease" is the only true hook, and everything else is simply a symptom of the hook's effects.

I see things exactly in reverse, and use the end result simply as a jumping-off point to uncover what truly matters.

For Meredith, the sharing of her story started at a very distinct point in time—on her actual birthday. It was during that week that her husband lost his job, she told me. The couple had young children and had recently bought a new home. A month before, they felt that they'd finally made it. And then, as if in an instant—anxiety about her husband's ability to find work and continue supporting their newly formed family took over. It was quickly joined by resentment, and fear. These were all new feelings for Meredith, and she didn't know how to cope. She was too embarrassed to share the news with her family, and the hiding and pretending made it worse. Her husband was struggling, too, and his insecurities made it impossible to talk to him about the situation.

Meredith felt trapped, and so she started leaning on alcohol more regularly. It worked to turn down the frightful anxiety that wouldn't let her get through the day. It gave her the space to sit next to her husband and not push and prod him about his job prospects. It made it easier to lie to her parents about what was going on. And no one noticed for years. Indeed, her husband liked it better when she was drunk, because he didn't need to deal with her anxieties on top of his.

But the situation kept devolving month by month, and year by year. Meredith's husband kept struggling with work, and their waning intimacy created deep fractures in the relationship. By the time they found me, they were on the brink of divorce. Meredith was drinking at least two bottles of wine every day in addition to taking anxiety medication.

She would pass out by six p.m., and periodically black out and embarrass herself and the family. The outcome seemed perplexing for such a high-functioning woman. But it made all the sense in the world when taken in the context of everything the family had been through.

Rather than focus on Meredith's drinking and her "alcoholism," I wanted to focus on fixing her relationship and opening up communication and intimacy with her husband and family members. She had lost all respect for her husband, he was struggling with depression and anxiety, and they were both losing hope daily. Alcohol saved their marriage as much as it was destroying their lives. They needed some deep work. I also wanted to find some quick real-world solutions to improve their overall situation.

Different approaches, without a doubt.

In the following section of this chapter, and the rest of Part 2 of the book, I will lead you through the SPARO and EAT processes. We will begin at the outcome, and then work on using specific tools to identify the most effective next stage of SPARO for you to focus on. Once you've completed the EAT process in the Outcome stage, you can keep reading along *or* jump directly to the SPARO stage that is most relevant to you, continuing your analysis there. Each person may have a different initial stage that most obviously needs attention. Typically, you will identify more than one potential stage for initial intervention. I recommend beginning with the stage that will provide you with the most immediate relief and change. Then, you can continue the process of evolution with this newfound relief serving as wind at your back, helping make the journey easier.

## APPLYING THE EAT PRINCIPLES TO THE OUTCOME STAGE

### Explore

If we are going to create sustainable, effective, long-term change, we have to begin by identifying your underlying hooks. That's what exploration is about here. It's important to approach exploration without judgment. This phase usually reveals unexpected factors that may have been driving your behavior. That's exactly the point. Don't hold back. Holding back and being anything less than as open as you can be will just slow us down.

To begin the Exploration process, you're going to look at your struggles from three different vantage points.

### A Bird's-Eye View

You'll start out by identifying the major low and high points in your life, as they relate to the struggles that brought you here. You'll specifically identify the initial appearance of major difficulties and the factors that were most relevant then, as well as identifying other times when your habits were at their worst. For instance, were you lonely? Did you experience a substantial trauma? Were you socially anxious and wanted to fit in with friends who were using? As you identify the factors related to all your low points, patterns will emerge. You should also identify points in your life when your struggle was least problematic (we'll use this to identify strengths and potential tools to use later). I've included an exercise called Mapping Your Struggle Journey in the SPARO Worksheets section (Appendix B) to help you in the identification process. So, please refer to it after you have finished reading this chapter. Doing this will offer you two very important experiences:

1. Better clarity about the factors that increase, and decrease, the likelihood of your struggles. Typically, this work helps us identify clear patterns that emerge quickly—specific circumstances and factors that are related to greater struggles or improved functioning. These factors will become important as you go about constructing a path forward.

2. A dismantling of the biggest and most damaging beliefs about addictive tendencies—that addiction problems only get worse over time. This "disease concept" belief is an important rationale behind the strict abstinence-only and

fear-based approach to addiction help. If things always get worse, you'd better stop now or there will be hell to pay. Most of the people I've worked with find that their journey is far less linear and straightforward, with struggles moving up and down in terms of severity over years.

This experience typically brings out stories that help clients connect to hooks related to their health, relationships, work, emotional well-being, family, and big life events. By the time we're done with the severity timeline (the Mapping Your Struggle Journey exercise, page 227), we have an incredible idea of exactly how clients got to struggling the way they have.

### *The Starting Point*
Next, you'll dive deeply into the very first point in your life when things got REALLY bad—you need to understand everything about what was going on during that point. You'll analyze the people in your life, the environment you were in, the experiences you were having around that time, and the reasons for making the choice you made to start the behavior. You need to understand the motivation, the purpose, and the benefit that your behavior first provided you with. Use examples from stories I told you about other clients to help you understand the level of detail you're looking for.

It's important for you to know where your struggles began. Go back to the very beginning and detail *everything* that made up your life and drove your decision to drink, use drugs, watch porn, gamble, lose yourself in video games or television, seek validation through affairs or cybersex, or start relying on ice cream and pizza to feel okay.

Did drinking help you overcome shyness? Did cannabis help you fit in or handle some other struggles? Did pills make your trouble at home disappear? Did porn or online sex satisfy your desire for physical intimacy despite your low self-esteem and fear of emotional connection?

In this portion of the work, I rely on one of my favorite techniques—
storytelling. So, go all the way to the very beginning. Pick a moment,
an experience that truly takes you back to those earliest days. Like my
first big drinking event, or Linda's first try of cannabis by the side of
the bus. What drove you to use? Take advantage of the Mapping Your
Struggle Journey exercise you completed to help you.

---

### A Note on Storytelling

Stories serve as powerful pathways to long-hidden facts about a person's
life. The storytelling part of exploration is my fact-finding mission, my information gathering phase, and it is crucial for the work. It's in this early phase
that I begin to get a clear look at the hooks that have been driving my clients' behavior. I can't ask for these directly because most clients don't know
their own hooks.

My typical initial question is often simply, "Tell me one of your most
important life stories, a story that explains what life was like for you before
we met." I make sure that clients understand I'm not searching for "good" or
"bad" stories, rather, for stories with meaning and relevance. It was through
the use of storytelling that the sexual abuse and family reaction story in
Aliyah's life came about. Storytelling allowed Jaylen to first connect to the
anxiety he felt whenever he visited his mother, which then exposed their
complex history and relationship. Until that point, his mother rarely featured
in his telling of his struggles. People repress many memories, but if you stay
curious and let them get started at the little bit of memory they have, then, as
with those strings of Christmas lights, they can unravel until the tangled web
of memories is laid out in front of them. And we find a place to start.

Once I learn about one story, I may ask for more, always looking for
common themes and facts to be explored more in depth in later stages.
Who was involved in this person's life? What have their relationships been
like? Have they undergone any serious traumatic experiences? Were they

supported as children or abandoned, controlled, or abused? Do they see life as generally good or bad? Are they connected to their feelings or only to the facts of their story? I keep exploring until I have a good feel for the person's life experience broadly, understanding that every first exploration journey is going to leave major gaps.

Patterns inevitably show up. There are blueprints hidden in the beliefs, themes, and assumptions that permeate every account my clients retrieve from their past. The details I pick up here become the fertile soil I use in the following phases.

### *Your Most Recent Struggles*

Finally, we'll analyze a recent scenario that ended in an outcome that made you, and those around you, believe that change was needed. This could be the specific event that made you want to pick up this book, something that happened last week, or a significant event from the last holiday season. It needs to be recent and meaningful. Identify all relevant aspects of the SPARO stages that were involved.

You can use an exercise called Rewriting Your Response Patterns (page 240), to work out this scenario, as well as process your earliest exposure experience (as outlined earlier).

Here's a quick example of how to use this exercise: Let's say you drank too much at dinner and you slurred your words in front of your family and said some inappropriate things that made your wife and cousins angry with you. If the inappropriate language happened at nine p.m., we'll mark that as the outcome, and note when it happened. When did the drinking start? If the drinking started at six p.m., what were you doing right before dinner?

What actually made you want to drink a lot by the time you got to your uncle's for dinner? Did you have a fight with your wife? A tough and stressful day at work? Are you going through financial problems and had a look at an outstanding bill at lunch that day? How far back do you have to go to identify the most proximal stimulus that made you want to lose yourself and forget about life that night? We'll use that as the starting point—the Stimulus.

Next, we'll need to look at your Perception—how did you internalize that stimulus? Did you take it as a sign your marriage is failing? A belief that you may lose your job? An image of having to give up your home because you can't pay for it? Remember that our perceptions of the world aren't necessarily true or objective, but your Perception of the Stimulus *is* what caused you to become activated.

Your Activation made you feel something—were you scared? Angry? Ashamed? Anxious? Hopeless? Was the feeling a familiar one or did it take you by surprise? If you struggle identifying your feeling, check out the Feelings Wheel in our resource page at adijaffe.com /unhooked.

Whatever they were, the feelings you had were uncomfortable and made you want to act to stop them from happening. The feelings made you create a Response to deal with them. How did you come up with the potential responses you took to stop the uncomfortable feelings? In the example I gave earlier, drinking was obviously one of the potential options. Were there other options? What made you choose drinking as the final response?

These are the set of questions I want you to think of when analyzing the recent event that made you behave in a manner that brought on the outcome you want to change. Obviously, there is more to drinking than the alcohol itself. The important thing here is to gain an understanding of the *factors* that brought you to the outcome.

---

**PRO TIP: Alignment and Inclusion**—Remember that the more points of view you get, the more clarity and knowledge you'll gain. If you want to have even better awareness into the parts of SPARO that you need to work on, this is a great opportunity to conduct some exploration with family members and loved ones. How do they see the timeline of your struggles? What do they remember in the past that you may not? There can be conflict and disagreement about certain facts and stories, but on the whole you'll typically find some agreement on your general path to "now." Creating consensus and team building at this phase is crucial to the future success of the entire process. Getting everyone on board early, if possible, is critical.

## Accept

As you may have already experienced, unraveling all this can be unnerving both for you and for those dear to you. I have never been part of a transformation process in which exploring one's journey doesn't trigger hooks and create discomfort in everyone involved. Addiction doesn't happen in a vacuum. You didn't develop your problematic habits without cause. Oftentimes, being silent and numb is simpler and easier than confronting and feeling. The Exploration phase brings up a lot for most people. Acceptance is about making peace with the feelings that come up and the path you have taken.

Typically, this initial Exploration phase reveals some difficult-to-accept hooks. Your road to this moment has been marked by painful truths. These include your own past misdeeds and consequences, long-repressed battles and scars, moral regrets, and deeply hidden relationship conflicts and controversies. It makes sense that your behavior is driven by such intense battles. The primary role of the addictive behavior has been to allow you to regain control and avoid pain. But understanding this alone does not make the reality of shame about the situation easier to deal with.

This is why Acceptance is so crucial for transformation. Too often, I see clients who want to rush immediately from exploration to transformation. Once they've uncovered the underlying reminders of pain, many people want to carve away at them. This makes sense, because pain is unpleasant, but it also rejects their humanity. It sends the message that "this part of me is damaged and I must purge it." Regrettably, ridding ourselves of parts we don't like is not possible.

We won't make that mistake here.

Your experiences have established you as you are. You may regret some of them, you may wish them away, and yet they remain forever within you. In the movie *Eternal Sunshine of the Spotless Mind*, we get a sense of how complex and terrible things can get when we try to erase parts of ourselves. The process of acceptance is an important step, as it allows you to gain approval, acknowledgment, and tolerance of a simple but powerful fact: *you have been doing your best.* If you knew better and were capable of more at the time, you'd have acted differently. But your past lack of knowledge does *not* need to limit your future actions.

This powerful realization allows you to make peace with aspects of yourself you may be critical of, allowing you to move forward and get better. If it's true that you've done your best to date, given what you know, then new knowledge, new practices, and new experiences will change what is possible for you. And the same logic applies to the misdeeds of others. Acceptance is about recognizing that others in your life were doing the best they could, too. Carrying on the pain will in no way serve you, or them.

*We succeed, or we learn.* This is the primary lesson I took away from my own experiences, my view into the lives of thousands, and my deep engagement in what it means to have a Growth Mindset. With this understanding cemented, you are better prepared to move toward true transformation.

I teach my clients that the primary value of past mistakes is to teach us, so that we can improve and move forward better equipped. The focus is *not* on the pain itself, but on the impact of the pain. You want to learn the lessons of the experience and identify the potential changes in your behavior that could lead to different outcomes. In this way, the Unhooked Method is about being proactive, solution focused, and judgment-free. This way of looking at current situations typically provides my clients with more hope than they've felt in decades.

For example, when it comes to Perception, there is plenty of research showing that a belief in powerlessness creates more disempowerment. For me, there's no place for it. This is why I stay away from calling people "addicts," "alcoholics," or any of those silly and limiting terms. We are not defined by our problems; we're defined by how we handle them. So, the goal of acceptance this early in the process is to allow you to accept your current Outcome as a learning opportunity and the natural result of "your best" to date. We want to connect to some appreciation of the journey through a less judgmental lens. In the process, you're injected with hope, awareness, and appreciation for the ways in which you have shown up in your life. If you can get there this early in the process, you are well poised to consider the changes that need to be made later.

### Transform

The goal of Transformation is to utilize the low-judgment, higher-awareness state created through Explore and Accept, to get into action.

Once you understand what brought you here from these three very different vantage points (bird's-eye, starting, and most recent), I want you to ask yourself a question: "In which of the SPARO stages am I likely to find the most effective starting point for changing myself in a way that will change my behavior?"

I do my best to help my clients pick the stages of the SPARO model that each of the factors they uncovered falls into:

1. Stimulus (Chapter 6)—Internal and external triggers and experiences that put things in motion
2. Perception (Chapter 7)—Beliefs, lenses, and interpretations of reality that filter your experience
3. Activation (Chapter 8)—Physiological and emotional reactions to your experiences
4. Response (Chapter 9)—The manner in which you choose a specific response from your available responses menu

Consider what you learned using all three vantage points. Is social influence showing up in all these examinations? If so, you may want to start with Stimulus. Are you finding that feelings of isolation or anxiety are always part of it? Then, starting with the Activation stage makes sense. If a victim mentality, lack of belief in your own self-worth, or not having a purpose are the problem, it could make sense to start with Perception. As you complete this exercise with each new learning cycle, you will only need to begin your exploration by looking at a recent Outcome to analyze. You will not need to go back and review your entire past again.

With your learnings bucketed, you can choose what you want to transform first.

I recommend exploring changes in no more than one or two stages at a time, and placing your efforts on those that are most likely to provide you with a quick initial path to change. This can help you gain momentum and even *more* motivation to keep going. One of the common mistakes I find at this point is that many clients have a difficult time choosing where to start.

To help ease this choice, I'd like to remind you of the importance of concentrating on things you can control. This concept is exemplified through the Spheres of Influence exercise, included on page 228, which provides you with a structured method to help divide your focus appropriately. The gist, for now, is this—too many people center much of their anxieties and concerns on areas of life that they exert no control over. If you can, split the universe into the following three categories:

1. Things you fully control
2. Things you have influence over
3. Things you don't influence at all

Many of the people I work with put far too much energy into factors that are completely outside their control, and need to rebalance their focus.

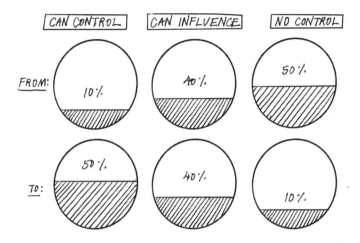

Throughout the following chapters and in each of the SPARO stages, you will use the Spheres of Influence exercise in the Transform stage to think about the fully controllable actions you can take to make a difference in your own life.

Now, it's time for you to make a choice: where will you go next? If you're not sure, move on to the next stage, Stimulus, and work things through from the beginning. But if another stage seems more relevant, head there now! And remember to use the exercises in Appendix B along the way.

# CHAPTER 6

# Stimulus

**O**n a recent flight back from a talk near Boston, while flying 35,000 feet above the earth, the plane started lightly shaking. I noticed the change and braced myself a bit. I don't like turbulence. It reminds me that I'm not on the ground. The guy sitting next to me gripped his armrest too. The shaking typically stops quickly in my experience, so I wasn't too concerned, even if I was a little nervous. But, this time things didn't calm down. Instead, the shaking continued getting worse. It's not an exaggeration to say that, within a minute, the plane felt like it was rocking 6 to 10 feet in all directions. Up, down, left, then back up again. The pilot's voice abruptly came on the speaker system, and simply said, "Everyone, please make sure your seatbelts are on and tightened." He then went silent again. My seatbelt was on, and I tightened it again. But I wasn't comforted. My heart was racing and my anxiety levels were high. I could almost taste the fear in my mouth. I could certainly feel myself shaking. It wasn't just the plane now.

I looked over, and my neighbor looked completely terrified as well. He was staring straight ahead, eyes fixed and hands white-knuckling the seat. My breath was short, and I wasn't seeing him breathing at all. I tried to look outside, but the sky was gray, dark, and thick. Suddenly, the plane dropped, making me levitate from my seat for what felt like a few seconds. Without the seatbelt, my head would have likely hit the overhead luggage compartment. Now, I was in full freak-out mode. I felt my breath shorten. I started thinking about whether I'd ever be able to talk to Sophie, or my kids, again. I was wondering what we were flying above right now, and whether the pilot could make an emergency landing. My mind was racing, and I couldn't get control of it. Again, the pilot came on the speaker system and let us know that we had "hit a rough patch of weather" and he was "taking us up to get above the storm." In a moment, we all felt the plane point up and start to rise. Within about ten seconds, the sky above us started becoming lighter, and the shaking was becoming less erratic. My breath was slowing down substantially. Within twenty seconds, we'd cleared the storm and the plane was flying smoothly through the sky. Inside the plane, it was silent. No one made a sound. We were all happy to be alive. I steadied my breath, looked over at the guy on my right, and gave a half-hearted smile. "I f*cking hate flying," he said to me.

We all hated flying in that moment.

We are most afraid of what we don't understand.[1] The monsters under the bed at night, thinking of death when we lose someone close, and flying 35,000 feet above the earth in a metal tube are all familiar parts of life that can leave us unnerved and troubled because we don't know enough about them. When the pilot told us to fasten our seatbelts, he didn't explain what was happening, and so his words put none of us at ease. But when he came back and explained that we'd hit weather and he was going up to avoid it, we got a bit of clarification. He also gave us an added dose of confidence of real, actionable steps he was taking. We could understand, which meant our fear could abate.

In life, as on that plane, we can stay afraid, or we can learn to better understand our situation.

When it comes to compulsive, addictive, and destructive habits, the fear of seeing ourselves behave in ways that make no sense to us and everyone around us can be terrifying. I often tell my clients' loved ones that, much as they struggle to understand the addiction battle, those who are struggling are often just as confused. We don't understand why we keep failing at trying to make things better.

Typically, once a client and I have undergone the first EAT loop, examining their outcome through the SPARO lens and starting to uncover their hooks, they begin feeling a bit better already. The reasons behind their actions have become clear in a way that resonates far more than the "alcoholic," "addict," or even "addictive personality" platitudes they've heard so many times before. Still, the work has only just begun.

While it's exciting, it's only after completing this phase that we are able to get into the meat of the actual behavioral change work. *Knowledge assuages fear, but it rarely changes behavior.* This is why no explanation of our mental health struggles can create true change. When we begin to understand our hooks, we're better able to explain *why* we behave in certain ways, but we're often no more able to behave differently.

Again, the process following the initial exploration is this:

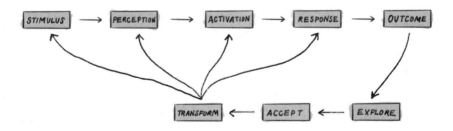

In the previous chapter, you worked on figuring out your hooks. Now it's time to break down the specific SPARO stages that are most relevant to, and most likely to help change, your behavior. The following pages start with Stimulus and move forward. If your analysis of your situation leads you to believe that a different stage may be more relevant to *your* hooks, feel free to go there directly.

## STIMULUS

All actions begin with a stimulus that sets things in motion. It doesn't matter whether you're dealing with an addiction to cocaine, a trip to the mall, or tonight's dinner. Every series of activity begins at this point—the Stimulus can be an object, an action, a thought, a feeling, something someone else does, or a natural event.

In fact, many of us would be surprised at the way in which the most minute details *and* the most involved and complex scenarios orchestrate changes in our behaviors. A certain color, a passing thought, an entire catalog of an artist's music, a specific family member, or a city block. There is nothing too big or too small when it comes to a stimulus.

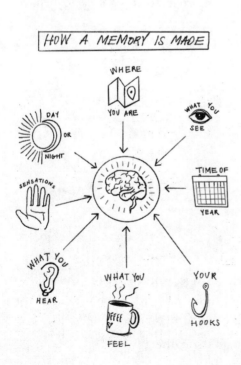

Many stimuli are connected to hooks. But, importantly, a stimulus is *not* typically the hook itself. Instead, stimuli are often simply reminders, or specific details that are connected, as if by a string, to the original hook.

If a street corner reminds you of a long-lost ex, that memory may trigger sadness and feelings of abandonment and loss. We can call the street corner the stimulus that activated the breakup memory and fear of abandonment hook, which led to your drinking at your favorite bar. This is how hooks tug and pull and affect us daily, even when we are unaware of any of it.

My client Michael watched his father nearly take his own life with a gun. The event took place in the backyard of his childhood home, while his father was sitting in a chair by the blowup pool. Michael was young and was eventually taken away from the scene by his sobbing mother. But, while standing there, he watched his father hold a gun to his head, looking straight into Michael's eyes, surrounded by petrified family members and quite a few police officers. Obviously, an event like this would be traumatizing to any of us, let alone to a young boy.

The hooks that this formative experience embedded in him were related to his experience in the moment—the memory of the experience, his abject terror, fear of abandonment, and fear for his father's life. He has done much to repress the terrible feelings he had that day in that backyard, and in the days and weeks to pass, as everyone tried to "get back to normal." Still, because the memory of the experience was seared eternally into his mind, *anything* that would even tangentially connect a present-day experience to this long-ago occurrence had the potential to trigger any thought or strong physical feeling he had in that moment.

Such is the power of memory. Research has shown us that a stimulus can be seen for an *incredibly* short period of time, as short as 4 milliseconds, and still affect our feeling and thinking. By comparison, it takes you 200 milliseconds to begin opening your eyes during a blink. This means that you can recognize a stimulus ten times faster than the blink of an eye.[2] Talk about a powerful but subconscious experience!

Michael came to me after collapsing on the floor of a courthouse building in which he had just won the biggest case of his life. He couldn't understand what was happening. There he went, from one of the most gratifying experiences he'd ever had, to one of the scariest moments he could ever imagine—all in ten minutes. He lay there on the floor, 100-foot vaulted ceilings above him, and people walking all around him, staring. He was certain he was having a heart attack and was about to die.

When we first spoke, he told me that sure, he'd been struggling with anxiety and stress for years, but never like this. Never to the point where he couldn't hold it together around others. He'd never had paramedics called to haul him off to the ER. It seemed ridiculous to him that this would be happening, and he had no explanation for it. "I'm getting everything I've ever wanted in my life," he told me. But when the panic attacks kept coming, he knew he had to do something about them. He couldn't keep living like this.

The thing is that, while a stimulus is processed the moment it's presented, the response to it isn't always. At least, not in a conscious way. That makes it even harder to identify the specific stimuli and hooks they activate. It also makes it more crucial to identify what happens between the stimulus and the response to it. Not only can the stimulus be tangentially and subliminally connected to the hooks it is tugging on, but it can be activated hours, days, or even weeks before the resultant action. This is one of the reasons that, although stress accumulates during working hours, many people resort to drinking, smoking, or taking pills only *after* work. The stress has been collecting all day, but the behavior emerges only hours later.

Sometimes, the trigger itself is so shaming, so painful to acknowledge, that we cast it aside and suppress it from our memory. When I began working with Michael, he wasn't clear about the true cause of the panic attacks. Even after an exhaustive three-hour life history and assessment session, the cause was far from clear. It was only later, in the middle of an intensive ceremonial medicine practice (we'll discuss specific versions in later chapters), that his biggest and most important hook came to light—the sight of his father with a gun to his head, surrounded by frightened family members and anxious police officers. It wasn't that Michael didn't remember that this experience had happened to him. But the connection to his current life, and the potential impact an experience like that might have had on him as a boy, were tossed in the psychological attic—stored but long forgotten.

We just had to figure out why that experience, that stimulus, triggered his recent panic attack in the office building lobby.

We like the analogy of a "trigger" for a stimulus because we associate it with the firing of a bullet. But the reality is that this isn't how a trigger works at all. In fact, as in us, a trigger merely starts a much more complex process. In a gun, the pulling of the trigger releases an internal spring mechanism, which discharges the stored energy in the spring. That spring then releases a hammer that strikes a primer and ignites the stored gunpowder. The explosion of the gunpowder then creates pressure that propels the bullet through the chamber. If any of these elements in the process are missing, damaged, or altered, the bullet will never fire. Depending on how you look at it, the trigger alone didn't make the bullet fire at all—but without the trigger, the rest of the process that caused the bullet to fire never would have happened.

HOW PEOPLE *think* TRIGGERS WORK

② BULLET
→ RELEASES

① PULL TRIGGER

Here's what makes the behavior of humans so perplexing. Most of us can look at a gun we've never seen before and identify the trigger pretty easily. But we can't get close to identifying most of the stimuli that activate us, let alone those around us, even after years or decades. These triggers are incredibly unique to each person, and there is almost no consistent and observable way to detect that a trigger has been pulled until long after the bullet has been propelled out of the gun.

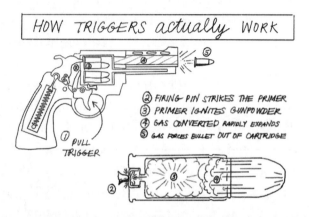

Here's an example. When I was in my second rehab, there was a guy by the name of Usman, who had moved to Los Angeles from North Africa. He was incredibly nice and jovial, the kind of guy you could listen to for hours as he told crazy stories, not only from his homeland, but also from his days in Los Angeles where, within a few years, he found himself addicted to smoking crack cocaine. We would go to meetings, walk to the nearest Starbucks with the other guys in the mornings, and spend hours together every day. By the time I'd met him, Usman was three months sober and had already served his jail time. I was still looking at jail time but had served a week before going to rehab, so we bonded over the experience. One day, at the usual time of our daily coffee run, I looked around the house for Usman but couldn't find him anywhere. After about fifteen minutes of searching, I gave up and decided to go by myself. On the way to the Starbucks, I ran into some of the other guys. It seems Usman had been walking with them to get coffee when a former friend/dealer of his drove by in a car, stopped, and called out for him. Usman engaged with the guy for ten seconds, then jumped into the car and they sped away. And he never came back. That's all it took. Ten seconds, barely a few words, and an ex-using stimulus became the trigger that made Usman give up three months of sobriety (not to mention a probation violation and the thousands of dollars he'd spent on treatment). This is why you can't rely on avoiding triggers to control your addictive behavior—because you never know where the stimulus might come from.

If you've discovered that you're being triggered frequently, and decided to work on the Stimulus stage, the following is a process that will help.

## APPLYING THE EAT PRINCIPLES TO THE STIMULUS STAGE

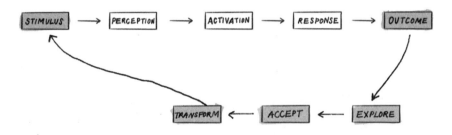

If you're working on exploring the Stimulus stage, it's because you're finding yourself heavily influenced by the people, places, weather, times, and other assorted elements of the environment you see, hear, touch, and interact with. Your use feels out of control and you feel you can't stop yourself from using if a triggering stimulus shows up.

The only way to interfere with stimuli themselves is by altering your behavior in a way that decreases your exposure to them. Indeed, this is one of the most commonly used techniques when it comes to addiction treatment—reduce your exposure to stimuli. This is a wonderful tool, if applied correctly, especially at the beginning of treatment when other recovery tools are underdeveloped.

When you don't have a lot of practice at stopping the impact of stimuli, not being exposed to them can provide some measure of safety.

Unfortunately, most of the people who struggle with addiction have never fully analyzed all the stimuli that trigger them in the first place. Sure, they may realize they're activated when they walk into a bar, or when they can't sleep, but oftentimes, those stimuli barely scrape the surface. As you've heard already, many of my clients first realize that a certain stimulus is triggering to them only after days, or weeks, of work. Some of the most beneficial aspects of working through identifying the stimuli that activate embedded hooks is the incredible access that it gives us to the associated stories and experiences that were remembered along with the hook itself. Let's explore.

### Explore

How do you develop an awareness of the things you've been repressing all around you for decades? For many of my clients, the triggering stimuli are all around—at home, on the street, on their phone's screen, in the expressions on loved ones' faces, in their family's kitchen, and inside their head. They are old and new reminders of past hooks, some from as far back as childhood, and not all explicitly remembered. This is why it's best to start conversations about stimuli with some primers.

Primers are little reminders that can activate your memory. I provide clients with lists of potential stimuli to choose from, and then encourage a conversation. (These primers have been provided to you as part of the Setting Up Your Trigger Chart exercise on page 229 in Appendix B.) Some items on the list are simple, such as "a specific location." Everyone has at least one or two places where they typically drink or use. For me, it used to be the couch in my recording studio, my car, or my bedroom. For some clients, it's a favorite bar or restaurant; for others, it's in the closet. Nearly everyone has some favorite spots; make sure to identify yours.

Two other common primers on my list are "with specific people" and "alone." Identify which of the two categories you fall into. If you are typically social when engaging in your behavior, identify the people who are commonly part of the experience. Be specific.

Whereas the earlier examples related to external stimuli (things happening outside of you), when it comes to internal stimuli, the primers include such terms as "stress," "anxiety," "boredom," "memories of past trauma," "being tired," and other internal states.

There is no right or wrong answer here, but I almost always find that using a primer list leads to realizations and new memories. These stimuli hold meaning for you, as we'll explore in later chapters, but you may need prodding to remember that they even exist.

For instance, early in my career, I sat down with Tim, a scrawny and slightly emo musician client of mine, who was struggling with this worksheet. He looked up at me and asked, "What does 'At a specific freeway exit' mean?"

"It's asking whether you get triggered when you pass by a specific exit on the freeway," I responded.

He thought for a moment, looking puzzled, then asked, slightly annoyed, "Why would a freeway exit trigger me?"

"Well," I said, "sometimes people have a specific area of town where they've bought drugs or have gone to use. Getting near those areas, either by getting off the freeway or turning down a specific street, can make them excited and activated."

"OH, SHIT!!!" Tim yelled out. "Hell, yeah, this makes so much sense. On my way home from work, I always pass by the Normandie exit right when I make it out of downtown. . . . When things are bad, I get off there and go score at a house about two minutes off the freeway. I have a whole ritual: stop at the gas station, get some cash, drive to the house, get the drugs, and then use in the car." The moment the trigger was activated, a whole chain of events spilled out of Tim without his even thinking.

Stimuli are powerful.

I spend time with new clients to fully outline every potential trigger we can identify. Use the Setting Up Your Trigger Chart exercise (page 229) to help you arrange these by their impact. It's important to note that stimuli don't usually show up independently of one another. So, it helps to create the most realistic representation of the true manner in which these stimuli play out in your life.

For instance, while a social environment with specific friends might be triggering, it may combine a number of elements:

- It typically happens at a specific time (e.g., 5 p.m.).
- It takes place in a specific environment (a favorite happy hour bar).
- It occurs while in a given psychological and biological state (e.g., being tired and stressed after work).
- It may occur only under specific circumstances (e.g., spouse is out of town).

It is this *unique* combination of stimuli that creates the true activation for the compulsive behavior. Once you develop an exhaustive list, you'll have a sense of the true impact of stimuli on *your* behavior. You're likely to find that your world is made up of a sort of virtual map of the world with triggering stimuli all around your daily life, directing and guiding you toward your problematic behavior. That awareness will give you a solid starting point to adjust your exposure.

### Expanding Awareness Through Psychedelic Medicine Work

Another very important technique I use for exploration of stimuli is psychedelic medicine work. This approach can be controversial, and the irony of getting back to this work nearly twenty years after going to jail for the sale of these drugs does not escape me. Nevertheless, I have found that psychedelic work can bring about massive awareness of memories and stimuli that have been repressed for decades. This is certainly not the only SPARO phase that will refer to psychedelic work, but the power of psychedelics is that they change the way the mind thinks. When trauma, time, and simple repression have cast aside important aspects of the self, the use of psyche-delic medicines often opens windows to these pasts, as if building bridges that clients can use to cross back in time to them. Upon this journeying, many return with long-lost memories and experiences. There are many psychedelic medicines that are useful in this context, but the best researched and most relevant to my work have been ketamine, psilocybin, and MDMA (a.k.a. molly or ecstasy).[3] When it comes to unravelling hidden stimuli, I have found the use of these, within guided therapeutic settings, to provide some almost unbelievable results. Each of these medicines opens awareness in different ways and allows a client to explore, identify, and connect with stimuli that may not be consciously obvious or that may feel unsafe to explore with-out the assistance of the medicine. We will discuss these medicines in more detail later in the book.

Completing the exploration of the triggering stimuli in your life can help you to feel more secure in your understanding of the way your behavior is affected by specific forces. This knowledge alone can create a sense of comfort on the one hand, but, on the other hand, it can also bring on anxiety, sadness, and even shame. This is why it is important to jump into the work of Acceptance next.

## Accept

Many of my clients are much more familiar with feeling shame than with feeling acceptance. This may be something you're famil-iar with as well. You may have been told you're worthless, damaged, hopeless, or worse. You may dislike this messaging, but you may also be comfortable feeling badly about yourself. If this is true and Acceptance is a foreign practice, it can feel easier to go along with the pain you know than to risk everything for an unfamiliar potential future.

When it comes to the discoveries they make during the Stimulus stage, many people report feeling disempowered ("Why would I let something so simple control my behavior?"), remorseful ("I can't believe I've let this person affect my life for so long!"), ashamed ("I've never told anyone about this before; just thinking about it makes me want to crawl into a hole"), or even angry ("I'm so mad that I've allowed these things to destroy my life"). You may feel it's unfair that you have been, and continue to be, affected by triggers that direct your life in this way.

Let me remind you that it isn't the stimuli themselves that hold the power. They are simply the activating point for hooks that set off an entire cascade of reactions. Remember, too, that this cascade makes all the sense in the world, when understood from the vantage point of the experiences that have led you to this point. If we revisit your personal history and reexplore the situations that first cemented these triggering stimuli in the first place, we can connect the dots. That's why I want you to adopt my "F*ck Shame!" motto. Shame isn't helpful when we are trying to make major life pivots. It holds us back and makes us feel powerless when what we really need is a bit of direction, some momentum and belief in ourselves.

It's also important to remember that we will never be completely free of triggers. This is a reality we all have to accept. It's also why simply trying to control triggers is never going to be a successful long-term recovery strategy. We must accept that we will continue to be exposed to triggering stimuli even as we work to avoid them.

It's how we react to them that makes all the difference.

And that's exactly what you're working to change.

With this understanding in place, I want you to allow at least the possibility that you aren't "damaged," "broken," or "sick." Your behaviors and responses make sense, given your experiences. The power of releasing shame and facing reality head-on is unbelievable when practiced properly. With shame cast aside, almost everyone is ready to move toward Transformation.

## Transform

By the time you reach the Transformation stage, you've gained a stronger understanding of the reasons behind your behavior through Exploration. And Acceptance has prepared you for the journey ahead by reducing the shame and guilt about the hooks that have been holding you back. Transformation is the stage where we apply actual tools and practices to the problems we've discovered, and this is where real long-term change gets cemented. During the Stimulus stage, we focus on triaging stimuli and either ridding ourselves of them or becoming more accustomed to their impact (sometimes called habituation or desensitization).

The overall approach to Transformation at this stage is simple: If you're only starting in your recovery process and are not feeling incredibly strong, it's best to avoid, or rid yourself of, any triggering stimuli that are highly activating. You can get rid of all the alcohol in the house, and stop spending time with friends who drink a lot or are otherwise strongly connected to your problematic behavior. If there are people, places, or experiences that create strong activations within you, place your exposure to these on hold. Not being exposed to strong triggers is one of the safest ways to avoid their influence, and a meaningful tool in early recovery.

Additionally, for any triggers you can't rid yourself of, it's important to make meaningful changes in the way you relate to them. For example, if you've rid your refrigerator of beer, complete the action by filling it up with other drinks that are safe—flavored waters, juices, nonalcoholic beers, or anything else that can replace the previous triggering stimuli. If there's a room that is usually paired with your problematic behavior, take on the project of changing the look and feel of the space. Paint the walls, move the furniture around (or replace it), or otherwise find ways to make the space look very different. If there's a time of day that is most difficult to resist, fill it with a new healthy habit, such as running, a positive social activity, or something of the sort. We'll discuss this powerful approach in more detail later, in the Response stage.

IMPORTANT: The changes made during this phase do not have to be permanent. But, if performed properly, doing this will make the next stages of the work much easier to complete. I say this because some clients find family members, work colleagues, or even good friends in the "Extremely Damaging" column. Relationships, in particular, are something we'll want to address, later on. For the time being, you may have to temporarily avoid triggers that you'll need to learn to face later on, so as to increase your odds of success at this early stage.

The focus of the Stimulus stage is simply to become aware of, and eliminate, exposure to obviously damaging and easy-to-address triggers. Unfortunately, this stage is typically nowhere near powerful, sustainable, or potent enough to induce real long-term life changes. As noted, sometimes it is just not possible to steer clear of them. Moreover, the complexity of avoiding triggers is that they're often not obvious, change based on setting, and can be impossible to predict ahead of time. That makes truly avoiding them for a lifetime essentially impossible.

But what if we could actually become much better at predicting what would happen once a trigger is activated? What if we could identify the mechanism that actually fires the bullet *after* the trigger is pulled? Wouldn't we be able to have additional opportunities to neutralize even a pulled trigger?

We would, and that's where we go next, with Perception.

CHAPTER 7

# Perception

STIMULUS ⟶ PERCEPTION ⟶ ACTIVATION ⟶ RESPONSE ⟶ OUTCOME

magine yourself on an afternoon hike. Heading up and down the
trails, you find yourself repeatedly engrossed in the beauty of the land-
scape around you. Massive pine trees cast shadows and cool the air. Squir-
rels scurry up and down the thick tree trunks, playing and searching for
cones to feast on. The trail isn't an especially difficult one, so you have more
than enough time to look around and appreciate the magnificence of it all.

These hikes are one of your favorite ways to recharge, and you enjoy
the way they allow you both the physical and mental space to expand
and stay grounded. About forty-five minutes into the hike, you come
up on a clearing in the woods and are faced with a simply breathtaking
scene. In front of you is the most exquisite mountain range. Astonished
by the wonder in front of you, you pause and take it all in, appreciating
the view and committing it to memory. A sort of mental image forms
in your mind, forever recording this special moment.

Later that evening, settled in at home, you and your partner are host-
ing some friends. Still moved by the experience you had that morning,

you share the tale of your hike with those around the table. Quickly, your friend realizes that he, too, has seen that view, appreciating it just as you had. However, he stands firm in correcting you on a few small details. You had mentioned that the mountain was snowcapped and that its left side was covered in fresh pines, wrapped in snow themselves. But the mountain had no snow on it, and the pines were evenly distributed around the base, your friend corrects you. Additionally, you mentioned a small lake at the base, slightly off to the right. But the lake was actually on the left side, and you'd forgotten to mention the beautiful foliage that surrounded it. You're a bit taken aback, since you are sure of what you saw. After all, this just happened this morning and you committed the whole thing to memory. You *know* what you saw. And so, you reassert yourself to your friend, making sure he understands that the details you shared were exactly as you had seen the mountain. The two of you go back and forth for a little while, never truly reaching an agreement on the actual scene. The whole experience puts a slight stain on the evening, with both you and your friend feeling misunderstood, disregarded, and a bit upset.

Three weeks later at a lunch meeting, you revisit the conversation with your friend. You discover that you and your friend had ended up on slightly different hiking trails. You were indeed both looking at the same mountain, but he was looking at it from about three miles northeast, and it hadn't snowed yet when he was there two days earlier.

Both you and your friend saw the same mountain from different vantage points, at different times. Your location affected your view, and hence your perspective, which became your perception of the mountain itself. Your perspective always affects your perception. And your perspective is rarely so *true* that it trumps all others. How many times have you found yourself arguing with others about the "right" and "wrong" way to think about a subject? To complete a task? To define a word? How many of those times did you find out that there was more than one way to think of the subject?

I have found that Perception is one of the most difficult aspects of the SPARO model for people to fully absorb. This is because our view of the world is so personal, its intimacy so consistently cemented and reinforced, that to admit that it might be "incorrect" is tremendously difficult. I've seen people take months, even years, to do so. It feels unnatural, even dangerous, to first admit to ourselves, and then eventually to others, that we may be "wrong" in the self-assured ways we see life.

In our hiking story, the different hiking paths you and your friend took represent the different life paths we all tread. None of us experiences life in the exact same way. There are no two people reading this book right now who've had the same life experience. We all take different hiking trails. We all look at the mountain from our own vantage point.

## THE WORLD CAN PLAY TRICKS ON YOU

A picture is worth a thousand words, and when we can *see* something happening it becomes so much easier, and clearer, to understand it. That's why a broken bone can immediately explain the friend's pain, but trying to recognize emotional pain is so much more challenging. But sometimes, even the visual can be perplexing. Like the following image. We know it is two-dimensional, since it's printed on a piece of paper. However, our brain gets tricked when we actually focus our eyes on the image and look at it for a few seconds.

The image makes you believe that the circles are radiating out, even spinning, and that the figure extends deep into the page. Obviously, you can't believe everything you see. You've heard that saying before. Still, it's easy to argue that black-and-white lines and circles on a page are far less complicated than human behavior and psychology. And, if you can't even believe everything you see, why on earth would we rely only on visible behavior to truly understand the inner workings of those around us?

Well, you shouldn't rely on what you see. What goes on inside our head is nuanced and delicate. Our reality is *not* objective, which is why it's simpler to rely on the seemingly objective—what we see—to describe it. Study after study has revealed hundreds of internal tricks and shortcuts by which our brain processes the real world. Here are some of these ways, biased and inaccurate as they are:

- **Confirmation bias:** We favor our existing knowledge and tend to ignore information that counters it.
- **Availability heuristic:** We give more weight to information that is readily available and greatly discount less common circumstances.
- **Fundamental attribution error:** We believe in our own control and changing motives, but see others as stuck in their ways and fixed in their personality.
- **Egocentric bias:** We project our beliefs onto other people.
- **Mere exposure effect:** We imagine that things we are familiar with are better.
- **Stereotype bias:** We edit our memories to reinforce our perception and takeaways.
- **Attribute substitution:** We favor simple options over more complex alternatives.
- **Hindsight bias:** We justify our actions and reject contradictory information after the fact.

## THE ME PERSPECTIVE

We are frequently told that the world doesn't revolve around us. While this is absolutely true objectively, our *personal* experience continues proving exactly the opposite. My world *does* revolve around me. Obviously, I recognize that your world doesn't revolve around me. But I see myself at the center of everything. When I turn, the world turns with me. The things I pay no attention to do not exist, for me. Without realizing it, we gradually develop a perspective of the world that is uniquely ours—affected by our experiences, our environment, and our beliefs. And this unique and biased perspective has a massive impact on all of our behavior—all our reactions and responses—always.

The reason that people respond so differently to stimuli has very little to do with the stimulus itself. It has to do with the *meaning* that these stimuli hold for each of us. A passing blue car may mean nothing to you, but for a person who was once assaulted in a blue car, even decades ago, it could mean the start of a panic attack that leads to all-night closet drinking.

What makes the difference here? Many factors are at play in creating this difference in perception. Without a doubt, the first factor that affects perception is attention.

## THE POWER OF ATTENTION

If you don't attend to what is happening in the first place, you won't register the event's existence, and so it is less likely to have an impact on you in the moment. This may sound obvious, but research has shown us that our attention is far more fickle than we suppose. We think we pay attention to what needs to be attended to, but that isn't so. You'd be amazed just how much we can miss.

One such effect is known as change blindness.[1] (Before I ruin this experiment for you forever, search the web for "change blindness basketball video" to see it for yourself, if you want more than just the education. DO NOT read further until you've watched the video.) Our brain becomes myopically task-focused and ignores even the most obvious things. In one study, participants watching a video were asked to focus on a simple task: counting the number of basketball passes among a group of students who were wearing a white T-shirt. While the participants focused on completing the task, a person dressed in a black gorilla suit walked across the frame, beat on his chest, and then walked out. Believe it or not, a full 65 percent of participants never even notice the gorilla![2] How is that possible? Similar studies have been undertaken with many different setups and scenarios. In driving simulation experiments, entire buildings, trees, or cars in a scene can disappear mid-driving, and the vast majority of people never notice![3] How does someone miss something so obvious and noticeable?

We miss it because we're focused elsewhere.

As you're reading this, you're likely certain you could never make a mistake like that. But I have news for you. We can only attend fully to one thing at a time, so our brain needs to make some choices, filtering out what seems unimportant.[4] It does this to save its efforts and resources for what seems truly relevant for us.[5] This is the first place where perception makes a difference. What your brain deems less important will get little attention. Or none. This may seem outrageous, but we all do it. And we're never aware that it's happening.

Over and over, we find ourselves remembering reality in ways that contradict the recollection of those around us. As in the earlier hiking story, we find ourselves arguing with loved ones about specific details that were, or were not, part of an experience. Who danced with whom at our wedding? Did we have a brown or black couch at that first apartment? What was the name of that nice person who lived next to us and helped us with our groceries? Or was it with our suitcases? And over and over, we trust with certainty that our recollection is correct.

Research shows us that our memory of events is profoundly influenced by what we pay attention to. Without attention, a trigger that would otherwise be incredibly activating won't reach your consciousness. And we aren't always consciously aware of all the stimuli our brain *does* process to make its decisions. In seeking to be efficient, some aspects of our environments that *are* actually processed and *that can* affect our thinking live outside of our explicit awareness.

So, you not only miss parts of reality that matter, but you also process other aspects that affect you without realizing it.

Whoa.

You may be asking yourself, "How will this help me?" when trying to change your own behavior. We can't necessarily control our attention to a specific trigger in an environment. But we can train ourselves, through mindfulness and related practices, to be intentional about where we put our focus. These practices are incredibly effective at allowing us to maintain control over our attention, and therefore our reactivity.[6] When you are better at attending to internal changes and fluctuations in your state, you can better prepare and respond. It's like the difference between being able to feel an earthquake because the walls are shaking or your having your own internal seismic detection device. The level of detail and precision you can register is endlessly greater and can give you a warning long before everything starts falling off the shelves. (We'll discuss specific techniques to increase mindfulness and attentional control later in the book.)

It's simpler than you think.

Our brain is an incredibly powerful association machine. Once we attend to a stimulus, it activates our associations and memories. Repetition and intensity are the biggest contributors to the retention of specific associations. To be able to understand this part of the SPARO process, it's important that we understand how a memory is formed.

## HEY, DO YOU REMEMBER ME?

Contrary to many people's conceptualization, memories are not maintained as "files" waiting to be pulled out of an imagined drawer in your brain. In actuality, memories are stored in a diffuse manner all over the brain.[7] Each segment of the brain that was active during the experience gets lit up like a Christmas tree whenever the memory of the experience is activated. This is why strong memories can make us feel almost as if they're occurring in real time. Ever find yourself feeling happier at the memory of the best family vacation you've had? Or sad at the memory of a bad breakup? That's because memories are actually *reactivations* of the brain in a way that is nearly identical to the original experience.

This is important for a few reasons:

1.  It should help explain why memories impact our behavior now, even though the experience itself happened in the past. This is especially true with memories of difficult and traumatizing events, but also for more common or joyful experiences.

2.  When the memory gets reactivated, it is also susceptible to being altered in the moment. This means we can actually change the past, at least insofar as it is related to our own *current* experience of past events.

3.  Memories are also context specific. What does that mean exactly? It means that the perception you'll have of specific stimuli depends on what is happening inside and around you. You'll experience a stimulus differently when you're at home vs. at the office, at your friend's house vs. the mall, when it's dark outside vs. in the full-sun afternoon. Internally, you will perceive things differently when you're stressed out vs. relaxed, highly focused vs. distracted, feeling warm vs. feeling cold.

For instance, did you know that you're more receptive to new information when holding a warm mug in your hand than a cold one?[8] Or how about the fact that you're more likely to see someone you consider good-looking as being smart?[9]

Most of us assume that our perception of what is happening around us is true even if it's colored by our past experiences. But, as we now know, research has shown us, over and over, that *our thinking is anything but objective.* The reason this lesson is so crucial is this: your perception of the world leads to your actual behavior. So … *if you can change your perception of a stimulus, you will change your response to it.* As Wayne Dyer said, "Change the way you look at things, and the things you look at change."[10]

And this is the idea behind the Perception part of the SPARO model: to create awareness of that which lies beyond our consciousness—our perceptions—so that we can change our behavior.

## I AM WHO I SAY I AM

Have you ever thought about how you identify yourself? For instance, even though I've lived in the United States for over twenty years, I still identify as Israeli. Most of us don't think about our "identity" much, but research has shown us that the labels and identities we ascribe to have *massive* influence over our thinking, feeling, and behavior. Your identity informs what you see as important, whom you feel close and similar to, and the most basic beliefs you hold about "right" and "wrong." Researchers have shown, time and time again, that what we believe is largely determined by considering the group(s) we belong to.[11] This bias also means that we align ourselves more closely with people who belong to the same group (our "in-group")—we reward them more,[12] see them as "better," and are more likely to take their side (and resist others—the "out-group"). In fact, research shows that we get uncomfortable when we find ourselves disagreeing with people we expect to agree with (members of our in-group). All of this is true even if the groups we belong to have been randomly created by the experimenters themselves! It's certainly true when we've selected to be members of the group, such as when we decide to use cannabis to fit in with a group of friends.

## WE FAVOR KNOWLEDGE THAT ALIGNS WITH OUR BELIEFS

Hundreds of studies show us that once you take a position on an issue (including yourself, others, the world, or even food choices), you make defending or justifying that position one of your primary purposes.[13] This Confirmation Bias means that you are actually far more biased *after* having a specific attitude on a topic than before you chose a position in the first place. And the first bits of information you are exposed to become the most relevant when making your initial decision on a topic, becoming a sort of anchor and impacting all information presented later, following something called the Anchoring Bias.[14] In fact, we make it nearly impossible to change our own opinions and expectations because we are sure of the "correctness" of our initial position. We then search for evidence, focusing almost exclusively on information that supports our view and ignoring everything else. We also surround ourselves with people who believe the same information we do, making it less likely that we'll be exposed to contradictory information.[15]

We believe what we believe, seek information that confirms our existing beliefs, and consider the little bit of opposing information we do allow in as being far less credible. This is why, when I work with those who struggle and are looking to change, I recommend adopting a state of curiosity and wonder. If you come in having a specific expectation or opinion, the odds of change are substantially lower. Expectations and opinions can completely block your awareness of reality itself. This is true *even* when you truly are motivated to change.

These ways of thinking affect us all, even if we don't believe that they do. For instance, research has shown that physicians are often much too confident about their diagnosis being correct. In one study, researchers examined a group of patients that doctors believed were 80 to 90 percent likely to have pneumonia, based on their own physical examination and assessment of the patients. However, later, lab and imaging testing revealed that only 20 percent of the patients actually did have pneumonia.[16] Doctors are also terrible at revising their previous diagnoses once they've come to a conclusion. They often dismiss tests that disconfirm their initial assessments as anomalies. And doctors are supposed to be trained in making correct assessments and diagnoses!

Now, imagine how this sort of bias impacts the way you think about yourself. First, you start out giving *far* too much weight to the initial information you're exposed to early in life. If you've been blessed with a nurturing and caring environment, chances are that you'll believe people are good, you have worth, and the world is safe for you. But if stress, anxiety, pain, or even physical danger is present in your early life, you are led in an opposing direction—toward a view that life is unsafe, miserable, and bleak. Due to the Anchoring Bias, the initial building blocks of your beliefs about yourself carry the most weight. So, if your starting point is difficult, you will believe yourself to be weak, unlovable, unworthy, and unstable. You continue absorbing and taking in any information that confirms this view while discounting most information that supports your worth and value, a process known as "positive discounting." Not seeing your own self-worth, you surround yourself with information and people that agree with your low sense of self. This means that you will be increasingly subjected to a negative view of yourself, making it even harder to escape. Even if someone does see your true worth, the fact that their view is unfamiliar and uncommon makes you discount it and pay less attention to it.

This loop will continue running daily unless broken by force.

When Aliyah was molested by a family member and no one believed her, it reinforced her sense of low self-worth. When she was set up with men who took advantage of her for sex in exchange for her mother having access to money and drugs, it drove her perception that her body, if not her entire being, was a commodity to be traded. This made her see all interactions in her life as transactional. And she kept finding more and more evidence that she was only worthy to someone else if she had something to give them. Once she identified what she could give, she expected her payment either in money or in drugs. If there was ever evidence that people saw more in her than just a commodity to be used up, she didn't see it. And if someone really tried to push through those blocks, she chose not to believe them or simply dismissed their virtuosity as a massive anomaly. Her life was full of people who reinforced her perception of herself, and she gradually isolated herself from anyone who could change her perspective.

## WE BELIEVE IN OUR OWN MOTIVES, BUT SEE OTHERS AS STUCK IN THEIR WAYS

In 1999, at the height of my drug-dealing career, I was surrounded by people all the time. I had moved on from the long days of 250-mile delivery routes, and had four or five guys selling drugs for me at all times. We'd spend all our days and nights together between deals. I was their manager, or employer, if you will. I was in charge of the five- and six-figure drug deals, which meant meeting new people and engaging in endless phone calls and texts all day. The more deals I made, the more money we all had and the bigger the deals got, driving the cycle forward. We had hundreds of customers, and many of them liked stopping by our hangout to get high, "talk" with like-minded others, get even higher, play music, and have sex. My life had become the grungy and dirty version of the clichéd "sex, drugs, and rock and roll" universe.

I developed a worldview that was cynical, distrustful, and manipulative toward everyone—including myself. This perspective had been reinforced numerous times by being robbed (including at gunpoint) and generally seeing people only when they needed something from me. I knew I was selling drugs and using them because I'd hated the life I had before. I wanted nothing to do with my parents' money, which they had held over me as a way to steer the ship of my life. So, my worldview remained fully guided by my experiences, never taking those of the people around me into consideration. I was quick to judge them, having no external information about them. I didn't put the effort toward getting to know them more holistically, nor did I believe I needed to. The Fundamental Attribution Error is when we judge others even though we don't know their circumstances and internal motivations; we view their behavior as representing their personality—who they *are*. But when it comes to our own actions, we rationalize them based on our circumstances. Here's the classic example of this: If you've ever been late to a meeting, or rushing to the hospital, you may have found yourself driving fast, changing lanes, and trying your best to get where you were going quickly. But if you've ever had someone cut you off in traffic, or see a person speeding by you on the freeway, you immediately think, "What an a\*\*hole!"

## I BELIEVE IT, SO YOU MUST TOO

We tend to believe that other people share our views of almost everything, including ourselves. We rarely verify this bit of projection, rarely questioning it. I have seen this play out countless times in the therapy groups we run. We've helped over five thousand people through our online platform, with many cutting down on their use by 50 or even 80 percent within a month or two. Interestingly, even with that level of success achieved, many people aren't happy about their progress. Why? Because the general societal understanding of addiction teaches us that complete abstinence is the *only* way to truly be "well." And so, over and over, those who experience incredible success on their recovery journey

find it difficult to share any of the stumbles and pitfalls they've experienced along the way. They think it proves they're failing.

Take Carol, for example. She once found herself crying when
another group participant shared that they were struggling. She shared
that, having done so well for an entire year, she believed she would be
judged by others if she confessed to having stumbled. She projected her
belief that her stumbles were a sign of her imperfection onto all of her
friends in the program, and the result was clear. She felt she needed to
disconnect from them because they looked down at her weakness. All
of this happened inside her head without even an attempt at communicating with the others. The feelings of shame, guilt, regret, and isolation
were overbearing and made the entire experience worse for Carol. But
the moment she was able to share this in the group, she was awarded
with empathetic and compassionate communication. The relief Carol
experienced at the disconfirmation of her negative self-beliefs is why we
practice acceptance at every turn. Having a safe and trustworthy community that opens us up to a broader perspective is vital.

## WE CAN BE PRIMED TO THINK IN SPECIFIC WAYS
## WITH NO AWARENESS

Just as we can completely ignore information we don't deem important, we can also be affected by information that we aren't even aware
of. These subperceptual bits of information can alter our perception
and judgment. We covered this in the previous chapter, but I think it
warrants repeating. A barely noticeable glimpse of a previous trauma-
related detail can make us tighten up, activating a state of fear. And all
this happens without us being aware.

These biases in our perception are important to understand because
they influence how the stimuli we are exposed to end up affecting us.

If you've found that your perceptions and beliefs are substantially
impacting your behavior, follow these steps.

## APPLYING THE EAT PRINCIPLES TO THE PERCEPTION STAGE

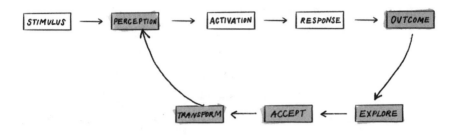

If you're working on exploring the Perception stage, it's because you're finding yourself stuck in negative thought patterns, have a hard time seeing your own self-worth, or spend your days constantly finding everything that's wrong with the world around you. You see the world as a dark place, have a hard time trusting people (and yourself), and expect the worst by default.

As I mentioned, the Perception stage of the SPARO model is often the most challenging phase. It's difficult to adjust your thinking about the world and recognize that all your beliefs, ideas, and truths are simply one set of possible ways of looking at life. It can be equally difficult to recognize that, if you want to live a different life, you may have to change much of what you've held to be true. In reality, the "truths" you've been holding on to may actually be some of the most deeply embedded hooks that have been keeping you back from the life you want. So, if you take the pressure off and move gently toward the change that is needed, it can make the entire process much easier to engage in.

### Explore

Use the Shaping Now exercise (page 244) to help with the exploration of the impact that important life events have had on your perception of the world. As you complete the exercise, you'll consider the following questions as they relate to your past experiences:

- What did you learn about yourself?
- What did you learn about other people?
- What did you learn about the world as a whole?
- What did you learn about the concept of asking for help?

This exercise can sometimes take hours, or even days, to complete. It is often the first time my clients are able to distinctly identify how closely their earlier life experiences are tied to their adult perceptions of who they are. Did you have a similar experience?

Whereas earlier, you may have described yourself as "slow," "lazy," "worthless," or "weak," can you now identify where and when this idea was first implanted? The realizations in this exercise often involve some tears, anxiety, and discomfort. I cannot overstate how gently you must explore the deep wounds that surround your self-perception. Curiosity, and not judgment, is your friend during this process. It isn't always easy to see behind the curtain, but the beauty of it is that, like Dorothy in Oz, once you take a peek, you can't unsee what you've seen.

Aliyah truly believed that she was untrustworthy, damaged, and worthless when we first met. But through this exercise, she was able to at least comprehend that those beliefs originated in the extremely traumatic and transactional ways in which she was raised. It's hard to see yourself as trustworthy when your family scolds and faults you for reporting a sexual assault. It's difficult to truly see your value and worth when you are traded effortlessly for a parent's needs.

Michael believed there was something wrong with his brain, or perhaps his body, that was causing him to collapse on the ground in panic. But through this exercise, he was able to see that his early childhood experiences changed the way he saw the world. They made him believe that the world was unsafe and that he needed to escape. They also showed him that others were not trustworthy and could abandon him at any time. His childhood experiences, not a mal-functioning brain or body, were the source of his deep fears. With every big deal he closed, he had to fight those inner fears. With every step up in his life, he was scared that if he screwed this particular deal up, he'd be right back with his suicidal father in that childhood home, fighting for his safety and being stuck forever with no way to escape.

The beliefs we carry generally fall into the first three categories I outlined through the questions in the Shaping Now exercise (page 244):

- Beliefs about self
- Beliefs about others
- Beliefs about the world

Other important beliefs may be relevant in specific situations. Still, most relate back to one of these three categories. Examples of other beliefs involve the value and availability of help, your self-determination, money, love, god or a greater power, justice/fairness, and failure/success. Once you have a full mapping of your beliefs and perceptions, you can progress into the Acceptance stage.

### Accept

Accepting your own damaging beliefs is something you have probably done all too well. Indeed, you've accepted them so fully, you forget that you can change them. For our purposes, acceptance in this phase plays two roles: accepting that you have these beliefs, and accepting the power you have over them.

To do the former, you must recognize the beliefs you have. The most damaging beliefs you discovered during the Exploration phase of the Perception stage typically fall into general "buckets":

*I am worthless/incapable/a loser who will never succeed.*
This belief typically arises where perfectionism thrives. I was surprised, when my work started exposing me to hundreds, and then thousands, of clients, how many of those I was working with struggle with

perfectionism. Perfectionism is *not* the same thing as striving for excellence, as Brené Brown writes in *Dare to Lead*.[17] Instead, perfectionism is about trying to prove to others that we are worthy of love. It means seeking validation through our performance, instead of through our connection with others and ourselves. Perfectionism leads to a never-ending shame cycle because real perfection is unattainable in the long term. And so, as we fail to reach perfection, perfectionism creates an ongoing cycle of self-hate, judgment, and comfort seeking. Perfectionism is a hook, convincing you that if nothing short of perfect is good enough, and you cannot attain perfection in your life, you may as well give up and disappear into your addiction of choice. I've seen it thousands of times.

People with this belief continue to see their shortfalls and failures, but ignore any evidence of their success. Ironically, some with this underlying belief about themselves develop a false sense of bravado and self-importance, to protect the inner fear of being a failure.

### *I am unlovable / alone and no one cares about me.*

This belief is intimately connected to early childhood attachment experiences. It is common when love at an early age was conditional OR when a child experienced being abandoned and neglected. Feeling insecure in their ability to connect to others, people with this belief develop a sense that they are doomed to be forever alone. This is often reinforced by rejected attempts to connect, often with ill-advised partners or through unhealthy behaviors. We humans are social animals, and so this belief, again, creates massive and persistent feelings of deep shame, isolation, and despair. The pain of this isolation leads to the numbing behavior so common in those who overdrink, overwork, overeat, overuse, and overspend. Those who hold this belief continue choosing relationships that further transmit this sense of an unlovable self, making it more and more difficult to believe in the availability of truly intimate, supportive, and loving relationships. In search of protection, some with this belief may outwardly seem to show that they don't need, or even want, to be close to others. If you don't search for connection, it's less likely you'll be disappointed when it doesn't show.

*I am hopeless / damaged / broken and my life will never improve.*
The belief of hopelessness robs us of our will to try for change. When you have had the belief instilled that you are *forever* damaged, every day can seem like a confirmation of the inevitable. We require hope to feel motivated, connected, and joyful. Without hope, there is no reason to change, because without hope of improvement, what would be the point? This is one of the main reasons that, in all my work, I do away with any language about disempowerment. We *must* believe in our potential to improve, even when facing incredible odds. No one is beyond repair, but no one can repair while feeling hopeless. We are all worthy of love, but when we have not had this concept modeled for us, or worse, have actively been unloved, it's very easy to identify opportunities to see the damage around us and not the beauty. Instead of outwardly displaying their dread, those with this belief may seem aloof, as if their circumstances do not trouble them at all. By seeming as if everything is fine, they ward off the concern and involvement of others, whom they don't see as capable of helping anyway.

*Others are untrustworthy / hurtful / cruel.*
We're supposed to be nurtured and cared for when we're young. Our vulnerable and delicate body and mind rely on the care and protection of those close to us as we develop. But many of the people I've worked with have had exactly the opposite experience—the people closest to them have often supplied them with the most pain. When your history shows you that the people you rely on will hurt you and take advantage of you, believing in the good of others can be hard. This belief arises from a need for protection, but in protecting yourself and "armoring up," you end up detaching yourself from the support you need. A mirror of the "I am unlovable" belief, this view of others continues reinforcing itself as you protect yourself more and more, avoiding

betrayal, but making real connection impossible. In defense of their worldview, individuals with this belief about the world may turn to being manipulative or hurtful themselves, thinking it unavoidable and the only way to not be taken advantage of.

### *The world is a scary / dark / empty place.*
When you believe that all existence is dangerous, dreaming of a better life is futile or even hazardous. Early life trauma is common for those who struggle with this worldview. The *fear* of a dark life that is devoid of hope, connection, worth, and purpose ends up creating an existence full of hopelessness, isolation, worthlessness, and apathy. Some with this view may completely detach from any social environment, or isolate remotely. Alternatively, they may develop a tough exterior that is itself dark and frightening, so as to fit into the bleak projection they see in the world.

Becoming immersed in a community that offers safety can feel like a mirage when you don't believe that a safe world exists. But this is a crucial step, as it can help provide consistent evidence that it is okay to engage with the world.

The notion that you can change your perception, and therefore your experiences, is a seemingly far-fetched one that can take some time to absorb. This is especially true when you believe that your perspective of the world is objective, realistic, and correct. When you've held on to a negative belief for so long that you no longer see it as an opinion, but as a fact, there is work to be done. It took me years to come to this realization, myself. But once I grasped it, I realized the power my old thinking had over me and wanted to make certain I'd never fall for that delusion again.

So, what do you do when you realize that you've been holding on to self-handicapping beliefs for years, and that you've actually had much more control over those beliefs than imagined? How do you accept this information? Many people go into denial or self-blame. If you're struggling believing that you can change the way you see the world, or feeling shame for the beliefs themselves or for your inability to shake them, you're not alone.

When you accept that you can't blindly trust your own thinking, any new idea, new belief, and new theory about life becomes suspect—"Why should I trust this new way of seeing the world when my old and trusty views have been proven suspicious?" My favorite part of this stage in the behavioral change process is the following realization:

*If old damaging beliefs kept me locked up in darkness, I can adopt new and empowering beliefs that will release me into the light.*

Accepting your own agency over your perception of the world allows you to do something about it. But with great power comes great responsibility. Once you realize, and accept, that you have power over these beliefs, you also have to accept responsibility for continuing to carry them. This can be a powerful motivator for change.

It's like climbing a mountain. Each step elevates your point of view, making it possible to see beyond what was feasible when you were standing at the bottom. It isn't that the world itself changed, but your perspective on it does. And that makes all the difference.

Through my own evolution, I was able to prove to myself that all was not lost. I started out seeing myself as a no-good loser who would be lucky to stay out of prison forever. It took time, and gradual progress, to change that. First, I was simply able to get admitted to a school; then, I achieved distinguished grades, which allowed me entrance into a respected doctoral program. Then, I graduated with a PhD, and eventually even taught at the university. Each step proved that more was possible and that there was hope. Then came more opportunities and challenges, and as I walked and stumbled and got back up, I learned how resilient and capable I really was. Eventually, I felt confident enough to strike out on my own, teaching others what had worked for me and helping thousands of others get better in the process. None of these feats would have been possible the day I got out of jail. But, as I continued progressing, I learned one *very* important fact: as we challenge our old beliefs, we grow and expand to accommodate our new capacities.

*You must accept that the limits you live within are the limits you place on yourself.* If your perception of reality was created through your earlier experience, then you can create your future reality by shifting your current and future thinking and beliefs. I now know this to be true more than ever.

Go back to your Spheres of Influence exercise and revisit what you control. If you hadn't placed your perceptions in the "Control" or "Influence" circles, it might be time to revisit this.

It's time to change the way you see the mountain.

### Transform

Most people recognize the need to change their behavior, but few come into this work recognizing the need to change their perceptions and beliefs. Since many of us carry beliefs we don't even recognize to be anything but "truth," it can be useful to begin by calling our views "assumptions."

You *assume* things to be a certain way because you have always seen, heard, and understood them to be that way. You don't see the specific assumptions that drive your problematic behavior as hooks that pull you back toward misery, because you don't see them as anything but unchangeable "truths." To fully understand just how changeable these assumptions are, you typically need to experience a substantial shift in your thinking.

You've changed your thinking before in this way; you just have a difficult time remembering it. Let me remind you: You used to believe in Santa Claus, or the Tooth Fairy, or the Easter Bunny, or some other such fantastical creature. You *knew* they existed and accepted it as *truth*. And then, one day, you stopped believing it. Whether it was because your friends told you, or you read about it in a book, or your parents finally owned up to the ruse, you changed your perception of what was true and what was false. You stopped believing in that particular gift-bearing friend and you've never looked back (unless you have kids, and then you played the same trick on them, most likely).

The analogy I use to explain the framework of changing our internal thought process is that of a sponge. When you first take a new sponge out of its packaging, it is clean, fresh, and untainted. Like a child. I don't know about you, but for me, there's something pleasing about a sparkling new sponge. It is ready and able to absorb anything you throw at it. As you use the sponge and clean with it, you expose it to different elements, which it readily absorbs. A brand-new sponge can take on a lot. At some point, the sponge becomes saturated. It's been filled up. At that point, the sponge that was able to take on so much is essentially incapable of taking on anything new.

That is how we function.

Research suggests that full "sponge" absorption happens by seven to ten years of age.[18] People vary, with some learning for a few more years, and some less, but the important thing to recognize is that this point of saturation happens early in our lives. Once a sponge is full, it cannot absorb much more. There are only two ways to change what has been absorbed—a squeeze, or gradual osmosis.

### The Squeeze

Once squeezed, the force applied releases much of the matter the sponge has been holding on to. As the pressure is released, the sponge returns to its original shape. It has also freed up space to absorb new matter.

### Gradual Osmosis

You may remember this concept from your high school biology class. When you take an object and place it into a different environment, the system will bring itself into balance. If you put a "dirty" sponge in clean water and wait long enough, the particles inside the sponge will "leak" out into the new water, and clean water from the surrounding environment will seep into the sponge. The speed and efficiency of this process depend on the difference in concentration between the two, and the permeability of the membrane that separates them.

So, how do the squeeze and osmosis processes relate to behavioral change and perception?

A *squeeze* equates with intensive therapeutic and transformational experiences. When you are figuratively loaded up with dirt and grime you want to get rid of, it can be useful to participate in intensive experiences to expel as much as possible. Examples of real-life squeeze efforts include the following:

- Going to inpatient rehab
- Going to therapy three times per week for ninety-minute sessions
- Participating in intensive guided psychedelic experiences
- Attending weeklong silent retreats

(These are all experiences I've participated in and have led people through.)

These experiences take focused time, effort, and often money. They are intensive and life-altering, but they are too taxing, time consuming, and expensive to take part in regularly.

Even without a squeeze, a sponge full of muck, placed into a clean bucket of water, will become less grimy through *gradual osmosis*. Osmosis is dependent on the environment you are placed in. The cleaner the new water surrounding the sponge, and the more porous its surface, the more quickly dirt will seep out and balance is achieved. In the human arena, the same can be seen. Put a person with massive negative self-beliefs into a supportive environment free of judgment, prejudice, and shame, and they will begin to change the way they see the world. This process doesn't create change as quickly as a squeeze, but it is easier to engage with over the long term. Just as with the sponge, the cleaner the water around the sponge (think: people, time, opportunity, reduced exposure to harmful stress), and the more porous it is (more ready for change, less resistant, more involved and engaged), the faster the process.

When Aliyah first joined my online program, her "sponge" was completely filled up with dirt. Her self-perception was damaged; her views of the world and of others were bleak. When she heard me speaking on the radio, something about the message felt different enough for her to pause and consider that there may be a different reality. When she first joined, she was in full "squeeze" mode. She attended all the groups, connected with me regularly offline, and generally was all-in on creating change. And it worked! Over three months, Aliyah was gradually able to quit her meth use and stay sober for the first time in years. She'd become one of our most diligent group participants and connected with the other members frequently. She was open, shared about her wins and her struggles, and really felt that she had turned the page in her life. It was beautiful.

And then, one day, Aliyah didn't show up for group. That same week, none of our coaches and counselors saw her attend. We reached out to her, but got no response. Two weeks later, she showed up again, but she kept her video camera off. In the chat, she admitted to us all that she had been using again. True to form, no one in the group judged or shamed her. We all expressed our support of her and our gratitude that she was there.

That day in group, I was using the analogy of a speeding car for addiction. I was equating the compulsive life many of us experience to driving a car, foot firmly on the gas pedal, heading up a mountain. Although we recognize we're going too fast, and are about to lose control and head straight off the road and into the abyss, many of us feel paralyzed. Our hands feel stuck firmly on the wheel, aiming straight. It's as if we've forgotten, I said, that we even have the power to turn the wheel at all. I urged everyone on the call—*at any moment, you can always turn the wheel.* The group ended, and I turned off my laptop.

It wasn't until a week later, when Aliyah made it back to group with her video camera on, that I learned the full story. The week before, while listening to the live group, she was at her drug dealer's house, waiting for some meth. She was there with a friend, and they'd been using together for a few weeks. Since Aliyah had some time, and she liked the groups she'd participated in, she decided to listen to the live group on her headphones. She even gave her friend one of the earbuds so she could listen in as well. Sitting there, on the dirty couch in her dealer's house, tired and beaten from two weeks of daily using, Aliyah and her friend listened in as I shared the metaphor of the car. As I told everyone in the group to remember that they always have the power to turn the wheel, Aliyah looked at her friend and said, "Let's get out of here. Let's turn the wheel right now." Her friend agreed. They got up, left the dealer's house, and never looked back.

That day marked a brand-new start to Aliyah that has now lasted years. It also marked the start of a brand-new life for her friend, who is now married and sober and happy. Aliyah's initial three-month combination of a squeeze (her high level of participation) and community involvement (her gradual osmosis process) changed enough about her view of the world that she was open to participating in it *even* at her lowest point. And that willingness opened the door to a transformation that no one had imagined was possible.

That story brings tears to my eyes every single time I tell it. For me, it encapsulates what can happen when a person learns to trust themselves and their community. It shows how even the most broken simply need the tools, and the kinship and support of others, to break free from an unimaginable darkness.

Miracles happen every day, but not by accident.

What most people don't realize is that the postsqueeze environment is crucial for true change. But think about it: If I place the sponge that

I just squeezed clean back into the same water it just released, what will happen? The sponge will simply take back all the grime it had released. This is why rehabs so often fail, and why the vast majority of efforts into behavioral change don't stand a chance. It's the mistaken idea that the only thing that matters is the sponge and what is in it. But the environmental influence matters more than most people realize. If Aliyah felt judged and put down after her relapse admission, she would have had a much harder time continuing her change process. For each of us, it is very important to pay attention to the environment into which we place the sponge (meaning ourselves) after a squeeze.

I have seen the squeeze and osmosis processes work wonders, and my preferred method of working with clients is to alternate between the two. There are a slew of techniques that behave like a squeeze and osmosis, positively impacting a person's beliefs, perspective, and self-awareness. The goal of these techniques is to challenge and remove old beliefs, and then replace them with other, more effective and constructive ones. The work can take time—months, or even years—to create long-lasting, even permanent change in one's core beliefs. But it can also happen quickly. Whether a client utilizes more traditional tools and therapies, such as cognitive behavioral therapy, dialectical behavioral therapy, and acceptance and commitment therapy, or more esoteric ones, such as plant medicine and Eastern practices (e.g., Kundalini yoga), I have personally seen thousands of transformations take place. In the end, regardless of the specific tools and the length of time, the outcome is always remarkable and worthwhile.

But when it comes to perceptual shifts and changes in core, I have rarely seen as powerful and rapid a "squeeze" as the following two scenarios:

- A life-changing "back-against-the-wall" moment that creates a mystical experience of willingness to open up and change, *or*
- A guided psychedelic experience, expertly tailored to the specific needs of a client

You've probably known someone who has experienced, or have personally experienced, a "do-or-die" moment. This is a point in life in which everything a person has believed, experienced, and assumed about life goes out the window and they rethink everything. Some call it "hitting rock bottom." My moment came as I was facing decades in prison and then went to jail for a year. I had, until that time, lived my life as if I were invincible. Being held up at gunpoint, having been robbed, facing cartel deals that could end in my death, going to jail four other times? None of it mattered.

It was only when I was faced with spending what seemed like the rest of my life behind bars, relegated afterward to a life that would surely leave me dead or back in prison, that I gave thought to truly changing. I had no idea how, but the moment offered a short opening of the previously locked door to the hallway of change. I bravely walked through it. It took me years to change. And my motivation gradually shifted from staying out of prison to reconnecting with my family, achieving success in school, creating my own family, and then helping change the world. It was slow, it took a lot of work, and it was all more than worth it.

I became involved in psychedelic therapy to help people make change even when it wasn't clear whether they'd hit rock bottom yet. It's always better when we can stop things before they get there. As I discussed in the previous chapter, these medicines can be a truly transformative tool.

Of course, there are no miracle cures that work for all. Nevertheless, with the right preparation, choice of medicine, and well-planned integration experiences, these medicines can change much of what we know about mental health. Some are fearful of these tools, believing them to be malicious and criminal. But again, that is simply a viewpoint. It's just another perspective.

In the end, the goal of transformation in the Perception stage is to create at least one credible alternative understanding of your view of the world. Then, you shake off the rigidity of belief in a single "truth" in favor of a more flexible and adaptable take on life.

This is crucial for your process because, as I stated at the outset of this chapter, we don't actually react to the stimuli that are presented. Instead, we react to the activation that our *perception* of these stimuli creates in us.

And Activation is where we will go next.

# CHAPTER 8

# Activation

STIMULUS ⟶ PERCEPTION ⟶ ACTIVATION ⟶ RESPONSE ⟶ OUTCOME

It was a crisp Saturday morning, and Mark was looking at the papers on his desk. He was a high-powered tax accountant, so staring at papers was something he was used to. Still, piles and piles of letters, bills, and various packages were stacked high and he needed to get through them. Even though he tried to ignore it, the mess was getting to him.

So, he set about clearing two hours in his schedule, and with a determined mind, began dealing with the piles one by one. He was feeling good about the work he was getting done... until he opened up that one letter. It was a bill for his mother's medical care, a stark, black-and-white reminder that she was slowly leaving him again, just as she had when he was a kid. Mark's mother had begun suffering with dementia about a year ago, and her situation was getting worse. In fact, over the past year things had gotten so bad that she no longer recognized him or his siblings. In a split second, Mark's entire demeanor changed, his breath became shallower, and his heart rate quickened.

He felt panicky. He didn't want to think about his mother dying. He didn't want to remember that he was supposed to deal with her taxes and put her house up for sale. As he thought about all this, his anxiety and stress became more and more pronounced. He got up from his desk, walked into the kitchen, and grabbed a bottle of Jack Daniels.

When you become aware of a stimulus and perceive it through your unique lens, your brain and body prepare their response. A stimulus is benign until it's interpreted. It's the interpretation that tells the body how to respond.[1] A *threatening* (perception) stimulus—a certain look or callout from a person on the street, or a peek at a letter reminding you of a fact you don't want to confront—may require you to defend yourself, escape, or pounce. But a *caring* (perception) stimulus—a glance or gesture from a friend or a close partner or a touching song that brings back good memories—can make you feel comfortable, relaxed, and safe.

Think about the two seemingly different activations of feeling "anxious" or "excited." In reality, the physical experience of the two is very similar—increased blood pressure, a quickened pulse, and sped-up breathing. If you're expecting something bad to happen, or are feeling uncertain, you're more likely to experience this as anxiety. If you're expecting a positive outcome, you'll experience excitement. The activation is created through thoughts and feelings, and you experience it somatically (in the body) and cerebrally (through the mind). The somatic, or physical, activation caused by the stimulus is often nearly immediate and beyond our explicit control.

This is why, when we first have an experience with any addictive behavior, it is typically the somatic experience we're drawn to—the way the alcohol reduces your anxiety, or how the shopping spree or postclimax porn binge distracts you and eases your stress. It's only later that we may understand the behavior as medicine. Sometimes, that recognition never comes. But the relief is still there.

As it did for Mark, negative activation often begins at a very basic level—a rising of our blood pressure, a tightening of the chest, a dampening of our spirit, or a pit in the depths of our stomach. The physical sensation tells us that something is happening—we're scared, happy, sad, angry, or in pain. It is trying to get us to pay attention. The responses are produced as a reaction to that signal.

Experiences that are perceived to support our well-being give us a sense of calm, joy, and fulfillment. We relax, become aroused, and feel free and exploratory. But situations perceived to threaten us cause us to get small, retract, flee, or shut down. No matter how old we are or how long ago the experiences occurred, if they were intense enough, meaningful enough, or repeated frequently enough, they stay with us and become the *learned* activation patterns associated with the experience.

You've likely heard this referred to as the fight, flight, or freeze response. The activation feels instinctive. It feels natural. It seems inevitable. But it's created by the association between outside events and internal physiological structures. These structures span our entire nervous system, as well as our hormonal mechanisms.

Adrenaline and cortisol get secreted into our bloodstream. Our pulse speeds up, pumping blood quickly out of our organs and inner tissue and flooding our extremities, readying us for action. If the perception is related to past trauma, as it was for Mark, the response becomes attached to the earlier experience that caused it. It pulls the memory back into the present moment in an instant and further energizes our response for fear of experiencing the pain again. Our vision gets disrupted and becomes more myopic. Our body's absolute focus on survival interrupts our ability to think rationally and reduces our capacity to pay attention to our environment. It's hard to think sensibly when you are under extreme stress.

There's a term for this. It's called *flooding*.

When you're flooded, your ability to think clearly is compromised. Your thinking reverts toward survival and what feels natural, or intuitive. It's harder to integrate new information and shift your thinking from its habitual ways. In the lab, this type of flooding can be created using physical means—such as having your hand placed in a bucket of ice water—or social/emotional ones—such as having your performance on a math task judged by others while being filmed. I'm sure you can imagine real-life situations that would mirror these uncomfortable physical and social scenarios. Under such conditions, you're more likely to cheat or lie, eat unhealthy foods, make quick judgments about people, and seek selfish immediate rewards or relief.[2]

This is why you find it harder to control your problematic behavior under stress—your brain *knows* that going back to the old standby will give you relief and it wants a quick, selfish solution. Integrating new coping while flooded is difficult.

It all just feels so automatic.

Think back to Michael's story: He knew that the experience of watching his father holding a gun to his head, threatening to take his own life, was a negative one. But he had no recollection of the way he felt about it. He *knew* (cerebral) the experience was "bad," but he had never processed his feelings. Indeed, his trauma had been so powerful that he'd completely repressed any memory of the feelings he had. And yet, anytime he perceived something in his environment that even tangentially reminded him of the experience, the feelings came up and he became flooded. All the responses were there—the anxiety, the stress, the tightening in his chest. Yet he hardly ever realized that his physiological responses had anything to do with those early experiences. When we first connected all of this in a session, he was already in his early forties, and had never told anyone about this event. As we worked through it, he became so uncomfortable that he wanted nothing but for the processing to end.

And who could blame him?

I can't think of any person I know who would willingly choose to sit and process the built-up negative emotions that would come up around the sight of his own father, staring back at him, gun in hand. Sheer terror, abandonment, massive anxiety, and the most profound sense of sadness must have hit Michael that afternoon in waves so big as to overwhelm the most hardened adult.

Except Michael was eight years old when this happened. He didn't have the mental capacity, the grit, or the support to process that sort of pain and discomfort. And no one in his life helped guide him along the path. That evening, everything in his household went back to "normal." Except it wasn't normal before and certainly never felt close to "normal" afterward.

It's important to point out that, in the backyard that afternoon, Michael was not in control. He was a child, there was distress and danger everywhere, and the person he expected to take care of him was compromised and completely unable to do anything of the sort. The only thing he could do at the moment was freeze and wait for someone to usher him out. His mother did just that within a few moments. But the traumatic moment had already occurred, and with no support to process it, time was passing quickly for resolving the experience in a way that wouldn't be damaging to Michael in the long term.

He didn't know it then, but the feelings of dread, the perception that he was alone and couldn't rely on anyone, including his own father, for safety, became a powerful hook that would anchor Michael's decisions for decades. He vowed to leave this life—his family, his father, his home, and the town he grew up in—behind him forever. He committed to doing everything he could to escape this hellhole. Nearly every moment after that day in the backyard was tethered to the *need* to reach safety on his own. Just about an average student before, Michael doubled down and became a star pupil. Although no one was around for him to model and emulate, he set his sights on being the first kid in his family to go to college. He knew there was a path out, and he was going to find it.

As with so many of my most successful clients, no one saw Michael's new obsession with achievement as a problem. Why would they? He was doing better than ever before and barely seemed fazed by the terrible events of that afternoon. Even his father's constant retreat to his bedroom, addled by medication that kept him sedated, didn't bother him. From school, to sports, to girls, Michael was on a winning streak.

He even made honor roll in high school. He was determined to make it out.

And he did! Becoming the first family member ever to attend college, Michael got into one of the most prestigious universities in the country. He even got a scholarship that fully paid for school, which was good, since his family couldn't even afford the cost of the dorms. When he got to school, he never mentioned his hometown or any other details of his experience growing up. He was resolved to leave his past behind, and erasing it from his stories was the next step. He rarely went back home for vacations and worked instead. He had girlfriends, but always made excuses as to why they couldn't meet his family. The name of his town, and everything else that went with his childhood, never crossed his lips. His escape was nearly complete.

Sure, he would have to get drunk regularly to repress the terrible doubt that crept into his mind daily. But everyone else drank like crazy here, too, so he didn't stick out. No matter how hungover or tired, he always made it to class, always did his work, and always did well in his classes.

It's incredible how powerfully a hook can pull you along.

The stress, anxiety, and fear of being stuck back in that crummy old town should have left him as he climbed the ladder, but it never did. In fact, the higher he went up, the greater his anxiety. The fear of being found out, of failing and ending up back at home, of realizing that he really never had a chance to escape, became constant. Even after starting to work in a successful law firm and becoming a successful lawyer, the anxiety never left. Even when he and his wife moved into their dream home, it was always there. He couldn't tell anyone about it because no one knew of his past, so he kept it all to himself.

Until that day in the courtroom, winning the biggest case of his life. The one that would take him higher than he could ever have imagined. When that trusty hook pulled him this time, Michael couldn't handle all the pressure. Walking out after hearing the verdict, he collapsed on the lobby floor and clutched his chest. He was sure he was dying.

## UNDERSTANDING ACTIVATION

To make the activation equation simpler to understand, I use the analogy of a thermometer. As negative activation amasses, creating more and more stress, our "temperature" rises. As more positive, relaxing, and enjoyable experiences accumulate, they counteract the negative, lowering our "temperature."

The absolute highest activation threshold is at the top. *Anyone* who reaches a 100-degree activation temperature becomes immediately flooded and unable to think logically. At this point, they may have a panic attack, rage, shut down, or otherwise fall into the fight, flight, or freeze response.

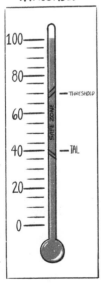

ACTIVATION THRESHOLD

At the bottom is absolute and complete relaxation. Imagine feeling no stress whatsoever and experiencing a complete sense of contentment.

None of us has a true 100-degree threshold, and none of us gets to experience actual 0-degree stress often. Navy SEALs, army rangers, Green Berets, Delta Force fighters, and other high-performing military units undergo *extreme* training to push their threshold as close to 100 degrees as possible.

This serves them well.

But for most of us, who can freak out at not finding a close enough parking spot, a much lower threshold of stress can easily send us into the flood zone. Each of our personal thresholds depends on experience, biology, and other relevant predictors. But let's pretend, for our purposes, that your specific threshold sits at about 70 degrees.

Since none of us really lives with 0 degrees of stress daily, let's use 40 degrees as the baseline temperature for what I call your *initial activation level (IAL)*. The area between your threshold and your initial activation level is what I call your *safe zone*. Your safe zone is the window of tolerance within which you get to operate every day before you get flooded and need to reset.

## ALL STRESS IS NOT THE SAME

Anything that happens in your day, inside your mind or out of it, can either raise your activation temperature or lower it. The specific type of stress, its duration, intensity, and predictability are all critical to sorting out its impact. There are four distinctions of stress and activation:

### Controllable vs. Uncontrollable Stress

When we perceive a stressor as controllable, we exhibit less activation than when we perceive it as uncontrollable.[3] Our immune, inflammatory, and hormonal responses are restrained. This makes controllable stressors less damaging to the body than uncontrollable stressors.

Some stress levels have been shown to be helpful for certain aspects of memory. But individuals exposed to uncontrollable stressors exhibit problems with executive functioning. This compromises our planning, behavioral control, decision-making, and attention. Research shows that chronic uncontrollable stress can actually damage the neuronal structure in the brain. A chronically stressed brain has less connectivity between important parts of the brain and makes fewer new neurons.[4]

These findings are incredibly concerning. They tell us that uncontrollable stress can damage our brain and make it harder to control ourselves, plan well, and make good decisions. The good news is that preparation can help reduce the negative impact. So, in the context of stopping ourselves from problematic behavior, going through the SPARO planning process and being better prepared for upcoming activations can, itself, help reduce the impact of any stress we experience!

### Acute vs. Chronic Stress

Our body is not meant to handle never-ending stress. That's the difference between acute (seconds to hours) and chronic (days to years) stress.

Acute stress is a short-term physiological response to a stressor, such as a sudden loud noise or a narrowly avoided accident. Acute stress activates our sympathetic nervous system, triggering the fight, flight, or freeze response, and causing an increase in heart rate, blood pressure, adrenaline, and cortisol. These changes are good. They help the body respond to the stressor effectively. But chronic stress is a long-term response to a persistent stressor or group of stressors. These could be related to ongoing home violence or stress related to work, poverty, or social issues. Chronic stress can also be created by something like long-term caregiving for a loved one. Chronic stress, and long-term activation of the stress response system, leads to wear and tear on the body.

The effects of acute stress on the body have been extensively studied in the lab. Too much exposure to acute stress, especially the uncontrollable kind, can lead to heart disease, stroke, diabetes, immune system issues, and other negative health outcomes.[5] It can also affect brain structure, leading to changes in short- and long-term memory as well as executive functioning and the spatial memory we use to understand directions and recognize our location.[6]

Aliyah's mother's drug addiction, the sexually inappropriate behaviors, and the poverty and violence that surrounded her were uncontrollable and ever-present—classic chronic stress. This, along with the disturbing memories of her individual traumas, explains why navigating complex decisions may have been difficult for her. And this was all made worse by the prevailing belief that Aliyah's future was hopeless and that she would be powerless forever.

Fortunately, we know that thinking was wrong. So, how do we reverse all of this?

## CONTROLLING THE UNCONTROLLABLE

Michael initially assumed that he couldn't control his stressors, anxieties, and ongoing changes in activation temperature. This is very common among the people I work with. It's a learned helplessness of sorts, acquired early in life. This is why, when he first contacted me, Michael was effectively clueless about the reasons for his attacks. "I don't know," he told me. "My life is perfect. I can't imagine why this keeps happening."

Many of those I work with react to the world as it happens. They try to "keep it together" throughout the day until they get to sleep and reset to start again. "Life is stressful, and our body will respond as it needs to," is the belief. But that thinking is wrong. The way we see, think about, and respond to stress is actually a learned behavior. With the proper practices in place, anyone can alter their current response and take control of their activation temperature. The military knows this and trains its members accordingly. Selective initial screening, followed by over a year of intense training, assures that, by the time they are awarded the coveted SEAL stamp, navy SEALs are some of the most capable warriors in the world.

The message from SEAL training is this: *even* for the most capable, there is incredible value in training and development to maximize ability. And for the rest of us, who may not be looking to take part in dangerous missions across the world, it is equally important to recognize that training and practice can produce massive changes in how our body responds to stress.

Sure, we still react to what life throws our way, but we are no longer at the whim of our initial capabilities and early life training. Instead, we can command our body to be thoughtful even in situations that would have historically produced flooding.

Navy SEALs *choose* to engage in highly stressful activations for the purpose of preparation and training. But when you think back to the stories of Aliyah, Linda, Jaylen, Mark, and Michael, you can see how uncontrollable stressors wreaked havoc in their lives. I have worked with thousands of individuals whose lives were crushed by uncontrollable stress at a young age. Their treatment requires both controlling the stressors themselves *and* learning how to shift their thinking about stress, so as to make it more manageable.

## APPLYING THE EAT PRINCIPLES TO THE ACTIVATION STAGE

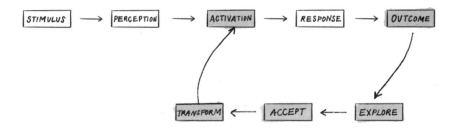

If you're working on exploring the Activation stage, it's because your anxiety, stress, sadness, loneliness, fear, or anger seems to control you. When strong feelings show up, you feel unable to wrangle them and manage your behavior. It likely feels unsafe to be so out of control, so you use the only coping tools that have worked—your problematic behavior.

To resolve struggles in the activation stage, you have to remember that you are never really reacting to the stimulus or trigger itself. Instead, you're reacting to *the perception of that stimulus.* Winning the activation game will come down to a few simple principles:

- Regularly control the controllable.
- Steady yourself for the uncontrollable.
- Train yourself to be comfortable with being uncomfortable.

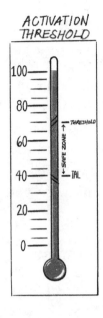

When you master those skills, there is little that can throw you off course.

Consider the thermometer example: You are trying to push up your threshold while lowering your initial activation level (IAL), creating a wider safe zone that provides you with a bigger window of tolerance for stress.

As someone who used to be heavily reactive and swayed by momentary changes in my world, let me assure you of this: The work you do here will help you far beyond resolving your addictive work, drinking, porn, drug, or gambling habits. These new rituals will change your life in all ways and will pay off quickly, once established.

As usual, we can't address what we don't know. This process will be iterative as you learn more and more about what truly activates you and stresses you out. And as you keep improving, you can revisit these practices and refine them.

### Explore

I typically start the Exploration part of the Activation stage with a simple question: "What are the three areas of life that are currently causing you the most stress?"

Most people will answer that question with a ready list of what they view as creating the most chronic and uncontrollable stress. They do this without any coaching, and without the benefit of having read this chapter. The reason is simple—as you've just read, the other sources of stress don't cause them much pain. Indeed, their other stress may actually feel empowering. Think of the physical stress of going for a run or a tight deadline at work—they're short-lived and can make you feel accomplished. But the uncontrolled stress has been so ever-present that my clients have both accepted it and grown to believe it to be genuinely impossible to overcome.

Here's a little example for context: Imagine you grow up in a very violent neighborhood. Going for walks outside is fear inducing and incredibly risky. You manage this by getting used to going outside only during the daytime (it's more dangerous at night) and, even then, only with a group of others, so as not to be alone. The stress of being stuck at home at night, of not being able to go outside at certain times, and of always needing others around for fear of being assaulted has caused you to have anxiety and depression. It's been this way for twelve years, though, and you can't see a way out. You have just enough money in your bank account to pack up the car and drive to a town far away, in which there is less violence. But you've become so accustomed to this way of living that you can't see a way out. And so you continue to choose the devil you know.

This story might be far-fetched for you, but let me remind you: How many of us stay too long in a job that causes us chronic stress? Or a marriage that has needed some serious help for twenty years? How many of us keep people in our lives who bring nothing but negativity and pain, but we do nothing about it for decades? And how many of us are resigned to a life of misery, discontent, and internal turmoil without picking up the phone, calling a therapist, and starting treatment, or asking for help in any way?

Those few examples describe most of the people I see every day. Except they don't come to me for those issues. No. They come for the drinking, the drug use, the obsessive work habits, or the porn use and sexual compulsions that they've been engaged in for years and have nearly destroyed their life.

Solving the wrong problem doesn't provide you with any real solution. It's time to look honestly at your own life.

Check out the Stress Thermometer exercise on page 231. What are the three areas of your life that are causing you the most stress? Look at the exercise and write them out for yourself, getting a bit clearer on the specific ways in which each of these is causing you chronic and uncontrolled stress. Is it that grueling schedule at work, or the overbearing boss you've been dealing with for a decade? Is it your husband's laziness and lack of focus or the fact that you haven't been intimate in five years? Is it your care for an elder parent?

The answers to these questions are important, because we have to be honest in our exploration before we can move forward.

For those who struggle with addictions and have dealt with substantial trauma in their lives, it is crucial to include trauma on this list. It's difficult to move beyond the mental health impact of trauma without dealing directly with the powerful activations that trauma can cause. A number of potent trauma-informed therapies can be employed in this context, and we'll discuss some of them later. Do not shy away from going after the dark forces that drive your addictive tendencies. It's exactly in that darkness that your salvation lies. Remember the cave Joseph Campbell referred to—the most challenging pursuits produce the most powerful results.[7]

Work, marriage, children, money, family, traumas, and internal self-doubt are the most common caves my clients are afraid to enter. Happiness and freedom are the treasures hidden within them.

### Accept

It's common for tears to begin flowing when I ask my clients about their top three areas of stress *if* I've created a safe enough environment for them to answer the question truthfully. It's not easy to take a look at the glaring darkness in your life. It's also not easy, for nearly everyone I work with, to realize how long, how painful, and how central to their lives these problems have become.

Nearly everybody beats themselves up for not doing more sooner.

Everyone wants to change the past. We feel enormous guilt and resentment toward aspects of our life that we would give anything to change.

And almost everyone has been so badly beaten by these ongoing, intractable waves of stress that they've lost hope that anything can truly be done.

Beating yourself up about not doing more or being better, hating yourself or someone else for past transgressions and mistakes, and believing the present to be unchangeable, will do nothing but keep you sliding backward. It's like a riptide ushering you out to sink in the ocean.

Acceptance is the only way out. Acceptance at this stage is about recognizing that:

1. You've done the best you could, given what you knew at the time.
2. There is no way to reverse course and change the past.
3. Your activation patterns can be changed with time and consistent effort.
4. There is a way to get out of this mess; you just have to find it.

It's a simple list, but it isn't easy for everyone to make peace with. Yes, you missed some opportunities to solve this earlier. Yes, this entire problem could have been unearthed many years ago. Yes, there are others who have wronged you and there are many mistakes you are responsible for. Yes, there are simple and complicated, easy and difficult decisions to be made to create change. And YES, you can do all of this now.

Doing anything else will just slow you down. And you don't have forever. If you're upset about not handling this ten years ago, how upset are you going to be in five years for not handling it now?

So, do not run from the pain. Sit with it, feel it, cry, scream, or bang on the floor. We've all screwed up before and we will all screw up again. But let's not mistake that with failure.

Failure is giving up.

And if you can get through this phase, stand up, and dust yourself off—you won't give up.

This may take real time, now that you know what needs to be done. Your old patterns might be hard to break, but they're not impossible. And you won't make the same mistakes again. Not without recognizing them and making changes. You WILL reach out for help when it's needed. You WILL practice the habits and tools in this chapter and wherever else you can learn them, so that you never find yourself here again. And you WILL let go of the shame, guilt, and resentment that have been holding you back.

You may still have hooks embedded, but by the time you're done with this stage, you will have done a lot to reduce the pain of their pull. You may even find yourself having completely rid yourself of a few.

## Transform

As mentioned, when it comes to dealing with Activation, we will focus on controlling what we can, letting go of what we cannot, and training our tolerance for discomfort. In all honesty, if you are able to focus on only one segment of this book, this one may be the one. It will be your deliverance.

Let's take on your goals, one by one:

### Controlling What You Can

As discussed, your body responds to stress differently when it's controllable versus when it is not. And so, we will first focus on eliminating as much of the uncontrollable stress as possible. We will then turn our attention to taking control of any stress that *is* controllable. Following are guidelines for controlling your biology, psychology, and environment:

**Biology.** Controlling your biological stress involves simple behaviors you've likely considered or even tried before. For some, maintaining these behaviors is a dragon to be slayed; for others, it is more like training their dog. Either way, you have to get this at least partially right; trust me, it will make things easier.

Broadly, you'll need to take care of your sleep, nutrition, breath, and movement.

I provide guidance related to sleep in the Crafting Daily Rituals exercise (page 232) and more are available online (see Resources, page 247), but I want you to think of your biology in this way: Your body is the engine of your machine, like a car's. If you don't take care of it as required, it will start making noises, breaking down, and eventually become unusable. These effects are your negative emotions, your overriding anxieties, and your sleepless nights. The right fuel, oil changes, filters, and care will help it all run more smoothly, and far longer. Your "Check Engine" light is on, and you need to take care of it. If the engine is damaged, it doesn't matter how good the tires are or how nice the sound system is.

**Psychology.** We like being in control, so we tend to look for risks and problems to be fixed instead of focusing on things that are working well. This can create a bias toward a negative experience of life.

The trick is that your brain responds to the questions you ask of it. So, if you ask yourself what needs to be fixed or corrected, your brain will always come up with answers. Along with the answers, you'll also experience anxiety, sadness, and fear. But, if you purposefully seek out the positive, asking yourself, "What am I grateful for?" your brain will scan for the answer to *that* question. In response, your experience will become more positive. I've provided tips for you to develop your own gratitude practice to help invoke this "positivity bias" in the Tips for Effective Gratitude Journaling exercise (page 234). Suffice it to say that, if you are reading your book, you likely have at least hundreds of things to be grateful for in this moment. It's just a matter of attending to them.

Since uncontrollable and unexpected stress causes us the most damage, you will also want to develop a way to plan ahead, reducing the chances of being caught off-guard by stress. Again, I've provided you with my method for doing this in the Defining Daily Success exercise (page 235). By controlling the predictability of stress, you'll also be better prepared to handle anything unexpected that does come up.

Finally, while a stimulus can bring about activation that feels incredibly powerful and permanent, in reality, most of the power in these psychological and physiological activations doesn't actually last as long as we're afraid it might. Getting familiar with the temporary nature of these activations can be accomplished through a mindfulness-based exercise called Urge Surfing (page 236), during which you can develop a better awareness of your internal experience from the start to the end of a triggering event.

**Environment.** Most people I work with massively neglect the influence of their environment on their activation. The reality is that changing your environmental influence can be one of *the* most effective ways to get massive shifts in your typical activation. Recognize that your physical and social environments occur in parallel. With only a few actions you can reduce much of the negative stress being caused regularly by both of these AND increase the positive activation you will experience in a given day to offset the negative stress.

The gist of this transformation is this: Clean up your physical and social environments. Make your physical space and the people you spend time with a source of inspiration and joy, not of negativity and stress. I've included the Enhancing Your Physical Environment for Recovery exercise (page 238) to help get you started.

### Letting Go of What You Cannot Control

The Spheres of Influence exercise you completed earlier is always there to remind you to shift as much of your focus as possible to what you *fully* control. The reality is that you are not in control of most of the events and experiences that surround you. Dealing with this on a daily basis is a matter of two distinct processes:

1.  Shifting your perspective and focus
2.  Developing tools to deal with the residue of discomfort

Hopefully, by now, you've experienced the massive relief, and impact, of focusing on the most controllable aspects of your life. The more of this experience you'll get, the easier it will become to ignore the rest. When it comes to dealing with the discomfort and anxiety you feel when events outside of your control cause you activation, I've included a Mindful Labeling Meditation exercise on page 237.

*Get More Comfortable with Being Uncomfortable*
Training *yourself* to be comfortable with being uncomfortable is the ultimate tool for regaining control over your activation. The message you send yourself by doing this work is this: "I am *not* afraid. Most people run from discomfort, but I don't have to because I am in control of it." You may not feel like a navy SEAL, but you *can* systematically train yourself to increase your activation threshold. These practices build self-esteem, resiliency, and self-control. I've included an exercise, Steps to Push Your Discomfort Threshold, on page 239.

Interestingly, if you try to stick to doing one uncomfortable thing for a while, you will quickly find that it stops being that uncomfortable. We are incredibly adaptable creatures, and you'll even get used to sober karaoke or a cold plunge if you do it frequently enough. The thing is, once that happens, you'll have to find another uncomfortable activity to engage in. *Push yourself* so that, like the navy SEALs, when life throws something at you that you weren't ready for, you'll be able to handle it with substantially more grit than before.

Being diligent about practices that can help you regulate your activation will pay dividends. You will experience improved clarity, sleep, energy, and motivation. You'll also make better choices, because you won't let stress derail your thinking.

It's this last effect that we care about most as we enter into the next stage of the SPARO model: Response. This is where your brain considers the available options and chooses the most appropriate response. Making that choice properly is crucial for success, because the wrong choice can lead us back toward negative outcomes.

So, let's learn how to avoid that.

# CHAPTER 9

# Response

STIMULUS ⟶ PERCEPTION ⟶ ACTIVATION ⟶ RESPONSE ⟶ OUTCOME

Aliyah had been to this particular dealer's house at least two dozen times. He didn't exactly have the best drugs, but he always had something, and that reliability was all she was looking for today. She'd often come alone, but every once in a while she'd show up with a friend—typically someone else who had money and also wanted to score. You could get a much better deal if you bought in larger quantities. It was like the family-size-cereal version of buying street drugs.

On this particular dark and gloomy winter day, Aliyah came to the dealer's house with Brenda. She was hoping to get an eight ball and have enough to make it through the weekend. She'd been trying out my online program and had done really well for the first few months. But then, those damn self-doubt and worthlessness hooks pulled at her, along with the misery about losing her daughters. She started using again. So there she was, in this familiar place, waiting to score. This time, she brought her friend and a pair of headphones. Aliyah had been honest with me and our online group about her recent relapses and, true to our promise, we didn't judge her return to using. So, on this Tuesday afternoon, at one p.m. as usual, she decided to join our group on her headphones while waiting with Brenda to score some meth.

Before this day, whenever Aliyah relapsed, she believed she couldn't return to her recovery support. She believed she wouldn't be welcome until she stopped using again. That's what she'd been told over and over. "Come back when you're ready…" they'd say, and she knew they meant to finish it off with "to stop forever." She never felt quite ready. On this particular Tuesday, Aliyah had a new option she'd never had before—to join her support group while waiting for her drugs. As you've already read about earlier, this unique new possibility ended up changing everything for her. Indeed, this is a necessary step in habit change—realizing that new, positive behaviors can replace old negative ones.

## THE REPLACEMENT CONCEPT

One of the most dramatic realizations I ever had about addiction treatment came early in my graduate school career, while attending a conference. I was having a casual conversation with a woman who sat next to me on the conference shuttle. It was cold outside, and we were passing time as the large bus filled up with other conference attendees who were headed to the massive Washington, DC, convention center. As we were talking about our respective research work, she blurted out one of the most important sentences I'd ever heard. "We're bad at getting people to stop doing anything, but we're much better at getting them to do something else instead," she told me. She was talking about her work on obesity in Massachusetts, where she happened to be a high-ranking official in the Department of Health and Human Services. Apparently, getting people to stop eating unhealthy foods that are terrible for them had proven nearly impossible over many decades. But getting them to replace the bad foods with healthier options proved much easier. She didn't realize the impact, but it was a godly revelation for someone focused on an industry that was essentially always trying to *stop* people from doing things.

What if changing addictive and compulsive tendencies wasn't about quitting them at all? It was time for me to learn more about how we make choices.

## THE RESPONSE PROCESS

Replacing an old behavior with a new one sounds simple enough. But when I studied the process required to perform a specific behavior, I realized that it was actually a bit more complex than expected. Once we are activated to produce a response, we undergo a two-step process:

1. **Response identification**—Identify the menu of potential response options suited to the current activation.
2. **Response selection**—Select the most appropriate response for the current situation and abilities.

I find that most people who struggle with addictive tendencies focus almost all their attention on the Response selection part of the process. In fact, they almost always try to eliminate their compulsive response—*not* drink, *not* use, *not* watch, *not* buy, *not* open the app. In this way, most people find themselves looping constantly between the Outcome and Response stages, using whatever Transformation techniques (usually willpower and avoidance) to try to stop themselves from acting.

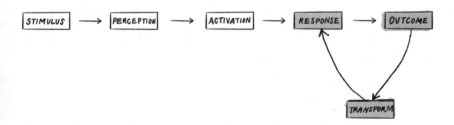

The problem with this approach is that *not* doing something leaves a void that has to be filled. In the SPARO loop, if there is negative activation that needs to be addressed, it's going to require a Response to resolve it. Otherwise, the activation, brought on by the hook, will continue causing pain. Not producing a response doesn't solve anything.

In this chapter, we will work on understanding, and expanding, your Response identification menu, as well as on methods to allow you to successfully select alternative Responses that provide coping without the damage.

## RESPONSE IDENTIFICATION

Think of the different ways you may handle anxiety—you may scroll on your phone, smoke cannabis, or perhaps isolate in your room. It's a bit like going to a restaurant with three items on the menu—the selection is limited. But, after you've become used to the same three items for years, or even decades, you grow accustomed to them and stop looking for new options. The current menu items are cheap (they don't require much effort), they're familiar, and so you keep going back.

Expanding your Response identification menu requires you to first develop a belief that there *are* other options available, and then search for them and practice them. It's about preparing you to "do something else instead." Unfortunately, many of my clients find themselves considering a very limited set of options when it comes to making choices. This is especially true when it comes to their strategies for coping with hooks. In fact, most people I work with have been told they're not in control for so long that they've come to believe it.

What is often missing from the conversation is a true recognition of how these behaviors were learned in the first place. The starting point for the choices you find on your menu is simple—you experimented with what was available and modeled what you saw others do.[1] Kids model the behavior of those around them, creating smaller versions of the people they grow up around. This is our earliest version of the Anchoring Bias, in that what we're exposed to first becomes the standard by which we assess everything that comes after.

And so, the Response stage may be *most* heavily influenced by early development experiences. Sure, Perception and Activation are also learned through exposure, but our Response identification often follows a near-direct "When _____, then _____" sort of script for children as they grow up. As children, we see what happens to those around us and how they react. We gradually collect our own scripts for the appropriate choices in different situations. For example, we may see our father following this script: "When I get home from work, I open the refrigerator, grab a beer, then sit on the couch in front of the television." Since we are unaware of the thoughts, feelings, and inner workings of those we are modeling, we tend to copy only their outward behavior. We don't know that Dad is drinking because he hates his job. We only see his drinking and withdrawing when he gets home. Sometimes, scripts are more directly handed down to us from family members. When we're told, "You better not cry once we leave this house," we see that as parental instructions for not showing negative emotion in public. "When we leave the house, then we make certain to never show that we're feeling badly." These scripts then become the programming that determines how we will behave as situations present themselves later.

One of my mentors, Bruce Lipton, writes that the period of this programming lasts from the third trimester of pregnancy to the age of eight.[2] There is no question that learning begins before we are born. The research I've seen suggests that, indeed, much of our learning is complete by the age of ten. Of course, learning continues into adulthood, but the vast majority of our understanding of how to handle ongoing, daily situations ends long before.

Recall our sponge analogy: When we are born, we are, in many ways, like an unused sponge taken from its packaging. Dry and ready to absorb, we are applied to the world, taking up all the water we can as well as the dirt. Especially early on in our development, we have little control over the water we take on, because our experiences are dictated by those around us. But, as we live and grow, our sponge fills up. We learn how to greet people. We learn what those around us consider good and bad. We understand how to disagree with others and when it's appropriate to do so. We know what we're expected to do when we grow up and what vocational, educational, and marital options we are to pursue.

We have been programmed for how to live.

Whether you are born into an evangelical Christian or a Hasidic Jewish home, a business-minded and money-oriented family or an Indigenous Inuit tribe—your programming for life has been handed down to you. Regardless of how you feel about them, you now have the scripts for your daily activities, which have become cemented: When _____, then _____.

When I get home from work, then I turn on the television.
OR
When I am anxious, then I smoke cannabis.

The modeling you perform early in your development affects your behavioral choices later in life. Your Response identification is almost entirely dependent on the environment you've spent your early life in.

You may not have realized it before, but when you react to situations, the response choices you are selecting from do not represent all the options you have available.

NOT EVEN CLOSE.

They are simply drawn from the responses you modeled, and the programming provided to you through that early life learning.

This thinking also applies to the way we learned our compulsive and addictive behaviors. For most of us, that learning happened quite a while ago, and was modeled as well. For example, many people begin drinking in high school. They've seen others drink (other teenagers, parents, relatives, celebrities in the media, actors in movies

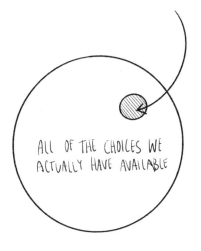

THE CHOICES WE THINK WE HAVE BECAUSE OF WHAT WE'VE SEEN AND LEARNED

ALL OF THE CHOICES WE ACTUALLY HAVE AVAILABLE

and on television), and so they try to model that behavior. But, having no context or real experience with drinking, teens aren't drinking wine to relax from a tough day at work or accentuate their evening meal. Instead, they're drinking to feel older and to imitate. And then they get drunk. Given their relatively small size and lack of experience, it doesn't usually take much alcohol to get teens drunk. And so, in high school, kids learn to drink to get as drunk as possible, usually while hiding their drinking from adults. As they move on to college, drinking becomes more and more public. It also happens to serve the role of an elixir for some. For those who drink to relieve the pull of underlying hooks that are causing emotional pain, drinking can become a more and more central pursuit. Eventually, some drinkers cross the line of what is seen as acceptable. They become labeled as a problem drinker or an alcoholic. Trying to stop, they realize they can't drink any other way. Without the alcohol, they feel lost and dysfunctional. They've found themselves stuck between a rock and a hard place—needing the relief provided by something they don't know how to use responsibly. They never had to develop other tools to deal with their hooks, because the drinking always worked so well. And that's a problem.

Expanding your Response identification menu is all about realizing the limitations of your past learning and identifying that there are other options available to you. As you expand your understanding of what's possible, you can begin to consider alternative responses, eventually finding ones that are a better fit. Then, you can practice them as replacements, until they become your new habits.

But Aliyah didn't know all this on that winter Tuesday as she was waiting to score.

## RESPONSE SELECTION BIAS IN ACTION

Throughout her childhood, Aliyah saw her mom addicted to drugs. She knew her dad had also struggled with drugs, though she didn't really remember him or how he behaved. One thing was clear to her—addicts and alcoholics can't get better, and the success of all their attempts depends on whether they can stay completely sober. Any relapse proves, once again, that they are hopeless and helpless. Aliyah hated the way her mother behaved and wanted nothing to do with the life she grew up around. Sadly, she found herself in the exact same situation when she became an adult. Following the scripts she'd learned growing up led to the exact same outcome for her that her mother had experienced. It felt terrible.

Aliyah didn't want this life for herself *or* her daughters. That's why she kept trying to get "clean," believing herself to be dirty and broken. But treatment after treatment didn't work, and life kept getting worse. After many previous relapse experiences and numerous evictions from rehabs for not doing things perfectly, Aliyah learned that she would be unwelcome in any help setting unless she was ready to stop using. She believed she didn't have the choice of getting help *while* using, because that's what she'd been told over and over.

They definitely wouldn't let you in while you're literally waiting for your drugs at your dealer's house.

But, because our program worked differently and took place virtually, Aliyah had seen us talking in a nonjudgmental way to people who had relapsed. And so, on this particular day, she found herself with a new choice of behavior—showing up to a meeting while waiting at her dealer's for the drugs. Aliyah put on her headphones and gave one earbud to Brenda. And so, as they waited for their meth, they listened in. I was sharing that anecdote I mentioned earlier, comparing our life in active addiction to a person driving a car on a windy mountain road. "As we head down the road, foot heavy on the pedal and traveling at full speed, many of us are aware of the cliff just ahead of us. Still, even as we see this cliff approaching, we feel paralyzed to do anything about our impending doom. We know we're headed straight off that cliff and that if we go off, we may die and never come back. But our hands, on the wheel, feel frozen and unmovable. We forget that, in an instant, we can make the choice to take that wheel and turn it hard—to the left or the right—and change course." I hadn't meant to get so close to the story of Aliyah on that freeway, driving her sister's car and looking for something to hit. "Sure, turning the wheel this way while traveling so fast isn't going to be fun. We may hit the mountainside, we may roll the car, we may still end up causing massive destruction and pain. But at least we'd have a chance at still making it, whereas we know we're done for if we keep heading toward that cliff. At any time, as soon as we realize it, it's up to us to grab that wheel and turn it. We are in control," I ended the story.

Sitting next to Brenda, listening to our meeting, and fully absorbing my message, Aliyah turned to her friend and said, "Let's get out of here." Brenda looked at her confused, trying to connect the dots. "Let's turn the wheel," Aliyah told her. "Let's just go." And so they did. They got up, walked out of that house, and never got that meth. Actually, they never got any more meth. Aliyah and Brenda stopped using that day, and the beginning of a whole new phase of their lives began. They've both remained sober ever since.

Such is the power of new response options.

You may have had an experience like this before, in your own life. Have you ever read a book, listened to a podcast, or watched a film or show that exposed you to an idea or behavior that you didn't even know existed? Have any of those moments ever produced an incredible "Aha" flash for you that changed how you looked at your entire life? If you have, you've experienced an expansion of your Response menu in that moment. With this new response option in place, you found new opportunities for behaviors that, until your Discovery, seemed impossible.

That same exact process can happen at any time for any behavior you're trying to change.

## RESPONSE SELECTION—SO MANY OPTIONS, ONLY ONE RESPONSE

When we address a stimulus that has activated us, most of us have at least a few options available on the Response menu. But no matter how many options we have available, we only get to produce one. And, yes, even doing nothing is choosing a specific option...inaction. So, how do you choose? As with Linda, who used weed to control her nausea, most people I've worked with either have no idea that they're choosing at all or believe they are in full control of their choices. But the reality of Response selection is more complex.

You select the most appropriate response by combining the influence of a large number of factors—some internal, many external—and they don't all point in the same direction. Whichever of your Response menu options has more factors pushing in its favor wins out. Here's an example: James was that local college president I'd mentioned earlier, who had a dark secret—he had a severe drinking problem. Sometimes, he would drink while on the job, but that was rare. Instead, his heavy drinking binges would usually start when he got home from work (as they do for so many). He didn't even binge every night after work. Instead, it would happen sporadically. He couldn't find a real pattern, which was frustrating to him, because it all seemed random. Once we combed James's history, a pattern emerged. As he drove home, he'd be processing the stress from his day (Stimulus). Especially difficult days—lots of fights, administrative BS, or terrible funding news—would make him anxious and afraid. Being the president of this college meant hundreds of parents were looking at him anytime there was trouble. He was afraid (Perception) of losing his job or screwing up and having everyone point him out as a failure. As the anxiety and fear mounted (Activation), the thought of getting some relief at home emerged. He could get a couple of drinks in him and calm down (Response identification). When he arrived home, if his wife's car was in the driveway, he knew he'd have to control his drinking (Response selection option 1). If her car wasn't there, he knew he could immediately start drinking (Response selection option 2). For James, the combination of an especially stressful day, severe fear of public failure and ridicule, and an empty home without his wife's probing presence created a perfect scenario for the start of a heavier drinking night. Each of those factors became a Promoter of heavy drinking for James.

Whether you realize it or not, many factors that have nothing to do with motivation or willpower dictate your chosen response at every moment. Responses vary given the environment, situation, and circumstance. Our brain is always searching for "correct" responses that will provide us with the best fit for a situation. In choosing a response, all the factors that become associated with our behavior join together and make it more likely (Promoters) or less likely (Inhibitors) that we produce a specific response.

Have you ever found yourself attending a dinner, fully intending to have a glass of wine or a beer, when the friend you're with orders a glass of water? Almost immediately, the drive to order a drink is reduced—your friend's choice of *not* drinking subdued your own drinking response (Inhibitor). Or how about the opposite scenario? Ever go to a dinner or an event, certain you didn't intend to consume any alcohol, but then saw the people around you ordering a drink and suddenly found yourself getting one as well? In this case, the social influence of the people around you was a Promoter of drinking.

Some factors that may have served as Promoters or Inhibitors in your past may have included the following:

- Time of day
- People present (or absent)
- Specific music
- A visual stimulus
- An internal feeling
- Seasons or holidays

and so many more.

In James's situation, an empty house, a stressful day, the time being four to five p.m., and severe anxiety were all drinking Promoters. But seeing his wife at home, having a calmer day, and experiencing no anxiety inhibited it.

### SETTING YOURSELF UP FOR RESPONSE
### SELECTION SUCCESS: THE P/I RATIO

I initially introduced the concept of the P/I Ratio in Chapter 3. Now that you understand the multiple forces that act on our behaviors, it makes sense to get a deeper understanding of how they work together.

Addiction thrives when the Promoters of the addictive behavior far outweigh the Inhibitors. This leads to constant and ongoing repetition. Without enough Inhibitors to counteract it, the behavior seems to go on, unchecked, until the chips get stacked in the other direction.

Fortunately, the P/I Ratio is something we can manipulate, and that's when behavioral change becomes evident (see the Assessing Your Promoters and Inhibitors [P/I Ratio] exercise on page 241).

Knowing the power of Promoters and Inhibitors in directing responses, you can put the pieces in place to support the behaviors you want. This can be crucial to your success, because it removes the need for strong willpower at every turn. Willpower waxes and wanes, but *consistency* is an absolute must for long-term change. Once you identify your Promoters and Inhibitors, you can begin arranging these factors in your life to support the direction you want to go in. *Change is inevitable, but you can either leave the direction of change to chance or take control of it.*

So, let's control as much as we can! For example, if James is serious about changing his after-work drinking, he could talk with his wife and ask to check in with her on video chat every day when he gets home. This way, he can reinforce the drinking Inhibitor to be more consistently present after work. If playing basketball with friends helps relieve his work pressure, he could do that a few times a week on his way home from work.

One of the most common Inhibitors for people I work with has to do with physical access. For instance, if you're working to limit or eliminate your drinking, get rid of the alcohol in your house. Not having alcohol available is a great Inhibitor to drinking because it makes the act of drinking more difficult. You can also promote a new habit by replacing the alcohol with a full stock of other things you like to drink.

Everyone reading this will have a different set of unique Promoters and Inhibitors. It's important to recognize those and recruit them in your quest for change.

Here's a simple example of how this may play out in a completely different context: Imagine walking up to a pull-up bar and deciding you'd like to be able to do a pull-up. With considerable effort, you jump up and hold the bar with both hands. You do your best to pull your body up, but you barely move. You try again but get the same result. By the second or third attempt, even holding on to the bar is difficult. Frustrated, you jump off, giving up. But just because you can't do a pull-up the first time you try it does not mean you're actually incapable of performing a pull-up. It simply means you don't know how to do this exercise and that your muscles are not strong enough. Yet. If you can't do a pull-up because you aren't strong enough, motivation and an available pull-up bar won't be enough to get you up there. You're going to have to use other tools to help you. To perform an actual pull-up, you could use workout bands, help from others, hanging resistance, or assisted pull-up machines (all Promoters of completing a pull-up). Each of those tools (Response identification) increases your ability to perform a pull-up, decreasing the chances that you'll do something else, such as hanging on the bar or quitting.

## MAXIMIZING THE PROBABILITY OF CREATING APPROPRIATE RESPONSES

To maximize the probability that you will choose your new behaviors over the old, habitual ones, do the following: Load up on Promoters that increase the likelihood of your new responses and eliminate Inhibitors for them. Then, do the opposite for your old behavior—maximize its Inhibitors and do your best to eliminate its Promoters. Eventually, a few things will happen. First of all, the Inhibitors and Promoters you've put in place will become more common in your life, making them a regular part of your environmental influence. This will make it even more likely that you'll stay on track. As you gain practice in the new behaviors and make them more habitual, you'll need less support to produce them. It's called the *flywheel effect*—it takes time to get started, but once you get going, it takes less and less effort to keep the wheel moving.

Think of a person who has three years of experience doing pull-ups. They can now do ten in a row, so help from workout bands or a helping friend is no longer required. This is related to the cliff metaphor I used in the last chapter. Using the Inhibitors and Promoters is like setting up guardrails around the cliff. With practice, as you get stronger, you find yourself moving away from the cliff itself. Then, the Inhibitors and Promoters become a protective fence around you. The fence is made up of such things as your social circle, your daily habits, and your commitments and skills (see the Social Circle Audit exercise on page 245). After enough practice and consistent application, you find yourself a mile away from the cliff, surrounded by this protective fence. Now, to "slip up" again, you would have to break through the fence, drive a mile, and hurl yourself off that cliff. It's a long and unlikely journey. But let's be clear: getting to this place in your life, where you have a wide repertoire of well-practiced behavior choices, will also require you to get comfortable with another concept—the difference between your desired outcomes and the actual results of your actions.

## THE BRIDGE BETWEEN INTENTION, RESPONSE, AND OUTCOMES

Once you select a response that you believe will deliver the best outcome, you have to go about performing it. This is often where reality and intention collide. If you're like me, there is sometimes a big difference between what you've committed to doing, what you think will happen, and how your actions appear in the world. This is an important distinction that most people don't consider. What it means is this: We have to make plans, because without plans we have no direction and no way to judge how we're doing. But plans are full of assumptions and faults and gaps. When you follow through on a plan, it will have to change, adjust, and conform to how it actually plays out in the real world.

This may sound counterintuitive if you remember our discussion of having control over our own behavior (see the Spheres of Influence exercise, page 228). But it simply reflects one of the realities of life. While we are relatively in control of the behavior we engage in (given all the limitations and constraints we put on the Perception → Activation → Response selection conversation), we have little control over what happens once we act. The moment I say something out loud, I leave its interpretation to those I am speaking to. Even when I buy a gift for my wife, I have no control over her reaction to it.

No matter our *intention* for an action, it is outside of our control once we put it out into the world. So, how do we know which response is "good" and which is "bad" until we see the outcome it produces?

And does the quality of our decision-making always depend on the outcome? Do good decisions always result in good outcomes? Unfortunately, the answer is often more complicated than we want it to be. And the exact same thing is true when it comes to bad habits and addictive behavior:

- When I chose to take that drink and it helped me finally feel comfortable around people, was the decision right or wrong?
- When Linda took a drag off that joint in high school to stop her nausea and it worked, was that a bad choice or exactly what she needed to join her peers and feel "normal"?
- When Aliyah turned to drugs to even out her terrible feelings of low self-worth, fear, and pain in her complicated and troubled life, was she making a mistake or doing her best to survive?
- When a successful lawyer like Michael hides traumatic experiences from his childhood, trying to distance himself and move on with his life, is he lying or being strong?
- When Jaylen uses porn instead of confronting his wife about his need for more physical intimacy, is he just taking care of his needs, or is he being selfish?

How do you judge what is good and bad when you haven't seen the result of the action? And what time frame are we supposed to use when making that judgment?

Over the years, I've learned that the vast majority of people I see have simply been trying to do their best at every single moment along their path. The judgments we make about others (true to such biases as the Anchoring Bias, Fundamental Attribution Error, Confirmation Bias, and others we've discussed) are based on our momentary perspectives and lack empathy, insight, and compassion for the relative context of their Response selection.

We need to understand that even the best Response selection may deliver imperfect results, given everything else that is involved. But, as we make better decisions and perform the most appropriate and effective responses, the results themselves will continue to improve. I have found this to be true over and over in my own life and the lives of thousands of others. Sometimes, the outcomes come quickly, sometimes slowly, but consistency and discipline will always win the day. I know that with certainty. I just can't tell you how long it will take.

## APPLYING THE EAT PRINCIPLES TO THE RESPONSE STAGE

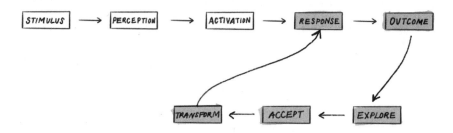

If you're exploring change at the Response stage, you're feeling completely controlled by your inability to change how you behave once you've been activated in specific ways. Your options for coping seem limited and you find yourself leaning on your unhealthy, addictive responses when the hooks create a big enough Activation.

By now, you have also developed a much deeper understanding and appreciation of the reasons behind the behaviors you've been so desperately trying to change.

You know that the reasons behind your behaviors have nothing to do with you being "damaged," "broken," or defective. Instead, you have been developing coping strategies to deal with the ongoing activation of past hooks in your life. Fully grasping the extent to which your past informs your present can provide you with a renewed sense of hope, or an increased feeling of desperation. On one side, you now understand that your past informed this present and that your actions actually make sense from that perspective. You may also feel as if it might be impossible to change this late in the game. Interestingly, I've heard this sort of thinking from people in their thirties, forties, fifties, and sixties. It isn't so much about age and experience. It's about a mindset.

There's a name for the mind-set you'll need to adopt. Dr. Carol Dweck, a champion of what she calls the Growth Mindset, defines it as the belief in our ability to change.[3] We'll discuss the Growth Mindset in more detail on pages 204–205. But let me assure you of this:

You *will* continue changing and learning and adapting forever. No one actually stays the same as they move through life. I've seen people from as young as twenty to as old as seventy change in meaningful and productive ways. Change is possible. Indeed, change is guaranteed.

The question here is simple: Do you want input and control *over* the change, or to continue letting it happen *to* you?

This is an important question.

If you want to control the direction of your change, you'll have to believe it is possible.

You will also have to do the work it requires.

There are no shortcuts and no hacks.

There are four progressive stages to shifting your Response: **Discovery**, **Selection**, **Experimentation**, and **Repetition**. In the following section, we'll map these across the Explore, Accept, and Transform process.

### Explore

You are going to use Exploration here to identify the existing repertoire of responses you currently have available to you, and then work on discovering new alternatives.

I've provided an exercise on page 246 in Appendix B to allow you to dive deeply into exploring your current Response Identification Menu. Here, I want to show you what a limited Response Identification Menu looks like, in practice:

- Stuck in a job you hate for years—quit, fight with your boss, just take it, or drink to forget.
- Unhappy in your marriage and in the middle of a fight— binge Netflix, hit your partner, call someone else for attention, or drink to stop caring.
- Bored, feeling disconnected and depressed—lie in bed all day hating life, scroll social media endlessly, drink or use drugs to make the experience less painful, or contemplate ending your life.

You can see that, in many of these situations, the drinking/using option is certainly not the worst. Sure, it's easy to intellectually think of additional alternative solutions. But things feel different when you're actually activated and having to come up with solutions in real time. Remember, when under stress, your decision-making is compromised. Depending on your experience and resources, if confronted with my three examples, you may not yet know how to

- Walk into your boss's office and have a challenging but crucial conversation.
- Come to your partner and emphatically declare that you feel a need to seriously pursue couples counseling.
- Get out into the world to connect to nature or other potentially exciting and enlivening options that the world has in store for you.

These alternative behaviors are challenging, even when you are well versed in them. If you're a novice or unfamiliar, they can seem damn near impossible—like a Mount Everest sort of climb.

What you have to remember is that you're currently relying on the limited menu of options you've learned. *You have to expand that limited menu.* But where are you going to find other potential responses? That's where the Discovery process comes in.

## Discovery

This first stage is all about searching outside your immediate knowledge base. You have to look out into the world, withhold judgment, and see what other potential responses might be available. This can be challenging for several reasons, but chief among those is the Confirmation Bias we discussed earlier. Your brain is much more likely to see, pay attention to, and remember information that supports your current knowledge. So, for example, if you struggle with watching too much porn (as many as 30 percent of men hide their porn use from their partner[4]), you may believe that all men secretly watch porn. To complete the first stage of expanding your Response selection, you will need to put this belief aside and ask, "Other than watching porn, what are some ways men in relationships deal with their anxiety, sexual frustration, or depression?" You will then go on a quest to discover what other options exist.

Where do you find this sort of knowledge?

You can discover this information in books, listen to podcasts, watch documentaries, or attend workshops, retreats, and seminars. In fact, the more varied and outside your usual comfort zone these sources of information are, the better. This is because the behaviors practiced

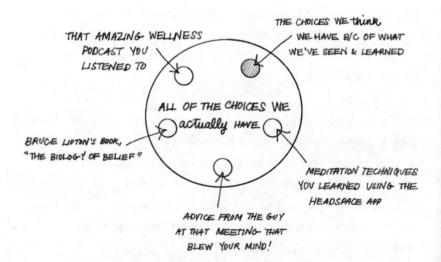

in different cultures, among people you don't know, and drawing on experiences and beliefs you don't hold, are more likely to be different than the options you already have.

Once you've gone on this exploratory hunt, you're ready to move to Selection.

## Selection

With a whole slew of new alternative response options, it's time to do some soul-searching. Which of these options seem most relevant for you? Which do you believe might help you change? Which are too difficult or out of step with your way of living? During this process, you'll narrow down options to a more manageable list of choices you're interested in pursuing. For example, you may find that some men have overcome their hidden porn use by reconnecting with religion. Others may have used cognitive behavioral therapy (CBT) or meditation. One of those options may feel more relevant for you than others. This is *your* life, and you need to make the choice about what options are appropriate for *you*. While Discovery is challenging due to preexisting biases and limited knowledge, some people get caught in analysis paralysis during Selection. With too many options, it's sometimes hard to make any choice at all. Research has shown us that having too many choices is confusing and makes decisions and motivation more difficult.[5] This is why creating a manageable list is important in the Selection stage. I like to recommend that clients focus on no more than five options they're interested in. If you find more options interesting, pick your top five.

The Discovery and Selection processes make up the Exploration stage. In this way, the Discovery part is like a fun scavenger hunt. How many new options can you find? It's important that you keep an open mind and not yet critique these new response options as appropriate, effective, or relevant to you.

Think of these like a literal menu expansion. Like Anthony Bourdain, Adam Richman, Andrew Zimmern, or Zac Efron, traveling the world in search of exotic, healthy, spicy, or just outright weird new dishes, you will experience a new menu that will have exciting new options for you to sample and try. You may even feel a little excitement at the new set of opportunities you have to improve your Response menu and create change.

The more open and curious you remain in the face of these new menu options, the better prepared you'll be to move into Acceptance.

**Accept**
The acceptance stage for Response requires you to make peace with two different concepts:

1. Your historical behavior pattern is not an indication that you're broken, but a natural result of the circumstances of your life.
2. Your exploration of new response options will be imperfect, take more time than you'd like, and include failures.

Many of those who struggle with bad habits beat themselves up for their historically damaging behavior, so the mere notion of making peace with the process it took to get there can be challenging. The problem is that until you accept that these behaviors were developed through experience and are not indications that you're broken, you will have difficulty fully recognizing the power of learning to change your future. If you think you're broken, you will have a hard time believing that you can become fixed.

When a child is taught to mistrust others at a young age, it makes sense that they will develop anxious or avoidant tendencies as an adult. Trust will be difficult to establish with close loved ones. This isn't a malfunction of the system. It's an appropriate response to the situation.

Once you understand that you're not damaged but are actually responding in precisely the way that made sense when the behaviors were learned, you recognize that you can adapt and learn new ways of responding. In this way, the Response stage can sometimes make it easier to accept our past learning. Because, more than only accepting the past, Acceptance here means taking responsibility for the required persistence, consistency, and discipline that are required to practice and become proficient in alternative behaviors. You're not focusing only on the primary behavior that is troubling you. You've identified alternative options that need reinforcing. Now, it is your responsibility to make the effort to practice them.

**PRO TIP:** I tell my clients often that, to do self-improvement well, you have to hold the following two opposing ideas in your mind at the same time: I am at peace with where I am and who I am at the moment AND I am always striving to get even better. Accepting only one of these will create either misery (failing to accept the first) or complacency (failing to accept the second). If we want to feel happy and joyous on our way to being better, the balanced holding of both will get us there.

When just starting out, you may have to both accept that you are terrible at your new behaviors *and* that you will one day master them. To "embrace the suck" means to consciously accept or appreciate something that is extremely unpleasant, because it is necessary to be able to move forward. You're going to have to learn how to do that. Get comfortable with being uncomfortable, because you know it's going to make you more comfortable in the long run. That's what winners learn to do. And you're a winner (only winners read and follow the Pro Tips).

Another area where some people need to practice acceptance has to do with what they feel is slow progress. We all want big wins, and we want them fast. You can have fast and easy change, but it probably won't last very long—think fad diets, the newest self-improvement gadget, or those pretty clothes that self-destruct after five to ten laundry cycles. If you want long-lasting change, it's going to take time and a consistent investment of effort. Acceptance is about learning to celebrate and acknowledge the progress on your way to the top of the mountain. You know you've mastered Acceptance when you can look at yourself, know you're giving everything you've got, and trust that you're on your way to your goal.

### Transform

You've discovered a whole slew of new alternative behaviors and have selected the ones you're most excited about trying out for yourself. How do you start performing them in a way that supports your progress, increases the odds that you will end up with the outcomes you want, and allows you to build confidence in your ongoing development?

You do this by performing the real Response transformation work—Experimentation and Repetition.

As I mentioned earlier, too many people make the mistake of simply trying to stop themselves from engaging in the behavior that troubles them. But replacing problematic behavior(s) with new options is a much more effective strategy. If, when you get into a terrible fight with your spouse, you see your options as screaming at them, leaving them, or taking a drink, drinking doesn't seem like such a terrible option. But if you learn to add some options—such as going on a thirty-minute walk on your own, taking two minutes to do some breathing, or saying to them before the fight breaks out, "I don't think I can hear you because I am getting angry. Let's stop the discussion right now and come back in an hour"—you now have new responses to practice, which reduces the probability of the other responses being performed. In this section, you'll learn how to increase the probability of producing the most appropriate responses!

You've expanded your available responses and selected a handful of them. Next will come practice and reflection. The big question is really about consistency and reliability. Can you manage this behavior over the long term? Does it seem to be moving you in the direction in which you were hoping to go?

The concept of the "1 percent principle" is very important for us here: even the smallest incremental progress toward our goal is to be celebrated as a win. And small successes build upon each other in a compounding manner, making them more powerful over time. We have to leave behind the nonsense notion that you must see massive change quickly to prove that you are on the right path. Success is rarely a straight line. There is no short fix for long-standing problems. But, as long as you can acknowledge your progress and keep moving, step by step by step, you will end up experiencing success. Take a moment to take this in fully. You can't lose fifty pounds without losing twelve pounds first. You can't get good at relationships without dealing with difficult conversations and conflict. You can't rescue yourself from trauma, depression, and decades of heavy drinking without first gaining awareness, experiencing subtle changes, and being diligent about walking up that mountain. Until you conquer it.

*Experimentation*

Once you select a smaller list (no more than five to start) of possibilities, it's time to commit and try one. This may sound simple, but it can become a place where many get stuck. You usually have to start by practicing a single new response. This means that you must again select from your narrowed list and choose the first behavior you want to experiment with.

To help with this final selection, ask yourself the following questions:

- What behavior holds my biggest potential for immediate change?
- What in my life will make these behaviors more likely (Promoters) and what will make them more difficult (Inhibitors)?
- What help might I need in cementing this new practice in my life? Who might be able to help me?

Unfortunately, even with the best preparation, your initial experimentation will likely not go perfectly. It may work immediately, but since you're not well practiced, it will likely produce suboptimal results. For many people, especially after numerous attempts at changing their behavior, engaging in yet another "failed" attempt can be disheartening. We don't like doing things we're not good at, and the reality of this process is that you will end up experimenting with behaviors you've never practiced before. That means you could start out performing poorly.

The goal of the Experimentation phase is to begin this process with a behavior you believe can become a replacement response for you. You must leave behind the inevitable expectations you will have about the results of these early experiments.

The Experimentation phase will give you some very valuable information:

- How easy is producing this behavior for me?
- How good is this behavior at helping address the Activation I'm experiencing?
- How committed and motivated am I to continue practicing this behavior?

Just because you can't do something well the first time you try it, does not mean the behavior is not worthwhile. Experiment with a few different behaviors and compare their relative "price." Ideally, you'll find a few that are easy to perform and produce substantial relief. Once you've found at least one behavior that fits this concept, it's time to move on.

*What stands in the way of improving your Response?*
Reading through this concept of the Response selection, you may be thinking to yourself one of two things:

- This sounds way too easy to be true.
- I've tried to do this before and it doesn't work.

Let me be clear: This process is not an easy one. Many factors and influences get in the way of expanding your Response selection. First, the options you will consider available and appropriate are heavily determined by the people around you. This includes your family, friends, culture, and colleagues. Most of these people are not *actively* seeking change, and are not incorporating new behaviors. For example, if you grew up in a house where rampant drinking and drug use were common, and you decide that you want to change your behavior as an adult, it is unlikely that anyone in your childhood home environment will be able to give you any new ideas or help. Indeed, they may even support your ongoing problematic behavior and enable it further.

Ironically, the same problem could occur in the opposite scenario, if you grew up in a family without any addiction struggles. In that environment, it is also unlikely that those close to you can provide new ideas for addressing any problems you may be having. They may simply offer solutions that have worked for them in the past, like the ubiquitous "This is bad for you! Just stop!" The Exploration process is, therefore, one that is either completely self-initiated or brought on by consultation with professionals or others who have struggled themselves.

The Discovery stage is also different when you have made numerous previous attempts at fixing the problem. Given the seeming failure of those previous attempts, you may point the finger at yourself, thinking, *There must be something wrong with me.* This thinking is incredibly damaging and relates back to the work of the Perception chapter. It is important to note that nobody can precisely predict what new behaviors will work for any specific person. You must select potential tools and techniques that you at least believe may be effective for you.

You may also be paralyzed by too many options, or become uncertain about the potential outcomes of any of the tools and techniques you've learned about. When you have a hundred options for which way to go, it can be difficult to choose one path. Remember to start your selection with a small, manageable number—no more than five.

Once you select a response, it is almost guaranteed that your initial attempts will be somewhat uncomfortable, more difficult to produce than anticipated, and less successful than you'd like. It is important that you go into the Experimentation stage understanding this, rather than expecting to hit a home run. Some people find useful tools on the first try, and others have to dig through dozens. This fact does not make the former group "better" or the latter group "worse." It's simply the reality of the search.

### Repetition

Once you have found a set of helpful tools, you must find the internal drive to keep practicing them even when they're difficult and seemingly produce only marginal improvement. Again, this is akin to a person who decides that they want to perform pull-ups and show up day after day unable to produce a single one. While it is guaranteed that, with practice, anyone can complete a pull-up, it is also incredibly common for most people to quit before reaching that goal. The same is true in behavioral change. Most people find it difficult to continuously find the motivation to keep showing up when change is slow. This is an excellent opportunity to practice the concept of *getting comfortable with being uncomfortable*. The better you are at showing up, experiencing failure, and then showing up again, the more likely you are to succeed.

Read that again—the more comfortable you are with experiencing the failures that occur along the way, the more likely you are to succeed.

In a way, this is one of the most important lessons for those seeking to change their lives—**failure is not the opposite of success; it's a necessary ingredient**. No one has ever succeeded in doing anything meaningful without first experiencing defeat. The only question is how you show up after you've failed.

Once you realize that you will be able to complete the coveted pull-up, the act of jumping back up on the bar is one of dogged commitment and discipline. The Repetition stage continues for any potential behavior, until you've practiced it enough for it to essentially become a new habit. In this way, repetition is the practice that gradually reduces the "price" of this particular menu item you've adopted. You are creating and reinforcing the new neural connections that reinforce a brand-new way of behaving when presented with specific Stimuli, Perceptions, and Activations. In short, you are training yourself to respond differently when your hooks begin pulling. These new response options will eventually replace your old habits.

## THE CHALLENGING IMPACT OF THOSE AROUND YOU

While you may be involved in trying to change, most people around you are probably not. This means that you will experience constant pressure to return to the way things were. At times, it will feel like a gravitational force pulling you back to the beginning. You may be surprised by how much resistance you seem to get from others, but most who change their behavior will experience it. Ironically, even the people in your life who want you to change can end up repeating the same cycles they are asking you to stop. There may even be relationships that are so unsupportive or damaging to your efforts that you will face the fundamental question of whether you need to let them go. Yes, you may even lose some people who have been important in your life.

I told you this may not be easy.

However, many of these unsupportive or damaging relationships will prove to be connected to the hooks that have been holding you back in the first place.

Letting these relationships go, or doing the hard work required to repair and redirect them, will be necessary if you want to experience long-term transformation. Humans are social animals. We need others in our lives. But our relationships also determine the quality of life we experience. So, we should be selective. We'll discuss relationships more fully later, but for now, know this: many of the clients I've worked with have had to retool substantial portions of their social ecosystem.

This isn't always a bad thing.

## THE SUCCESS INDEX

Next, you'll have to have a way to measure your progress. I think that the biggest mistake many people make here is relying on a single measure, and often the wrong one. As I mentioned before, when it comes to addictive tendencies, the most common way to measure success has to do with measuring the number of "consecutive days abstinent"—how many days you haven't had a drink, taken pills, used porn, or played video games. I've already pointed out the limitations of this way of measuring success. I will discuss what to measure more comprehensively on pages 210–211, but I want to give you an important start right here.

First, we have to measure our progress on the new habits we are trying to build, not just the bad habits we are trying to stop. If we measure both, even better! So, for instance, if in doing this work you've realized that you experience substantial social anxiety and are working to rid yourself of it, you have to measure your progress in this area. If you've begun practicing meditation or have taken on a gratitude-list morning habit, or if you've started practicing yoga, or seeing a therapist, or connecting with a like-minded group of supportive peers, let's measure your growth in these areas.

If you realized that your marriage is suffering and that you need to work on the relationship, you'll have to measure that. How often are you fighting? How long are the fights lasting? How often do you feel that you've had a good day in the relationship? How long does it take to recover after a fight? How many date nights have you gone on? How many times have you touched, kissed, hugged, had sex? On a scale of 1 to 10, how would you rate your relationship overall? It is these aspects of improvement that we care about, not only whether you are still drinking.

Regarding the addictive behavior itself, you should incorporate more nuance into your progress assessment: How much are you using on average on days when you do use? How many days of not using have you had in the past week/month/year? How often are you being honest about your use versus hiding it? How often is the using affecting other areas of your life? How often are you using more than you'd like? How long is it taking you to recover from instances of using? In using these more nuanced and complex ways of measuring progress, you may find you are absolutely moving forward in your quest for improvement, even if getting thirty days full sober is still eluding you. When Terry came in, she was a heavy drinker, drinking two bottles of wine (approximately ten drinks) per day. After thirty days, she experienced the following results: drinking half as much as usual, drinking four days per week instead of daily, and not hiding her drinking from others. Wouldn't you call that massive progress? I would!

## TERRY'S JOURNEY THROUGH THE EAT PROCESS IN RESPONSE

In a strained relationship, with her husband gone weekly and no apparent tools or hope for things to improve, Terry finds herself depressed, alone, and hopeless. How might she use the four stages outlined: Discovery, Selection, Experimentation, Repetition?

Terry uses her daily drinking to make the time go by, connect with some of her friends, and help her feel that she hasn't lost out entirely in life. When her husband is home, things go terribly. They fight daily, and it generally ends in screaming in front of the kids. Terry's husband hasn't hit her, but she's hit him a few times. When she's drunk, she doesn't care as much and the fights don't feel as bad. She can pass out at night, making falling asleep easier given all her anxiety. This has been happening for years with no seeming end. But now Terry's husband is insisting that she stop drinking. She's tried to cut down or stop for the past three years, but it hasn't worked. She feels out of options. She's sure she's an "alcoholic" and feels desperate.

**Terry's Discovery**

Terry feels like she only has a few options when she's anxious and upset in her marriage:

- Fight with her husband
- Hold her feelings in and feel anxious and panicked
- Dream of leaving her marriage behind
- Drink herself into oblivion

She chooses to drink most days, but sometimes one of the other three options wins out. None of these options actually allows her to feel good. Sometimes, she feels better when the family is on vacation, but nothing else really works. When it comes to exploring new options, Terry could try Discovery by listening to podcasts, reading books, or attending workshops. But on what topics?

At first, she'd begin with books and podcasts on how to drink less. But slowly these sources expose her to new options. Although listening to podcasts on drinking is fine, Terry's real difficulty lies in her marriage and her feeling of loss about where life has taken her (she had such a promising future before the kids and her husband's constant travel schedule for work!). Her true need was to take in content about marriage, relationships, communication, and female empowerment.

In opening herself up to new knowledge, she could have found Dr. Andrew Huberman's work on morning rituals for improved daily functioning. She may have been exposed to Lisa Bilyeu's podcast on female empowerment and general badassery. Her sadness and frustration in life could have been helped by Mel Robbins's books and content on happiness and finding yourself. In these, Terry would have discovered dozens of new thoughts, activities, concepts, and approaches for living her life.

Among these may be

- Imago couples therapy
- Mindfulness and meditation practices

- Gardening in her backyard
- A powerful morning routine she'd practice before the kids woke up
- Going back to playing tennis with friends
- Getting a sitter during the daytime, to allow her to take a midday workout class
- Cold exposure therapy
- Gut- and microbiome-balancing supplements
- Ideas about programs for returning to school

There could be hundreds of options and ideas that Terry had either never heard of or seriously considered. These would all go on her list of potential new response options.

### Terry's Selection

Now came the filtering part, which is crucial. Terry needed to identify five options (no more) she would seriously consider implementing, focusing on feasibility and ease.

Couples therapy was out of the question. Unfortunately, her husband was not interested. So, on her list of options, we put down

- Going to her own therapy
- Establishing a more substantial and consistent self-care routine
- Relying more on her sitter during the day
- Adopting a meditation practice, along with her sister
- Taking some workshops on parenting practices to reduce overwhelm

With three children, there was undoubtedly ongoing tension. She needed to have daily tools to handle her stress. She also began looking into doing some legal work in a local law office and thought about going back to school (she had been studying law before having kids).

Finally, Terry started a conversation with an attorney about potential separation from her husband. Yes, this step was a difficult and more controversial one, but it was relevant, given her partner's unwillingness to work on the relationship. At this stage, she was just choosing which options she could dive into further, not actually selecting what she'd follow through on in the end.

We used the Spheres of Influence exercise (page 228) to help Terry get laser focused on the aspects of her life she fully controlled. She exerted control by choosing the subset of behaviors she wanted to actually test out.

### Terry's Experimentation

Now it was time for Terry to actually try some of the behaviors she'd selected.

She was nervous; I reminded her that experimentation is not necessarily going to be enjoyable or very effective, initially.

I also recommended that she try to have some fun in the Experimentation stage, and not take herself, or the results of each small experiment, too seriously. She was—as you will be—there to see how these practices actually showed up in her life. Taking up hiking as a morning practice may have sounded like a great way to clear her head, until she realized that she lived too far from a proper hiking spot.

Once Terry had her list, we had to take away judgment and start experimenting. She started with one practice at a time. She didn't have to rush—and neither do you.

Terry experimented with going to therapy and practicing meditation with her sister. Having a weekly place to process her emotions and thoughts gave her more insight than ever before. She'd been avoiding therapy because she thought it would make her feel worse to talk about her trouble. But it actually provided some measure of the escape she could only find in alcohol just weeks before. And meditation allowed her to connect to her sister and learn to control her Activations. She was getting some initial relief simply by engaging in these new behaviors. She was becoming *hopeful.*

### Terry's Repetition

In the Growth Mindset literature, the kind of Repetition we want is known as Deliberate Practice, coined by psychologist Anders Ericsson. Deliberate Practice has specific requirements:[6]

- Identify the behaviors that you could perform better. These are the options you've picked in the Selection phase (see page 171).
- Set aside specific time to practice the behaviors you are specifically *not* good at.
- Get feedback on your performance.
- Adjust your practice based on feedback and then practice more.

Terry ended up reducing her drinking from two bottles of wine per day to two bottles per week. This reduction of 85 percent in her drinking and her move from daily drinking to one to three days per week was an enormous success. But she didn't have a full month of not drinking yet, and so her therapist couldn't see her progress. What a way to sabotage incredible success and create shame! Remember, if you focus on measuring the more complete picture of your progress, you'll be much more likely to follow through on the things that are working. Terry did just that.

I want you to carefully consider your Experimentation phase for early results. Are there any promising practices you've experimented with? Are there any practices that have moved you in a positive direction, even if they're incredibly challenging? Have you found any new responses that have made you grow? If you have, make note and focus on Deliberately Practicing these—they could be an essential part of your new toolkit.

Clients ask me an important question:

*"If doing the things that are bad for me creates stress, tension, and discomfort, but so does practicing the things that are actually good for me, how can I tell the difference?"*

Here is the key.

Ask yourself, "If I project into the future and imagine myself practicing this behavior until I become an expert in it, will my life have moved in the direction I want it to?"

If the answer is a resounding "YES!" then keep going and committing to the work, no matter how difficult or uncomfortable. If you're unsure, ask for advice from someone you trust. If it's a "No," drop it like a bad habit… it probably is.

## A FINAL WORD ON THE RESPONSE STAGE

If you have been diligent about this stage, you will have found a handful of very promising new practices that have the potential to completely change your life. The list can be nearly endless. There is no way for me to know which are most relevant for you without diving more deeply into your circumstances and going through Experimentation. But you will know, and if this does prove too challenging, feel free to seek help or join one of our programs and get actual hand-holding and guidance. *You can't beat your addictions without replacing your responses.*

As you go through practice and Repetition, you will hone and make habitual these new practices that will completely change how you behave after Activation by hooks that previously controlled you. To increase the odds that you will perform these responses consistently, you will have put in place Promoters that drive them, while introducing Inhibitors that make your old, unhelpful Responses less likely. You will measure your success holistically, so that you have a clear idea of your improvement as you practice. Gradually, these new options will become well-practiced habits, and the outcomes in your life will change significantly.

To review the changes you can expect, we'll have to go right back to where we started, only better informed. The new Outcome stage comes up next.

## CHAPTER 10

# Revisiting Outcomes

It was September 2016, and I was driving home after a long day of work. With a long commute, my workdays were a fourteen-hour affair. Sophie and I wanted more room than our little two-bedroom apartment afforded us, so we moved to the San Fernando Valley. "The Valley" was long known as the seedier, more affordable, and slightly more boring outpost of Los Angeles. I would have to wake up at five thirty a.m. every day to get out of the house before six a.m. If I left the house any later, my commute would double, from forty-five minutes to an hour and a half.

I wasn't used to waking up this early, but in life you sometimes have to sacrifice. I would leave the house before six a.m., and be at the office by seven. I would work until about six p.m., waiting for traffic to slightly ease, and then leave at around six thirty for my hour-and-a-half commute home. I'd walk in the door by eight p.m. Those were long days.

I had cofounded a rehab center with another psychologist, and the work was grueling yet meaningful. We were helping people and were starting to experience some success. But I was new to business and I had to learn a lot on the fly. It was stressful. I was managing a real team for the first time in my life, all while seeing clients, sometimes painting walls, and trying to keep it together. It was hard.

And so, on one particular September day, walking into the house at eight p.m., I put down my bag, headed straight to the kitchen, grabbed a double glass and my bottle of bourbon, and poured myself a drink. As I put the bottle back up in the cabinet, I heard Sophie say, "You've been drinking a lot more than usual recently."

I paused.

I was taken aback.

I took her words in and let them settle.

Had I been drinking more than usual? Was she right?

I started looking back at the last few days. Then, the last few weeks. Within less than a minute of self-reflection, I realized that there was at least some truth to her words. For the past few months, I'd been drinking four or five days a week. On each of those days, I'd have at least one of those double pours of bourbon. On many nights, I had more than one. I also drank on the weekends. I may not have regularly made it all the way to a "heavy drinker." (Our health authorities define that as having fourteen or more drinks per week for a man.) But I sure was cutting it close.

Damn.

Here I was, the owner of a drug rehabilitation center, going home every day and drinking. How did I not catch this earlier? Did anyone else know? Was this affecting my work? Was I slipping back into my old addiction?

I immediately poured out the bourbon, turned to Sophie, and started a conversation . . .

## RECONSIDERING OUR OUTCOMES

Every single one of us will end up experiencing outcomes we don't like. I didn't like feeling like a fraud, running a treatment center yet drinking regularly. Aliyah didn't like coming to and realizing she'd lost her daughters because of her behavior. Jaylen dreaded nearly destroying his marriage because of his sexual acting out. Linda was frustrated finding out she couldn't get a job she wanted because she couldn't stop smoking weed. Terry hated being yelled at by her husband for another night of uncontrollable drinking. Michael couldn't handle collapsing in front of his clients and embarrassing himself. Every single one of the stories you heard in this book began with a negative experience.

But ending up with outcomes we don't like isn't the problem—it's a reality. Whatever we do, no matter how well prepared, cautious, and well intentioned we may be, the world will deliver us struggles to deal with. You see, problems are things you can fix, while realities are things you have to learn to live with. As I learned from one of my first-ever coaches, **we spend too much time trying to fix problems that are actually realities**.

The question isn't how to stop bad things from happening, it's what to do about them when they do happen. Michael Jordan has famously said that the reason he became such a great player is not only because of his tenacious commitment to practicing (though it certainly did have to do with that). A big part of Jordan's success came because he was willing to take the risk of failure. Every time he took a last-second shot to try to win a game, he risked failing. Indeed, Michael Jordan, the best player in the history of basketball, failed more times than he succeeded at winning the game with a last-second shot. Jordan took a total of fifty-one last-second game-winning shots. He scored, and won the game, on twenty-five of those occasions.

He missed, and lost, on twenty-six.

I want you to stop and consider that for a second. The best player in the history of basketball failed more than half of the times he took a game-determining last-second shot. So, why is it that so many of us beat ourselves up when we fail to get things right 100 percent of the time? In fact, so many of us react to every failure as if it is somehow a judgment of our entire self-worth. We believe a negative outcome says something terrible about who we *are*. But it does no such thing. Jordan understood that you have to be willing to fail in order to be great. It's your mindset and what you do after the failure that matter most.

## HAVING A GROWTH AND DEVELOPMENT MINDSET

Carol Dweck published her book *Mindset* in 2006.[1] Back then, it was believed that execution was the most important thing in business. Capable people execute well, it was thought. And the harder you work, and more precisely you execute, the better the outcomes. But Dr. Dweck's work showcased that how you went about your work—your mind-set—has a lot to do with your results. Dr. Dweck found that having a Growth Mindset—the belief that people can change, grow, and improve—was essential for long-term success. In a Growth Mindset, you focus on learning as a way to get better in any area of potential improvement. Without a Growth Mindset, Dr. Dweck found, people would get stuck in what she termed a Fixed Mindset. A Fixed Mindset has people believing that their skills and capacities are innate and unchangeable. Whether they believe they're gifted or weak, those with a Fixed Mindset don't believe they can change.

And that single difference—between a Growth and a Fixed Mindset—impacts a whole slew of work- and life-related outcomes. If you've been reading this book, you can tell that Dr. Dweck's Growth Mindset is very much aligned with my belief that **anyone can beat their addiction to anything, they just have to become someone who isn't addicted**.

To create that change, you have to have two important ingredients:

- You have to believe change is possible.
- You have to do the work to create it.

Thankfully, this book is providing you the recipe for the work. I hope that the stories within it have made it easier to believe that it's possible.

Aliyah is now meth-free and has been so for years. Jaylen is happily married with two beautiful children. Linda hasn't smoked weed in years and is thriving. Terry has continued drinking less than 20 percent of her long-ago levels and is regularly experiencing long periods of abstinence. Michael hasn't experienced a panic attack in years. There's success everywhere. People do change.

## HOW I USED THIS EXACT PROCESS TO CHANGE MY LIFE

By this point in the book, you can recognize the process I went through when Sophie told me that she thought I'd been drinking too much. I paused, considered her words, realized that there was at least some truth to what she was saying, and then went about figuring out what exactly was going on.

I didn't panic and start believing that I had thrown my life away.

I didn't get scared and wonder whether I have to run to a meeting.

I didn't slam down the drink and pour myself another, trying to push away my anxiety.

I did that thing I've been training myself to do for fifteen years—I decided to take a very deliberate look at how exactly I had gotten there.

It was obvious to me that I had missed the shot. The question was why.

And so I went about going through my own EAT cycle, which I want to use as an example here, so you can follow along:

### Explore

The first part of my exploration was to look at the hook(s) that were underneath this drinking. I also wanted to explore how long this had been going on. In my exploration, I found that I'd been escalating my drinking over the course of about a year or so. This alone was an interesting discovery because it had been going on for longer than I'd initially realized. I'd become very fond of whiskey and bourbon, in particular. To make things feel more "appropriate," I'd even become somewhat discerning about them, drinking slightly more expensive and "refined" brown liquor and learning about its history and such. I was a whiskey and bourbon snob. In my exploration, it became clear to me that developing those tastes was part of the escalation of my drinking. How did I know this? Because I'd never been a drinker before, not really. Not since my second year of college, when I discovered drugs, did I care about alcohol. My return to drinking was unusual. Developing some sophistication in that subject made me feel better about it.

When it came to looking for my hooks, the "why" behind my drinking, it took me a little longer. I had to dig back a bit, but once I started looking, it wasn't hard to find. I realized that I was falling back on something I'd learned from my father decades ago: that being busy and working yourself ragged was the way you show you're serious and responsible. I had become incredibly stressed and resentful of my daily life. I was in over my head at work—running a rehab doing $1.5 million and managing a staff of fifteen while also seeing clients there and teaching two courses at UCLA. I also had that two-hour commute every day. This meant I had been working fourteen-hour days, prepping materials for class on the weekends, and taking client calls whenever it was necessary—for over two years. To make matters worse, the partnerships at the rehab were starting to really suffer. We weren't making enough money to take anything home, even though we were working like dogs. I had to fire one partner, who was now suing us, and the other was causing trouble with the staff. These were more recent developments, and they were adding a massive amount of stress. I hated admitting it, but once I took a look, it was clear.

I actually hated my own business.

I was resentful of it all the time.

This was a tough pill to swallow. But it was true. My dream had become a nightmare. And it is better for us to realize difficult truths than to easily swallow lies. I knew I'd have to do something about this.

The thing was that, when it came to work, I had learned from my own upbringing that you could never work hard enough. I barely knew my own dad before the age of fourteen, because he worked two jobs most of his life, and he was working three before I entered junior high. He did what he felt was necessary to support the family, but the result was that we literally never saw him. The message was clear: do what you have to; no costs are too high. I realized that I was paying the costs in my own life now, being gone from sunrise to nightfall. I was repeating my dad's cycle, but adding alcohol to the fire to deal with the stress (my father never drank).

I knew things would blow up soon if I didn't do something about it.

## Accept

The next step in my process was to accept what I'd just learned. There was A LOT for me to accept here. First and foremost was accepting that I could screw this up badly. Here I was, the owner of a drug rehab center, previously addicted to meth and facing more than a decade in prison, and I was drinking heavily. It was hypocritical, to say the least. It might even be dangerous. How could I have let things get this bad? It was a lot for me to process. I had to remind myself that I am human, and that I'll make mistakes. I had to remind myself that I believe enough in my capacity to change. That I know I'll make it to the other side of this. I'd been here before, and this was nothing compared to my past; I thought, "*I will figure this out.*"

I also had to accept the fact that I had disappointed my wife. She must have been thinking this for a while, watching me from the side and wondering whether I was going to keep heading down my old path. It must have been scary for her, and we had been having a lot more trouble recently. I didn't like letting her down, and I was sure I was also showing up differently for my two boys. This wasn't who I wanted to be as a husband or a father. Feelings of being a failure and of not being good enough washed over me regularly. I reminded myself that I was doing everything I could *now in the moment* to make things better.

Finally, I had to accept that I may not be able to save my business. This was one of the hardest things for me, personally. I had a lot of my identity invested in this project, and I felt that I would end up disappointing so many others if I had to shut it down. My partner and I weren't getting along, there was constant stress and pain behind closed doors, and it was the most stressful thing I'd ever tried to do. But we were also helping dozens of people who were relying on us. How was I going to let those people down? I wasn't really sure what I wanted to do about the business yet. But getting to accept that my life, my family, and my future were more important than this particular project took some time. I agonized over it for weeks. The voice of my father, always telling me to do more work (he had passed by this point, so I couldn't actually talk to him) kept egging me on. Eventually, it dawned on me. Like everything else in my life, the survival of this business wasn't all up to me. I had to deal with the hard things, present the best options I could find to my partners, and see how things moved forward. All I could do was my best—the rest would work itself out.

That realization finally allowed me to truly accept what had happened. I had been stressed for the past two years, but as the stress built up, I began handling it by having a drink here and there. With drinking as an option, I leaned on it whenever possible. When things at work took a turn for the worse, I had a ready answer—drink more. And it worked, at least to reduce my momentary stress, by making me care less. And so I'd let things get out of hand both at home—with my daily drinking—and at work. At work, I didn't have the hard conversations that were necessary, and I didn't do the hard things that were required. Instead, I relied on my evening alcohol as a stress reliever to make me feel better. That's how I'd gotten to this place. Now it was time to do something about it.

### Transform

There was a lot of work to do now. First, I had grown used to having my evening drink, and I was going to have to do something about that habit. Next, now that I'd realized how stressed I had become because of all my work, I needed to begin doing something about that as well.

The former was easier and more in my control—I got rid of the bourbon. When it came to the latter, things were more complicated. I was teaching two classes at UCLA, on top of my forty hours at the rehab and the endless phone calls and emails before and after all of that. And then there was that two-hour daily commute. This would have to be dissected slowly. Finally, there were all of the issues with the partners and managing the business. I couldn't just walk in there and shut things down because it was stressful. Technically, that would have been an option, but it wasn't one I was interested in.

I set about changing my life in small, incremental steps. I added exercise to my morning routine. In my drinking haze, I had gotten used to feeling slow and groggy in the mornings, which meant working out wasn't happening. Now, I committed to heading to the gym on my way to work. Ten minutes from the office was a gym, and I signed up and made a commitment. This meant I would spend about one hour less at work every day, and use that time to take care of myself instead.

Next, I decided to reduce my teaching load at UCLA from two classes to one. I let the department know that I'd be looking to reduce my commitment by half. Surprisingly, just knowing that relief was a few months away, already made me less stressed. The light at the end of the tunnel was coming into view.

Now, I had to tackle the hardest challenge—the business. I set a meeting with the three remaining partners and resolved to either fix or dissolve our partnership. This required many meetings over many months. We first resolved to get one partner to leave. He would scream at the staff, especially when I wasn't around; it was obvious he wasn't happy working with us and no one felt safe coming to work around him. It took a lot of uncomfortable conversations, but eventually we got him to leave. Fixing my relationship with my main partner proved to be much more difficult. There were dozens of reasons that things weren't working out, many of which I take the blame for. In the end, it turned out that going our separate ways was best. In April 2017, about a year and a half after that September night in the kitchen, we ended up closing the office. It was one of the most difficult, but necessary, decisions I'd made in my life.

It felt like failure. I felt like a failure. It also felt unavoidable. I blamed myself, and there were a lot of other people who were more than willing to blame me too.

But I was out. I could breathe. I had absolutely no idea what I was going to do next, but I had choice, whereas a year earlier, I felt completely trapped. If you've ever felt this way, you know how terrifying it can be. Humans are programmed to want freedom. In fact, our brain tells us we want the things we can't have more than it does those that are readily available.

The grass is always greener...

In about a year, I went from working eighty-hour weeks to having almost no work whatsoever. A few clients followed me, but UCLA was about ready to shut down for summer and I wasn't teaching. I was about to have three full months of nothing but time. I was nervous, but also hopeful and excited. It was time to dream.

My books, my online programs, the podcast, and so much more, all came from the dreaming that took place over those next few months. I won't lie to you by pretending it was easy. But it has been an incredible journey. I've been able to reach tens of thousands of people and build a company that has already helped thousands more, and will help millions by the time we're done. I've also been fortunate to bring our work to prisons and to people who find themselves on parole or probation, as I had been all those years ago. If someone had tried to tell me, eight years ago as we were closing the Alternatives clinic, that there was *this* much impact waiting for me at the end of that difficult decision, I wouldn't have believed it.

But here we are.

Oh, and I haven't struggled with drinking since.

Because I got to the root of the problem and did that hard work of fixing it.

## HOW TO REVISIT OUTCOMES IN YOUR LIFE TO MAXIMIZE YOUR POTENTIAL

Too many of us want things to be easy. We want simple solutions that are guaranteed. We want to be told, "Do A, and B will happen," or "Stop drinking, and everything will be perfect." But that's not how life works. It doesn't work that way for anyone. The most successful people in the world aren't necessarily better, smarter, luckier, better looking, or less damaged than you. They simply don't quit when things go wrong. Instead, they try again, adjusting a little (or a lot) based on what they've learned. Eventually, they find success. If you keep trying long enough, odds are you'll find success. Sadly, most people aren't willing to try that many times.

Thomas Edison, in his push to create the world's first electric light, took years and resorted to reaching out to all of his contacts worldwide. He was already a world-famous inventor, but he staked his name on lighting up the night sky with electricity. When he and his entire forty-person workforce kept failing, he famously said, "I haven't failed, I've just found ten thousand ways that don't work." In all, his team created 1,200 experiments to create the first functional lightbulb. The project he believed would take three to four months ended up taking almost a year and a half.

Would you try 1,200 times to create something you'd be remembered for?

That's how you guarantee success. You don't quit.

As we said at the outset, you're here because your life hasn't turned out the way you'd hoped. Your specific problems could be related to money, relationships, your health, your success and status, or even your freedom and safety.

Odds are that, before you read this book, you believed that much of what you've experienced has been the result of your addiction struggles. But now, you know there's much more to this. Hopefully, you also recognize the extreme level of influence and control that you can have in determining where you go from here.

Just like me, you can have a say in the direction your life takes. Just like me, this will probably involve your changing substantial elements of your life. The good news is that, as you do this, your life will get better. Your addictions will diminish. Your self-esteem and self-perception will change.

But you have to start out with a belief that you *can* change.

I challenge you to let go of the old, and mistaken, notion that people who struggle with drugs, alcohol, technology, work, or sex addictions can't change. Change is everywhere around you. All you have to do is use the process and tools you've been reading about to help you identify what is, and what isn't, working in your life. Then, by adopting a Growth Mindset and focusing on learning how to get better, you can continuously apply your new learnings and improve.

This is what getting unhooked is all about—it's not about bemoaning our past, nor is it about ignoring it. It's about learning from our experiences, and the experience of others, and using the knowledge to release ourselves from anything that is holding us back.

I hope you use the tools in this book to create the life you deserve. I can't wait to see what you become!

# From This Point Forward

Throughout this book, I've done my best to challenge and dismantle the basic assumptions you've been handed about any bad habits, or addiction, you've been fighting to break.

Struggling with addiction is not abnormal—how could something that a third to half of adults in the US experience be considered abnormal?

Addiction does not mean your brain is broken or your genes are a mess—in fact, your physical machine created these habits in a way that very much proves they functioned as they were meant to.

Addiction is not a permanent problem—from the dozen or so examples I've shared with you, to the millions who have fully recovered, it's clear that addiction can be defeated.

You're not hooked on alcohol, porn, cocaine, work, shopping, or sugar—the real hooks are embedded inside you and are responses to experiences you've had. The addiction has been your way of escaping the pain of these hooks.

From this point forward, you'll never see your struggles through the same lens again, and you know the truth—that anyone can break their addiction to anything; they just have to become someone who isn't addicted.

The process is simple, but it isn't easy. It will require work, time, and effort.

Remember that no one truly goes through change because they hate their habits. You didn't pick up this book because you wanted to stop your addictive habits. You picked it up because the life you found yourself living was full of outcomes, consequences, and situations that make you suffer. The way out of that suffering is through the work. And as you move forward, the suffering will subside and will be replaced by satisfaction.

You will discover your best self when you remove the hooks that have been pulling you back and keeping you down, small, and in pain. When you no longer spend your days escaping the pain of your old hooks, you'll instead spend them building the life that you want.

That is my promise to you.

Again, I have seen this come true over and over.

Remember that the work is ongoing, as are the rewards. Every time you take yourself through a SPARO loop, using the EAT cycle to uncover the parts of your life that aren't serving you, your life will improve. The change will be incremental, but it will be continual. There is no end to how great of a life you can have, if you stay the course.

So, go on. Get started now, if you haven't already. Pick up the end of the sparkling string that is inside you and begin the untangling. And when you find yourself untangled and unhooked, don't forget to pay it forward. Share with others and help everyone around you find their ultimate light.

That is what makes a life worth living.

# Unhooked for Life

## Key Strategies and Practices

B y this point, you've come to understand the SPARO model of behavior analysis and change. You have also gained the benefit of practice in the Explore, Accept, Transform cycle for learning. This means you're ready to begin the journey of implementing specific tools that you will plug into the EAT cycle. These will help you create tangible outcomes that propel your life toward fulfillment and enjoyment and away from hopelessness and compulsive coping behaviors.

Sounds great, right?

While we discussed a slew of techniques and approaches in the main body of the book, I wanted to leave you with the gift of a reference guide. Outlined here are some of the most foundational, important, and powerful tools for behavioral change that I have come across. I have used these myself, and I've seen each one of them work wonders for my clients.

I am not overpromising when I say this—implementing any one of these techniques and practices in your life *will* deliver outstanding results and shifts. The question is this: Which are the best and most appropriate techniques for *you*? I've paired each technique with one or more SPARO stages. Your task is to experiment and then refine your practices over time. I've provided more information, including worksheets for some of these techniques (you can find them here as well as at adijaffe.com/unhooked).

Remember: To get started you just need to act. To get good, you have to practice. To become great, you have to make it a habit. Find the practices that resonate with you and integrate them so deeply into your life that they become part of you.

Now, it's your turn to become.

### Adopt a Growth Mindset

Carol Dweck's seminal book *Mindset: The New Psychology of Success*[1] introduced one of the most powerful ideas in business over the past twenty years: the Growth Mindset. It emphasizes the belief that we can grow in our abilities and intelligence and change through dedication and practice.

In addiction recovery, a Growth Mindset supports the belief that change is attainable, regardless of past mistakes. Individuals with a Growth Mindset are more likely to engage actively in the treatment and recovery processes. That's because they perceive their abilities as malleable rather than fixed or stuck. This perspective encourages individuals in recovery to use tools and strategies to learn, grow, and, ultimately, to succeed in changing their behavior. Learning, going to therapy, and joining support groups are not admissions of weakness, but steps toward growth.

The Growth Mindset approach aligns seamlessly with the principles in this book. It advocates for a nonjudgmental and compassionate approach to change, viewing failures not as dead ends but as opportunities for learning and improvement. By promoting resilience, persistence, and a commitment to lifelong learning and growth, we increase the odds of success for those who seek help.[2]

A part of the Growth Mindset is also learning to embrace failure. Too many of us become so scared of failing that we end up fearing anything that challenges us at all. This fear keeps us stuck in a Fixed Mindset. We are afraid of failure because we believe that failing means that we *are* failures. I teach all of my clients the following concept: between here and your ultimate success are a whole slew of failed attempts. We don't judge ourselves by the attempts that didn't work. We judge ourselves by the lessons we learn from them and the opportunities they present to find methods and tools that work!

*No one has ever succeeded in doing anything worthwhile without failing over and over again.* Remember the story about Thomas Edison? "I have not failed. I just found ten thousand ways that won't work."

You must not only stop being afraid of failure, but you must *embrace* failure as something you must experience to reach your ultimate goals. In the context of getting help for your addiction and struggles, it's going to look something like this: You're going to try a few different approaches, a few meetings, a few therapists, or a few tools. You're going to like some of what you learn and dislike a whole lot of it. You'll take breaks, and may relapse. You'll reduce your use, but then have a bad day. It's all a natural part of the process for many. It's not necessary, but it's common. Continue working on finding more and more approaches that help you. String them together. Eventually, you'll find yourself with a whole toolkit that regularly works to keep your life moving in the right direction.

### SPARO Stages Best Applied To

**Perception.** A Growth Mindset will allow you to fully accept, and believe, that you can change the way you see the world with the right tools, effort, and feedback. This belief is *crucial* for changing your perceptions. For example: Letting go of your perception that failing means *you* are a failure will go a long way toward allowing you to find your way to success.

**Outcome.** A Growth Mindset will allow you to see negative outcomes as simply a form of *feedback*, which is crucial for learning. Those with a Growth Mindset understand that it is precisely through practice in *weak* areas that they will achieve ultimate success. Seeing failure as a learning opportunity will allow you to embrace imperfect outcomes as opportunities to learn, improve, and grow.

## Create a Daily Ritual/Routine

Establishing daily rituals, especially morning and evening routines, holds transformative potential for anyone, but especially for those of us navigating the delicate journey of addiction recovery. Until I got this right, I was functioning at 50 to 60 percent of my capacity, even while free of my addiction. But with my own daily rituals in place, I began stacking successes and improving in areas I thought were impossible to develop. Daily rituals provide structure, predictability, a sense of purpose, and direction in an often chaotic world. They serve as positive anchors, setting firmly the habitual actions that help create your new destiny.

A morning ritual sets the tone for the day ahead. By dedicating time each morning to activities that nourish the mind, body, and soul, you can cultivate a proactive mind-set, preparing yourself for the challenges and opportunities the day may present. This could include such practices as meditation, gratitude journaling, exercise, or setting intentions for the day. For someone in recovery, a consistent morning routine can act as a daily reaffirmation of their commitment to self-development and personal growth. It serves as a reminder of the progress made and the goals yet to be achieved. My morning routine has been instrumental in improving my focus, reducing my attention issues, and providing me with more discipline than I've ever had.

On the other hand, an evening ritual provides an opportunity for reflection and relaxation, allowing you to wind down and process the events of the day. This can involve such activities as reading, reviewing the day, taking a warm bath/shower, or deep breathing exercises (see the Box Breathing exercise on page 233). For those who struggle with compulsive habits, the evening can be a vulnerable time, often filled with triggers and cravings. An evening routine offers a protective shield, redirecting the mind and body toward constructive and calming activities. My evening rituals have helped improve my sleep, reducing my anxiety and helping me connect with my wife and children.

In essence, daily rituals act as bookends to your day, offering moments of grounding and centeredness in the face of the unpredictability of life. Over time, as these rituals become ingrained, they serve as lifelines—powerful tools in your toolkit of coping strategies, bolstering your capacity to navigate the complexities of progress and recovery with grace and determination. You'll find a sample Crafting Daily Rituals for Stress Management checklist on page 232.

### *SPARO Stages Best Applied To*
**Stimulus.** By creating a consistent morning and evening ritual, you'll gain better control over the stimuli that trigger you. Your morning rituals will keep you away from negative stimuli and move you toward positive stimuli that entice productive habits. Your evening ritual will help you get better sleep and avoid connecting to stimuli that disrupt your self-care and healthy behavior.

**Activation.** If you remember the thermometer metaphor, a set of rituals and habits are like the blanket that keeps you warm when the temperature gets too low, and a salve that cools you when it gets too hot. With these rituals in place, it will become substantially easier to regulate your activation level, no matter what the day throws at you.

### Seek Accountability
While we're struggling, many of us run away from and grow to despise accountability. This is, to some extent, understandable because the accountability we've been exposed to has historically been paired with punishment.

Here is the thing: you're going to have blind spots and you're going to screw up sometimes. Since biases make us somewhat blind to our own actions and realities, you won't always realize you're screwing up immediately. So, let me ask you a question: If you really want to succeed in building a life you are proud of, would you like to know sooner or later that you're straying off path?

This is where accountability comes in.

If we have regular opportunities to check in on our progress, we are more likely to correct course and improve in time to change direction. Think about athletes—they have accountability at practices and at every competitive event. If you're a wide receiver for an NFL team, how quickly did you run the route? How many catches did you make and drop? How many touchdowns did you score? Each of those measures allows a receiver to understand how they're performing. If their performance suffers, they can use their stats to help identify the skills that require attention. At work, you have accountability to your boss and colleagues—did you finish the task on time? Was its quality up to par? Are you getting back to your colleagues in a timely manner? Start falling behind on any of these and there will be consequences. Ignore the consequences too long and you'll get fired.

Accountability is a good thing.

One way to do this is to create a *personal advisory board (PAB)*. In business, an advisory board is a group of experts who provide advice and support to the management team. Similarly, in the context of addiction recovery, a personal advisory board is a selected group of trusted individuals who offer guidance, support, and perspective on your journey.

Load up your personal advisory board with people who understand the challenges of addiction, mental health, and other life areas where you want to learn and grow. They can offer diverse perspectives and insights to help you navigate complex decisions and situations. This board can consist of trusted friends, family members, mentors, and peers who have your best interest at heart. You can be accountable to your spouse, your parents, or any other supportive adult. Each member will bring a unique set of experiences, knowledge, and skills to the table. You will gain an all-around support system that can enhance your ability to make informed and balanced decisions.

Important: DO NOT make your child a member of your personal advisory board or your accountability partner. It is not their job. Don't make an ex romantic partner a member of your personal advisory board or your accountability partner unless you are on great terms and they're not an ongoing trigger. The same holds for your boss, unless you're sure it won't lead to losing your job if you slip up.

This collaborative approach provides emotional and psychological support. This is especially true when you encounter difficult decisions or uncertainties on your journey. And you will. In essence, your personal advisory board acts as a protective confidante, offering a safe space for you to express concerns, share successes, and seek advice. Create one as soon as possible. You can start with one or two members and expand as needed.

When seeking accountability, do not focus *only* on your problematic behavior. Sure, you should seek accountability around your primary struggle, but also around your self-care, your work performance, your finances, the state of your home, and/or your mental health. Become accountable around anything that would be on your Success Index and drive you toward success.

### *SPARO Stages Best Applied To*
**Response.** Having accountability will keep you more consistent and disciplined. Once you embrace accountability, it helps improve motivation. During the Response phase, your motivation is focused on continuing to search for new potential replacement behaviors. Being accountable to someone during the Response phase is like having a personal trainer at the gym. They push you when you're feeling sluggish and make you more likely to show up to practice when you'd rather stay at home. Deliberate Practice is made vastly more powerful when you get feedback on your performance, and your personal advisory board can provide that feedback.

**Outcome.** In the end, we're trying to improve our outcomes. It may take a while, and your progress in performing new behaviors might be obvious long before long-term outcomes improve. Being accountable to those around you will make it substantially more likely you'll continue practicing until you've mastered your new behaviors. For instance, being honest with at least a few people in your life about a recent slip-up will not only help you get back on track, but will also show those you trust that they can trust you back.

## Develop Your Own Success Index

It may be hard to believe right now, but as you progress and move forward, you will forget how bad things were at the outset. Yes, it's not always comfortable to look at ourselves at our lowest point, but get an initial overall assessment of your level of functioning and struggle completed early and you'll always have a starting point to measure against.

A comprehensive assessment can help you identify the areas that are causing the most pain and discomfort right now. If you're not ready to go for the biggest problems yet, start smaller, in areas of life that aren't completely troubled but still need help. These may seem to have nothing to do with your addictive habit. I typically recommend focusing on two or three areas of life to improve. Any more than that, and you could easily get overwhelmed.

Set clear goals for improvement on your addictive behavior, given your starting point. Your goal could be completely stopping the habit or reducing it. Be specific. Set a goal and a timeline for reaching it. If you're going for abstinence, are you going to stop immediately? If you're going to reduce, are you aiming for a 50 percent reduction or 80 percent? Lastly, identify the ways to measure your success. Sure, you can use the "X number days of abstinence in a row" measure, but I urge you to include others. Here are some examples (alcohol examples are used here, but you can substitute any other behavior):

- Percent of days abstinent out of last week or 30 days (goal to increase)
- Longest abstinence streak in past 30 days (goal to increase)
- Most drinks consumed on any drinking day in past 30 days (goal to reduce)
- Number of days drinking below average in past week or 30 days (goal to increase)
- Average number of drinks in past week or 30 days (goal to reduce)

Get at least one outside measure of your success. Use your personal advisory board or accountability partner to regularly give you an assessment of *their* sense of how you're doing. If you want to grow, you need outside feedback on your performance. Like a teacher helping you by grading your homework and correcting your mistakes, this feedback can be the greatest source of learning for you.

Combine these different assessments to create your success index on a regular basis. I recommend you do this *at least* monthly. Combine this with a Growth Mindset and committed, consistent work on self-improvement, and there is no way you will fail. If you want help with this, check out our free assessment resources at adijaffe.com/unhooked.

### SPARO Stages Best Applied To

**Response identification.** Knowing how to measure your progress on each of the habits you're practicing could make or break your motivation. Find the right ways to measure your progress as you move forward. Will you focus on reliability (how regularly you can perform the behavior when tried), perseverance (how long you've been practicing and how consistent you are in your practice), skill level (how good you are at the actual skill), or all of them?

**Outcome.** Here you'll want to measure how your progress is affecting your quality of life. Besides reductions in your compulsive behavior, there should be other clear indicators that your progress is moving you in the right direction. You can fill out our simple Wheel of Life (see chart on page 243), use our online assessment, or use another tool, but be sure to focus on life factors you care about.

## Master the P/I Ratio

Gaining control over the Promoters and Inhibitors that drive your positive behavior while at the same time aligning them to minimize your problematic behavior is a crucial skill. Once mastered, it will make even the most difficult behavior change easy.

To do this, I like to split up the forces that impact our Response selection into four categories: Psychology, Biology, Environment, and Spirituality. And while the categories are separate, we continue to uncover how interwoven these systems truly are. Our biological machine, our mind, and the environments within which they operate (be they physical or social) constantly affect each other as they change and shift.

Remember the P/I Ratio: If you want a behavior to be more likely, you have to place strong Promoters for it and remove as many of its Inhibitors as possible. If you want a behavior to become unlikely, do the opposite.

You can use the Assessing Your Promoters and Inhibitors (P/I Ratio) worksheet on page 241 to break down the specific Promoters and Inhibitors for any given behavior. Spend some time focusing your attention on what has worked in the past. Use the Mapping Your Struggle Journey exercise (page 227) you completed to find factors that have already revealed themselves to affect your behavior.

If you drink alone, late at night, on stressful days, you'll have to create social (in-person or virtual) opportunities (Inhibitors) to reduce the likelihood of finding yourself in those compromising, isolated situations. But you'll also want to put in place Promoters of stress-reducing behaviors that will make your evening more conducive to rest and sleep—like the evening rituals discussed earlier.

If you find yourself scrolling endlessly for hours when you're feeling anxious or depressed, you may want to use screen-limiting apps or even lockable cellphone holders (Inhibitors) to make it harder to access your device. But you'll also want to use Promoters to increase the likelihood that you'll have something else enjoyable to do instead.

Remember: Don't work only on reducing the problem. Work equally diligently on increasing alternative solutions. You can turn to your personal advisory board and your accountability partners for help. You'll find some powerful replacement activities to promote below.

### *SPARO Stages Best Applied To*

**Response.** The P/I Ratio is a powerful tool for Response change. Instead of being reactive, it allows you to be proactive, thoughtful, and strategic about your actions. The changes won't necessarily be easy, but they'll be effective, so remember to measure your progress in a way that captures your continued improvement and adjust the Promoters and Inhibitors as you go.

### Establish Boundaries

There is no better tool for changing the impact that relationships have on your well-being, happiness, and feelings of control than establishing boundaries.

Many of us struggle with asserting our needs, communicating our preferences and uneasiness, or engaging in conflict. These difficulties can lead us to stay in relationships that don't serve us, while also causing us increased stress and reduced feelings of self-worth.

Boundaries exist in many areas of our lives—social, work, family and friends, romantic partnerships, money, physical touch, and more. While many of us can tell something is wrong when our boundaries have been crossed, we're not great at knowing what to do about it. Often, we're not even very clear about what our boundaries themselves may be.

The simplest process I know for helping with this includes four simple steps:

1. **Define your own boundaries.** If you don't know what your boundaries are, it will be difficult to protect and respect them. Spend some time clarifying for yourself what you are comfortable with and what is out of bounds. We all have "red lines" we don't want crossed; make sure you're clear on those.

2. **Communicate your boundaries to others.** Once you're clear on your own boundaries, you need to communicate them to others you're close to. Make sure to let them in on the best way to respect and protect your well-being and the relationship. The best way to do this is to be clear; use "I" language (e.g., "I would appreciate it if, moving forward, you would let me know when you're going to come home late, because it makes me anxious when I don't know where you are.").

3. **Protect communicated boundaries.** Given the relative lack of boundaries we've displayed in the past, it's unreasonable to expect others to perfectly adhere to our newly communicated boundaries. When others encroach on or break boundaries you've communicated, you'll have to remind them of the new agreement and be firm in getting them to respect it.

4. **Maintain and adjust your boundaries over time.** Your boundaries will change over time. It can be important to revisit your defined boundaries periodically and make any necessary adjustments as you change. Don't forget to communicate these changes once you've established them for yourself.

As you go through this process, you'll gain more self-awareness and understanding, and also become better practiced at communicating your needs to others. Over time, being clear and protective of your boundaries will pay dividends in improving your relationships and your mental health.

Finally, if you're going to be asking others to be respectful of your own boundaries, it's important that you model the same to them—respect the needs of others and be careful not to break their comfort and trust.

### SPARO Stages Best Applied To

**Activation.** When your boundaries are violated and breached, you become activated in negative ways. You develop resentment, feel anxious, become frightened, or are otherwise made to suffer internally. Doing boundary work will help you experience less activation, which will translate to reducing the strength of the forces that make you want to act out.

**Response.** By reducing your activation, and making you feel more in control of your emotional state, setting and maintaining boundaries will give you a calmer and more controlled ability when it comes to Response selection. When less stressed, you can do a better job of choosing the behaviors that you want to perform, instead of falling back on habits that feel natural and easy. You will be less reactive and more proactive about your behavioral choices. And that's what this is all about.

### Try Abstinence Sampling

*Abstinence sampling* is the practice of removing the drug or behavior of choice from your life for a limited amount of time. It's an easy way to set short, attainable goals (vs. the goal of long-term 100 percent perfection) and practice success like any other habit.

The idea behind abstinence sampling is simple: take the possibility of drinking or using off the table for an hour, a day, an entire week, or a month and pay attention to what comes up. After doing this with tens of thousands of others, I can promise you this—issues that you haven't realized are bothering you in life will bubble up once you take the coping strategy you've been using to escape from them off the table.

I use abstinence sampling with my clients to help them become more aware of the driving forces behind their addiction. The key is to pay attention to what's happening in the present moment. Are you in a relationship full of conflict and drinking all night to ignore reality? Do you hate your job so much that the only thing getting you through the day is looking forward to watching porn when you get home? Is stress in your life eating you up and making you run to your phone for endless scrolling to numb and avoid? These types of scenarios will be exposed through abstinence sampling. If you don't have that daily drink or other escape after work, you're going to be activated and experience the unpleasant emotions that you've been repressing. Instead of reaching for that bottle, I want you to actually sit with that discomfort and ask yourself, *"What about this situation is making me want to drink?"*

Combine that curiosity with the ongoing practice of sitting with your discomfort for longer and longer periods of time, and you will perfect abstinence sampling. I've seen clients get from barely being able to have seven days of abstinence to entire months in a relatively short while, even after decades of trying to quit unsuccessfully.

*SPARO Stages Best Applied To*

**Activation.** Abstinence sampling is one of the fastest ways to become acutely aware of activations that you have been hiding, even from yourself, for a long time. By removing your favorite coping mechanism, these uncomfortable feelings will bubble to the surface quickly. In the process, you'll develop awareness of the discomfort, and if you pay special attention, even of the beliefs and perceptions that drive them. This can be a quick path to uncovering some of your most basic hooks and provide you with more actionable options to work on for even long-term success.

**Response.** If you do abstinence sampling right, you will focus not only on the bubbling discomfort, but also make this a perfect opportunity to practice some of the replacement behaviors you're experimenting with. Without the need to commit to long-term change, these periods of abstinence can become your best opportunity to test new coping strategies and responses. As you get better at being uncomfortable, and at practicing your new replacement responses, your abstinence lengths will increase and you will find an easier path to success.

## Be of Service

There is plenty of research showing that focusing on the struggle of others and supporting their needs helps reduce our own suffering. It makes our life feel meaningful and gives us perspective.

People who give their time and attention to helping others have greater self-esteem and experience less depression and lower stress levels.[3] Engaging in acts of kindness can lead to what is sometimes called a "helper's high," a surge of positive emotions following prosocial actions. There is even research that shows brain changes when we choose to help others,[4] with anxiety centers in the brain becoming less active. Other studies have shown that when we donate to charitable causes, we activate a key part of our reward system (the ventral striatum).[5] Helping others not only improves their well-being, it also helps *you* feel less anxious or depressed and more connected and secure.

One of my own preferred methods of helping involves random acts of kindness, or volunteering. You should find the most relevant forms of helping for you. Here's the bottom line: try to do something helpful for others every day, and never let a week go by when you didn't take time to help others. Trust me.

### SPARO Stages Best Applied To

**Perception.** One of the quickest ways to gain a different perspective on your life is to go help someone else in need. If you want to maximize the impact, go help people who are struggling in areas of life you take for granted. This will help rebalance your feeling of lack.

**Response.** Being of service is, in itself, a replacement behavior. Imagine reaching out to someone who could use your help whenever you are anxious, or aching for a drink. The act of service will help those you're being of service to and yourself. When you're in service to others, it serves as an Inhibitor of your problematic behavior and as a Promotor of your best behaviors, because it makes you even more motivated to serve as an example. Being of service is the ultimate gift to the world.

## Establishing a Gratitude Practice

A gratitude practice helps recalibrate the way we look at the world. Having a good gratitude practice (which is more than the simple repetition of a few things you're grateful for) will forever alter the Perception stage of your SPARO behavioral loop and therefore impact almost every single decision and action you take in life.

Let me explain.

Most of us seek to avoid or fix what is wrong with the world. But when we need everything to be "perfect" to be able to experience joy, we spend our entire life in misery. A gratitude practice can help counter this.

As you read these next few lines, I want you to think of three things you are currently grateful for. They can be incredibly significant (winning the lottery, buying a new house, getting married), noteworthy (getting a raise, finishing a big project, buying a new car), or minor (finishing your homework, a beautiful sunny day, having shoes that fit). As you create this list of three aspects of your life you feel grateful for, I want you to pause, close your eyes, and visualize them.

How do you feel? Did a little smile creep onto your face unannounced? Do you feel a little warmth in your chest? Is your breath a bit more relaxed?

This is the joy of gratitude.

If you do this regularly in your life, you can start having this feeling every day.

Here's what is going to happen if you truly begin practicing this regularly: As you continue to pick three things to be grateful for every day, and then spend a few moments reflecting and truly meditating on your gratitude, your brain will change in important ways. Firstly, you will begin creating an internal "Rolodex" of "things I am grateful for." Start this gratitude practice and within one year, you will have been grateful for roughly one thousand different things. As your mental gratitude archive grows, the things you've expressed gratitude for in your practice will become "gratitude beacons" in your everyday life. The sun hitting your face, your kid's smiles, that cup of coffee, and your boss who gave you a raise will all become reminders of what is good. In this way, a regular gratitude practice is the best tool to create a Positivity Bias to counter the Negativity Bias (or perfectionism) most of us have been cursed/blessed with.

Trust me, you want to start doing this (see the Tips for Effective Gratitude Journaling exercise on page 234).

### *SPARO Stages Best Applied To*

**Perception.** The entire goal of a gratitude practice is to shift your perception of the world from one focused on lack to one focused on abundance. But it goes deeper than that. A gratitude practice shifts your attention in a consistent way so that you learn to attend to things you'd historically ignored.

**Activation.** When your attention shifts to the positive on a regular basis, your activation level is lowered as your parasympathetic nervous system becomes more frequently activated.

**Response.** Your gratitude practice will become one of the potential behaviors you can pull from when you're activated and trying to control your activation. Since gratitude can reduce stress and anxiety, it's a very useful tool to practice getting well.

### Find a Purpose

I like to tell my clients, "If you don't have a purpose, make it your purpose to identify your purpose." It may sound dramatic, but I swear it's true. Here's the thing—your purpose doesn't have to remain static; you can adjust and change your purpose over time.

Just don't get stuck without one.

Simon Sinek, in his best-selling book and incredibly popular TEDx lecture,[6] talks about purpose as the idea that you have to "Start with Why." Why are you doing this? Why is it important to you? Why will you keep going when it gets hard? Your "Why" doesn't have to be big and dramatic like saving the world, or curing cancer. What truly matters is that *your* "Why" resonates for you and feels authentic. Your "Why" could be that you want to support your family and be the best husband and father you can be. It could be that you want to make the lives of a certain group of people better.

*Ikigai* is a beautiful Japanese concept that is helpful for finding your purpose (you can get a downloadable version of this exercise at adijaffe.com/resources). Ikigai is seen as the intersection of what you're good at, what you love to do, and what the world needs. Think of it as your purpose. If you're hoping to turn your purpose to your work, as I have, your ikigai is also what people will pay you for doing. See page 242 for the What's Your Ikigai? exercise.

I promise you this: If you can spend the time to identify your purpose, even the hardest work and the longest days will simply feel like part of your path. You won't mind challenges as much if they are in service to your calling. You'll resent your days less and feel less stressed and depressed. Those changes, in turn, will play right into your SPARO loop by causing less negative activation that may lead you to the problematic behavior you are trying to change!

### *SPARO Stages Best Applied To*
**Perception.** With a purpose identified, your view of the world aligns in ways that support your discovered calling. This alignment gives meaning to actions that seemed meaningless, hope where there was none, and direction instead of aimlessness. It's also harder to feel useless when you're serving a higher purpose.

**Response.** The directionality provided by a sense of purpose can add new behaviors to your repertoire that align with your long-term vision and goals. Additionally, having a sense of purpose provides motivation that can be helpful in selecting between a specific set of available behaviors to practice. *And* a sense of purpose, like helping others, provides strong Promotor support for pro-purpose behaviors (those that move you toward your purpose or are aligned with it). It also helps you inhibit negative behaviors, as those typically interfere with serving your purpose.

### Utilize Trauma-Informed Somatic Therapies
Somatic (as in body-oriented) therapies emphasize the connection between the mind and body, aiming to address the physical symptoms and sensations associated with trauma. As mentioned throughout the book, groundbreaking work from such experts as Drs. Bessel van der Kolk, Peter Levine, Pat Ogden, and Stephen Porges has made it clear that trauma does not live in your head alone. The understanding that trauma often manifests in bodily symptoms has created an entire field focused on helping you unhook not through traditional talk therapy,

but through the integration of movement, emotion, and thinking. Find a trained practitioner that can help you somatically. Here are some that I recommend to my clients: EMDR, Brainspotting, Somatic Experiencing (SE), and Sensorimotor Psychotherapy (SP). You can find more information on these modalities at adijaffe.com/unhooked.

### SPARO Stages Best Applied To

**Perception.** When you discover that your past experiences have left physiological and somatic "fingerprints" that have affected your experience of the world, it can provide relief from the false impression that you are broken or damaged. When you see somatic work making a difference in your life, it can help release the perception that you are forever stuck or hopeless.

**Activation.** Somatic therapies specifically aim to change the relationship between your experience of triggering stimuli and the internal activation they create. As you become practiced in these therapeutic approaches, they will likely release some of the stored-up "energy" that has been fused to your hooks.

**Response.** These tools can become some of your favorite in-the-moment approaches to address activation as it happens in real time. By reducing activation and becoming part of your arsenal of potential responses, somatic therapies can become a primary replacement response. In this way, you can end up adopting a stress-reduction or internal-awareness practice to replace an escapist coping strategy. A pretty good trade, if you ask me.

### Psychedelic Medicine

The use of psychedelic medicine for healing spans many cultures and hundreds, if not thousands, of years. Shamans and guides have used these medicines in different rituals and practices to connect to spirits, find answers, and provide healing. No longer fringe, there is a resurgence of interest in their potential for treating a range of mental health disorders including depression, anxiety, PTSD, and addiction.[7] The research is compelling and suggests that these approaches could provide help specifically where Western medicine has failed. Importantly, research is showing us that, when combined with appropriate therapeutic support, these medicines can help in some of the most resistant cases of depression or the most persistent instances of PTSD.

As it stands, hundreds of studies have either been completed or are examining and showcasing the potential of these approaches.[8] The federal government is on track to finally change the legal standing of these medicines to allow for their use more broadly. When used in the proper ways, with therapeutic support and helpers who know what they're doing, they can be powerful.

Truth be told, I was resistant to doing this work, let alone talk about it publicly, given my background and the fear of criminal consequences. But, having seen the power of these medicines for improving the lives of so many of my clients, I decided I had to commit to doing the best I could by them. These medicines have played a role in helping clients unhook in the deepest ways. I can't ignore the reality—these medicines can work wonders when used appropriately.

I have been trained in and have worked with ketamine, psilocybin, and MDMA. I have personally seen incredible, life-altering results with these practices, and know many other practitioners who have experienced the same. You can find more information on these three psychedelics, as well as other medicines, at adijaffe.com/unhooked.

### SPARO Stages Best Applied To
**Perception.** I tell my clients that the experience of psychedelic medicine is like opening a window to a part of the mind you hadn't seen before. Once you look outside the window, your view of the world will be changed forever. Sometimes, the change is grand, and at other times, more subtle. With the right guidance and integration, this

new thinking can have incredible effects on your overall experience of life.

**Activation.** Research has shown that psychedelic medicine experience can change the way people react to stimuli that have been historically triggering. Reductions in depression and trauma symptoms, lower suicide rates, and improved mood and outlook during end-of-life treatment showcase the power of these medicines.

## Medication-Assisted Treatment

There are a number of traditional prescription medications combined with good therapeutic support that can offer an easier first step in getting someone started on the path to healing. If you're struggling to get started, or find yourself continuously starting but then losing steam in your attempts to recover, these medications may offer some help. While they do not truly resolve the hooks we discussed throughout this book, they can provide the extra bit of support that one may need to have the ability to engage in treatment more fully. These medications include naltrexone, buprenorphine, acamprosate (commonly known by its brand name Campral), and buspirone (often marketed as Buspar). You can find more information on these treatments at adijaffe.com /unhooked.

Note: In addiction treatment, it's important to emphasize that while these medications offer significant benefits, their effectiveness is maximized when integrated into a comprehensive treatment approach that includes behavioral therapies, counseling, and ongoing support. You will want to consult with a prescribing physician or psychiatrist to find the best medication for your specific struggle.

### SPARO Stages Best Applied To

**Stimulus.** Some of these medicines reduce the power of stimuli to generate cravings in the first place. Others may even make the stimulus itself less palatable or effective.

**Activation.** Most medications used for addictions and compulsive habits may block or blunt the effect of the behavior or substance they're specified for. They may simulate the original effect and therefore reduce cravings for the original behavior. Or they may act on your overall level of activation, by alleviating anxiety for instance, reducing the need for the addictive coping.

## MAPPING YOUR STRUGGLE JOURNEY

**1** **Draft Your Timeline**

Draw a timeline that shows the history of your addiction, from the beginning to today. Mark important positive & negative events/periods.

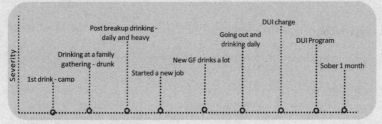

**2** **Date the Events**

Write down when (approximately) specific experiences happened.

**3** **Rate the Severity**

Look over your timeline and rate the level of addictive struggle from 0 to 10.

**4** **Analyze the Context**

Think about what was happening in your life around the time of each event on your timeline. What were you feeling before, during, and after these times?

**5** **Identify the Themes**

Look for patterns in the most problematic and less problematic times you identified.

- What typically sets off a bigger problem?
- Did certain things make it easier to cope?

These factors will prove crucial in future exercises, including Spheres of Influence, Triggers, and more.

# SPHERES OF INFLUENCE

**Can Control**
- The words you speak
- Your daily routine

**Can Influence**
- A friend's behavior
- Workplace environment

**Outside of Control**
- Past traumas
- The economy
- Political climate

**❶ Assess Your Current Status**
Fill the circles with what currently takes up your focus & energy in each sphere. Note the percentage of attention in each sphere.

**❷ Shift Focus Toward Control**
Try removing concerns from your "Outside of Control" sphere and adding more items to your "Can Control" or "Can Influence" spheres.

Try to shift your pattern from the typical:
- **Can Control:** 10% of energy
- **Can Influence:** 40% of energy
- **Outside of Control:** 50% of energy

To a more effective:
- **Can Control:** 50% of energy
- **Can Influence:** 40% of energy
- **Outside of Control:** 10% of energy

**❸ Reflect**
Think about what you need to let go of and what you should focus more on to achieve this new balance.

As you go throughout your week, refer back to your Spheres of Influence and remind yourself of what should be taking your energy and what should not.

# SETTING UP YOUR TRIGGER CHART

**1** **Prepare Your Chart**
Create a 4x4-cell chart on a piece of paper or your computer. List the rows and columns as you see below.

**2** **Sort Your Triggers**
Use the trigger list as a starting point. Add any others that are relevant to your specific situation and behavior. Place each one into the right cell in your chart.

**3** **Review and Plan**
Your aim is to reduce or totally avoid the triggers in the "Extremely Damaging" column to help you stay on track with your recovery. Create a plan that can help you avoid these triggers, like turning to meditation when you feel a lack of self-control or taking a different driving route to avoid a certain casino.

The more awareness and preparation you put into avoiding your triggers, the better you will be able to apply your plan in the moment.

| | EXTREMELY DAMAGING | SOMEWHAT DAMAGING | NEUTRAL |
|---|---|---|---|
| **ENVIRONMENT** | Driving by bar where I used to drink most weeknights | Seeing empty single-serving bottles on street | Watching someone drink on a TV show or in movie |
| **PSYCHOLOGY** | Experiencing a major stressor, like big financial debt | Fear about my GF leaving me | Feeling restless |
| **BIOLOGY** | Insomnia/being unable to sleep | Feeling anxious/stressed after workday | Waking up tired |
| **SPIRITUALITY** | Feeling no purpose, that what I do "doesn't matter" | Skipping my gratitude and meditation practices | Talking about religion |

# TRIGGER PRIMING LIST

 **Internal Triggers**

Think about the emotions you experience that immediately make you consider using substances or falling back into addictive habits. Write down these emotions. Here are some common internal triggers to consider:

| | | | | |
|---|---|---|---|---|
| JEALOUSY | EXHAUSTION | FEAR | LONELINESS | FRUSTRATION |
| ANGER | NEGLECT | GUILT | CONFIDENCE | NERVOUSNESS |
| HAPPINESS | CRITICISM | PASSION | INADEQUACY | DEPRESSION |
| PRESSURE | INTEREST | HUMILIATION | RELAXATION | IRRITATION |
| EXCITEMENT | SADNESS | BOREDOM | ANXIETY | REJECTION |
| REGRET | GRIEF | PRIDE | LOVE | INSPIRATION |

**2  External Triggers**

Consider whether there are any specific external circumstances that lead to thoughts of your addiction. Write down these external triggers. Here are some examples to guide you:

| | | | | |
|---|---|---|---|---|
| **LOCATIONS** | Friend's home | Bars/Clubs | Concerts | Sporting events |
| **SITUATIONS** | Driving | Home alone | During a date | Before family event |
| **PLACES/TIMES** | Before bed | After payday | Before/after work | Before/after sexual activities |
| **EVENTS** | Celebrating milestones | Weddings | Funerals | On a trip |
| **OTHER** | Social media scrolling | Online dating | With certain friends | While watching a movie/show with addiction |

# YOUR STRESS THERMOMETER

**1** **Identify Chronic Stress Areas**
Write down three areas in life that consistently cause you stress. Choose aspects that you find particularly uncontrollable or overwhelming.

**2** **Detail the Stress Impact**
For each area listed in Step 1, describe how it contributes to your stress. Be specific about the physical and emotional effects.

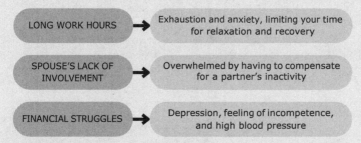

| | |
|---|---|
| LONG WORK HOURS → | Exhaustion and anxiety, limiting your time for relaxation and recovery |
| SPOUSE'S LACK OF INVOLVEMENT → | Overwhelmed by having to compensate for a partner's inactivity |
| FINANCIAL STRUGGLES → | Depression, feeling of incompetence, and high blood pressure |

**3** **Analyze Addiction as a Stress Coping Response**
How often do the identified stress factors contribute to you operating outside your "safe zone"?

Using the thermometer metaphor, reducing the occurrence and impact of these existing activations will create space for you to operate in the "safe zone."

Threshold

Safe Zone

Initial
Activation
Level

# CRAFTING DAILY RITUALS FOR
# STRESS MANAGEMENT

**Morning Ritual Checklist**
Creating a morning routine sets a positive tone for the day, helps stabilize your mood, lowers initial activation level, and gets you focused.

✓ Avoid using technology for the first 30 minutes.

✓ Drink a glass of water with a pinch of salt, to replenish electrolytes.

✓ Spend time outside or near a window, to get natural light.

✓ Engage in at least 30 minutes of physical movement. If mornings are too rushed, shifting this to another time of day is perfectly fine.

**Bedtime Ritual Checklist**
A soothing nighttime routine can significantly improve your sleep quality, lowering stress and enhancing your resilience.

✓ Ensure your sleeping area is cool, dark, and quiet. Replace white lights with warm, or even red lights.

✓ Avoid all screens (phones, TV, tablets) at least an hour before bed.

✓ Incorporate relaxing activities, such as drinking chamomile tea, taking a warm bath, or reading a book.

✓ Aim to go to bed and wake up at the same times every day, allowing for 7 to 9 hours of restful sleep.

## BOX BREATHING EXERCISE

Called Box Breathing for its symmetric pattern, this practice helps engage the parasympathetic nervous system to feel calmer and more relaxed. This practice can help lower your heart rate and blood pressure when you need a reset.

## STEP 1

Inhale through the nose for **4 counts**.

## STEP 2

Hold your inhale for **4 counts**.

## STEP 3

Exhale through the nose for **4 counts**.

## STEP 4

Hold the exhale for **4 counts**.

Repeat this box breath 4 times or as many times as you'd like to bring the body into a calm, restful state.

# TIPS FOR EFFECTIVE GRATITUDE JOURNALING

### Be Consistent
Every morning, write down three things you are grateful for. Try to make gratitude journaling a daily habit. Even a few minutes each day can make a significant difference.

### Go for Depth Over Breadth
Instead of merely listing superficial items, choose two to three things each day and explore them in depth—people, experiences, feelings.

### Be Specific
Rather than writing general statements like "I'm grateful for my friends," specify an instance or quality that made you feel grateful, such as "I'm grateful for my friend Sarah, who called me today to check how I was feeling."

### Avoid Repetition
Challenge yourself to think of new things to be grateful for each day. Challenge yourself to look beyond the obvious.

### Reflect on Challenges
Include entries on challenges or difficulties and what they taught you or how they helped you grow. Lessons are gifts, too.

# DEFINING DAILY SUCCESS

**1** **Organize Your Day**
Review your schedule and daily tasks. Write everything down, from small chores to major meetings, and use a calendar or a digital tool to keep everything organized.

**2** **Prioritize Your Tasks**
Identify the tasks that are the most important and rank them (#1 to #3). Prioritizing can increase predictability, help control your schedule, and identify what is truly important.

**3** **Set Your Criteria for Success**
Looking at your schedule and prioritized task list, think about three to four things that would make today successful. Success is more than completing a to-do list; it can involve the way you show up, the way you feel, and more. For instance:

- Maintaining calm throughout the day
- Participating in online support groups
- Connecting with your family/spouse

**IMPORTANTLY . . . Focus on Positive Actions**
Define success by what you actively plan to do rather than what you aim to avoid.

For example, instead of "Today will be successful if I don't drink," say, "Today will be successful when I exercise for thirty minutes and drink seltzer water throughout the day."

**4** **Make It a Habit**
Repeat this practice every day to set yourself up for daily success.

# URGE SURFING

Urge surfing is a powerful mindfulness technique that helps manage cravings and is particularly effective when you start to feel the onset of an urge.

**1** **Recognize the Urge**
Acknowledge the presence of the craving without judgment as soon as you feel it. Record the time.

**2** **Ground Yourself**
Connect to the feeling of your feet firmly on the ground and close your eyes, if possible. Focus on the physical sensations that accompany the urge, such as a tightness in your chest or a quickening heartbeat. Label these feelings in your mind.

**3** **Visualize the Urge as a Wave**
Picture the urge as an ocean wave. See it in your mind's eye as growing larger as the craving intensifies, peaks, and then gradually fades.

**4** **Breathe Deeply**
Breathe slowly and deeply through your nose. Imagine each breath as a calming force that takes the strength out of the wave.

**5** **Let the Wave Pass**
Continue to breathe deeply and allow the "wave" of craving to pass on its own. Most cravings are brief, typically lasting just a few minutes.

**6** **Reflect on the Experience**
Once the urge has passed, reflect on the experience and record the time—note its length, and see whether practice helps you shorten cravings.

# MINDFUL LABELING MEDITATION

**1 Find Space**
Find a quiet spot to sit or lie comfortably. Close your eyes, and take deep breaths through the nose to settle yourself.

**2 Engage with the Present**
Focus on the now by noting any sensations, sounds, or smells. Experience these elements without attempting to change them.

**3 Label Your Experiences**
As thoughts or feelings arise, label them with a word or short phrase that fits, such as "thinking," or "cold," or "work worry." Use simple terms that naturally come to mind.

**4 Return to Your Breath**
After labeling, release the thought and gently redirect your focus back to your breath. Do your best not to judge the thought as "good" or "bad."

**5 Maintain the Practice**
Continue this process of observing, labeling, and returning to your breath for 5 to 15 minutes. You can extend the time as you become more familiar and comfortable with the practice itself.

## ENHANCING YOUR PHYSICAL ENVIRONMENT FOR RECOVERY

**Develop a Daily Improvement Habit**
Commit to a 14-day plan focused on small, daily improvements to make your space more supportive of your healing.

| DAILY MPROVEMENTS | |
| --- | --- |
| DAY 1 | Clean bedding |
| DAY 2 | Do the dishes |
| DAY 3 | Open windows to let in fresh air |

**Spend Time in Peaceful Places**
Regularly visit places that calm you and enhance your well-being. Whether it's a quiet morning at the beach, a reflective walk in a nearby park, a rejuvenating hike, or enjoying a cup of coffee at your favorite café, these outings can significantly lower your stress and help stabilize your mood.

**Modify Problematic Environments**
Identify and alter spaces that trigger addictive behaviors. If your home office becomes a spot where you're prone to drinking while working late, consider making changes to disrupt this pattern. You could rearrange the furniture, paint the walls, or improve the lighting. These changes can trick your brain into breaking old associations with the space, making it less likely to trigger unwanted behaviors.

# STEPS TO PUSH YOUR
# DISCOMFORT THRESHOLD

**1  Identify Your Challenge & Threshold Tasks**
List 10 activities (examples follow) that push you out of your comfort zone. List behaviors you can realistically integrate into your life.

☐ Take on cold exposure

☐ Talk to a stranger

☐ Sing karaoke sober

**2  Plan Your Specific Commitment**
Choose one to three activities from your list to start incorporating into your life. For example, if you select cold exposure, do you want to go for a 2- to 3-minute cold plunge or begin with a 30-second cold shower?

Commit to starting and get specific.

Once you've mastered these activities, move on to the other items on your list. The goal is to do at least one challenging activity daily.

**3  Reflect on Your Experience**
After each activity, take time to reflect on how it felt. Note your initial reactions and any changes over time.

It's natural to feel uncomfortable at first, that's the whole point. But with regular practice, you will grow to cherish and appreciate these challenges and their effect on your confidence and stress.

## REWRITING YOUR RESPONSE PATTERNS

**① Choose an Outcome**
Reflect on a recent negative outcome linked to your addictive behaviors.

**② Identify the Stimulus**
Identify the initial stimulus that triggered this negative spiral. Record the time.

**③ Analyze Your Perception**
How was the stimulus perceived? What thoughts did it trigger? How did it relate to your self-view?

**④ Recognize Activation**
Determine the emotional response this perception triggered in you, such as anxiety, fear, or anger.

**⑤ Examine Your Usual Response**
Reflect on your typical reactions when feeling this way. These are the responses you usually rely on, including unhealthy coping behaviors.

**⑥ Go Through the EAT Process**
Brainstorm any alternative perceptions, activations, and responses that could have led to a more positive outcome.

What Transform techniques can you use to adjust future experiences?

STIMULUS

↓

PERCEPTION

↓

ACTIVATION

↓

RESPONSE

↓

OUTCOME

# ASSESSING YOUR PROMOTERS AND INHIBITORS (P/I RATIO)

**1  List Your Promoters**
Identify and list the people, places, things, and events that tend to trigger or increase the likelihood of your addictive behaviors.

**2  List Your Inhibitors**
Conversely, write down the people, places, things, and events that help reduce or prevent your addictive behaviors.

**3  Rank Each Factor**
Evaluate the strength of each Promoter and Inhibitor on a scale from 1 to 10, where 10 indicates a very strong influence.

| PROMOTERS | STRENGTH | INHIBITORS | STRENGTH |
|---|---|---|---|
| Friends that drink a lot | 7 | A favorite hobby | 4 |
| Stressful work situations | 5 | Low-stress days | 6 |
| Fighting with spouse | 9 | Support group meetings | 8 |
| Being hungover | 7 | A good therapy session | 9 |

**4  Calculate Your P/I Ratio**

**P/I Ratio**
Total Promoter Strength / Total Inhibitor Strength

Example: *A stressful workday (P = 5) where you engaged in a favorite hobby (I = 4) and went to support meetings (I = 8)*

**P/I Ratio** - 5/12 = Inhibitors 2.4 times greater than Promoters

**5  Adjust for Optimal Balance**
Aim for a P/I Ratio where your Inhibitors are two to three times greater than your Promoters (1:2 or 1:3). Consider steps to enhance this balance (flip this balance if working on a positive behavior).

# WHAT'S YOUR IKIGAI?

**1** **Build Your Diagram**
Draw your diagram and fill in each of the four sections with activities, skills, or behaviors that fit that section's description.

**2** **Find Intersections**
Examine the areas where the circles overlap and write down any themes or insights you notice:

 **Passion**
Activities that provide personal satisfaction.

 **Profession**
Marketable skills that get you paid.

 **Vocation**
Making a living by helping fulfill needs.

 **Mission**
A gratifying path that honors goodwill & altruism.

**3** **Discover Your Ikigai**
Identify the activities or behaviors that are relevant to all of the four circles. This intersection represents your ikigai, where passion, mission, profession, and vocation converge.

How can you align your daily activities and long-term goals more closely with your ikigai?

# WHEEL OF LIFE

**1** **Create Your Wheel**
Draw a wheel like the one below with all ten categories.

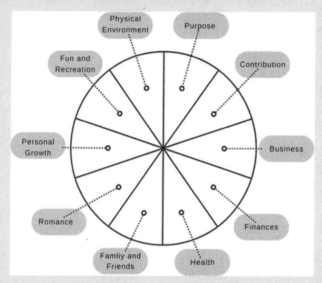

**2** **Rate Each Category**
Review each category and rate your current level of satisfaction on a scale from 0 (very dissatisfied) to 10 (fully satisfied).

**3** **Reflect on Your Scores**
Look at your scores for each category and choose one or two with the lowest satisfaction scores to focus on. These are likely helping to drive your problematic behavior. Focus on improving these low-scoring categories on your Wheel of Life.

You can find an interactive version of the Wheel of Life on the book resource page at www.adijaffe.com/unhooked

## SHAPING NOW

**1 Identify Key Life Experiences**
Reflect on the most significant experiences in your life (positive or negative). List two or three of the most important and memorable ones and create detailed stories that truly lay out these moments as you experienced them at the time. Be as detailed as possible, as this will help you connect to the past.

**2 Reflect on Self-Perception**
For each life event, write down how these experiences affected your

Core beliefs about yourself

↓

Fears about yourself and your capabilities

**3 Examine Views on Others**
For each life event, write down the following:

Core beliefs about others

↓

Fears about others and your relationships

**4 Analyze Perceptions of Getting Help**
For each life event, write down the following:

Core beliefs about the idea of asking for help

↓

Fears about getting, or needing, help

**5 Review These Beliefs and Perceptions**
Examine how these beliefs showed up in your severity timeline and whether they currently play a role in your behavior.

# SOCIAL CIRCLE AUDIT

**1** **Assess Your Social Environments**

Reflect on the various social settings you are part of. Determine factors within each environment that are both positive and negative for your mental and emotional health.

**2** **Shift Negative Environments**

For each environment, think of ways to reduce the negative factors and increase the positive factors.

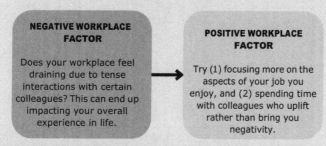

**3** **Identify Key Influencers**

In each of these environments, identify the individuals who have the most impact on you, both positively and negatively. Make a list of the top three most positive and the top three most negative people across all your social settings.

**4** **Foster Positive Connections**

Get active in strengthening your relationships with the three most positive influencers in your social environment—how can you create stronger connections and spend more time with them?

# RESPONSE IDENTIFICATION MENU

**1** **Identify Your Common Activation**
Begin by pinpointing a frequent trigger or activation that leads to the addictive behavior you're working to change. You can refer back to your "Trigger Chart" or "Trigger Priming List" from previous exercises, for insights.

**2** **List Your Typical Responses**
Write down the usual ways you respond when this activation occurs. Be as specific and honest as possible about these behaviors.

**3** **Identify Primary Response Behaviors**
From the list you've created, circle the one or two most common behaviors. These are the responses that most frequently occur and thus hold significant potential for change.

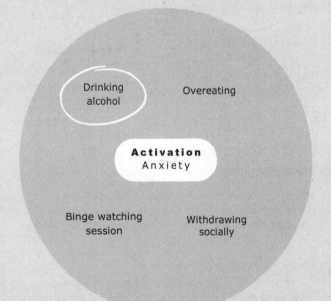

# RESOURCES

**Get Unhooked Online**

Visit https://www.adijaffe.com/unhooked for more information, including additional support and resources for your unhooked journey.

# ACKNOWLEDGMENTS

This book took an army of people to make it into the world. Thank you to John Kim, who introduced me to my agent, Laura Yorke, who believed in it from our first conversation and then helped me edit it into shape. Thank you also to Renée Sedliar of Hachette, who decided to take the leap with me and actually buy this book, giving it life.

Thank you to my personal support team, which has gone through many iterations over the past few years, but has included Maddy Hishan, Rei McCormick, Brian Moseley, and Alex Mitchell.

Thank you to the home team, which of course includes my wife, Sophie, who had to give me so much space to get this done in the midst of our full and often chaotic life—I love you. Thank you to Dawn and Daniella, for all the support at home that made it possible to clear enough space to write. Thank you to my amazing kids—Kai, Leo, and Noa, for providing me the inspiration and the purpose to keep writing and showing up in life—you're my heart and my everything.

Thank you to the IGNTD team, Jennifer Brogan, Fred Lastar, Pierce Baugh, Rachel Azaroff, Desiree Grin, Chavel Chambers, Francis Ndiritu, Shagay Graham, Alvin Nichols, Trevor Hansley, Alyssa Castillo, and many more. You make the ship run even when my life is too crazy to steer it.

Thank you to my academic mentors—from Dennis Fisher to David Jentsch, to Peter Bentler, and everyone else who was part of my journey from the bottom to the life I get to live. You were shining examples of what's possible when you put in the work, and your support meant the world.

Thank you to my clients, who have trusted me over the years and allowed me to develop and hone my skills, culminating in this method. Being part of your lives has meant the world to me and has been one of the most gratifying parts of my own journey.

Thank you to Miki Ash, for the amazing help with the illustrations. I know they made the book better, and probably helped explain some things I couldn't in mere words.

Thank you, Stacey Root, for help with finalizing the exercises in the book, making the concepts and principles become useful for all those who read this.

Thank you to Zinque, John O'Groates, Superba, and the many other coffee shops, diners, Soho House locations, and Delta airplane lounges I found myself writing in for hours, days, and weeks.

Thank you to the tens of thousands who read my first book, *The Abstinence Myth*, and gave me the belief that I could actually write a book that would make a difference in people's lives. I hope you find this book at least as helpful and that you continue allowing me to be part of your journey.

And thank you, for picking this book up and becoming part of my life's purpose.

# NOTES

## Introduction

1. National Center for Drug Use Statistics, 2023; Administration, Substance Abuse and Mental Health Services, "National Survey of Drug Use and Health," 2021.

2. D. N. Greenfield, "Psychological Characteristics of Compulsive Internet Use: A Preliminary Analysis," *Cyberpsychology, Behavior, and Social Networking* 2, no. 5 (1999): 403–412.

3. A. N. Gearhardt et al., "Social, Clinical, and Policy Implications of Ultra-processed Food Addiction," *BMJ* 383 (2023): e075354.

4. National Center for Drug Use Statistics, 2023.

5. A. Athey, B. Kilmer, and J. Cerel, "An Overlooked Emergency: More Than One in Eight US Adults Have Had Their Lives Disrupted by Drug Overdose Deaths," *American Journal of Public Health* 114, no. 3 (2024): 276–279.

6. Gearhardt, "Social, Clinical, and Policy Implications."

7. T. L. Rowell-Cunsolo et al., "Return to Illicit Drug Use Post-incarceration Among Formerly Incarcerated Black Americans," *Drugs* (Abingdon, UK) 25, no. 3 (2018): 234–240.

8. National Institute on Drug Abuse, "Costs of Substance Abuse," 2013, accessed 2/26/2024, available from https://archives.nida.nih.gov/research-topics/trends-statistics/costs-substance-abuse.

9. C. Florence, F. Luo, and K. Rice, "The Economic Burden of Opioid Use Disorder and Fatal Opioid Overdose in the United States, 2017," *Drug and Alcohol Dependence* 2018 (2021): 108350.

10. N. D. Volkow, J. A. Gordon, and G. F. Koob, "Choosing Appropriate Language to Reduce the Stigma Around Mental Illness and Substance Use Disorders," *Neuropsychopharmacology* 46, no. 13 (2021): 2230–2232; R. D. Ashford, A. M. Brown, and B. Curtis, "Substance Use, Recovery, and Linguistics: The Impact of Word Choice on Explicit and Implicit Bias," *Drug and Alcohol Dependence* 189 (2018): 131–138; L. M. Broyles et al., "Confronting Inadvertent Stigma and Pejorative Language in Addiction Scholarship: A Recognition and Response," *Substance Abuse* 35, no. 3 (2014): 217–221; R. D. Ashford, A. M. Brown, and B. Curtis, "Abusing Addiction: Our Language Still Isn't Good Enough," *Alcoholism Treatment Quarterly* 37, no. 2 (2019): 257–272.

## Chapter 1: We Change When It Hurts

1. Association of American Medical Colleges, "21 Million Americans Suffer from Addiction. Just 3,000 Physicians Are Specially Trained to Treat Them," 2019, accessed 2/29/24, available from https://www.aamc.org/news-insights/21-million-americans-suffer-addiction-just-3000-physicians-are-specially-trained-treat-them; Caron Treatment Center, "Drug Use: Drug Use Statistics and Demographics," 2024, accessed 2/29/24, available from https://www.caron.org/addiction-101/drug-use/statistics-and-demographics; National Safety Council, "Injury Facts: All Injuries," 2021, accessed 2/29/24, available from https://injuryfacts.nsc.org/all-injuries/deaths-by-demographics/top-10-preventable-injuries.

2. L. R. Gowing et al., "Global Statistics on Addictive Behaviours: 2014 Status Report," *Addiction* 110, no. 6 (2015): 904–919; B. Mann, "There Is Life After Addiction. Most People Recover," 2022, accessed 2/29/24, available from https://www.npr.org/2022/01/15/1071282194/addiction-substance-recovery-treatment.

3. Mann, "There Is Life After Addiction. Most People Recover."

4. M. A. Faria Jr., "Violence, Mental Illness, and the Brain—A Brief History of Psychosurgery: Part 1—From Trephination to Lobotomy," *Surgical Neurology International* 4 (2013); Encyclopedia.com, "Mental Illness During the Middle Ages," 2019, accessed 2/29/24, available from https://www.encyclopedia.com/science/encyclopedias-almanacs-transcripts-and-maps/mental-illness-during-middle-ages; *The American Experience*, "Treatments for Mental Illness," 2024, accessed 2/29/24, available from https://www.pbs.org/wgbh/americanexperience/features/nash-treatments-mental-illness/.

5. *American Experience*, "Treatments for Mental Illness"; Lehigh Center, "A Timeline of Mental Health Treatment," 2022, accessed 2024, available from https://www.lehighcenter.com/history/a-timeline-of-mental-health-treatment/.

6. M. Solinas et al., "Dopamine and Addiction: What Have We Learned from 40 Years of Research," *Journal of Neural Transmission* (Vienna) 126, no. 4 (2019): 481–516; E. J. Nestler, "Cellular Basis of Memory for Addiction," *Dialogues in Clinical Neuroscience* 15, no. 4 (2013): 431–443; R. A. Wise and M. A. Robble, "Dopamine and Addiction," *Annual Review of Psychology* 71 (2020): 79–106.

7. B. J. Everitt and T. W. Robbins, "From the Ventral to the Dorsal Striatum: Devolving Views of Their Roles in Drug Addiction," *Neuroscience & Biobehavioral Reviews* 37, no. 9, pt. A (2013): 1946–1954; K. C. Young-Wolff et al., "Mood-Related Drinking Motives Mediate the Familial Association Between Major Depression and Alcohol Dependence," *Alcoholism: Clinical and Experimental Research* 33, no. 8 (2009): 1476–1486; L. M. Najavits, R. D. Weiss, and S. R. Shaw, "The Link Between Substance Abuse and Posttraumatic Stress Disorder in Women: A Research Review," *American Journal on Addictions* 6, no. 4 (1997): 273–283; S. R. Dube et al., "Childhood Abuse, Neglect, and Household Dysfunction and the Risk of Illicit Drug Use: The Adverse Childhood Experiences Study," *Pediatrics* 111, no. 3 (2003): 564–572.

8. R. Room, "Stigma, Social Inequality and Alcohol and Drug Use," *Drug and Alcohol Review* 24, no. 2 (2005): 143–155; Y. Hser et al., "A 33-Year Follow-Up of Narcotics Addicts," *Archives of General Psychiatry* 58 (2001): 503–508; M. E. Patrick et al.,

"Socioeconomic Status and Substance Use Among Young Adults: A Comparison Across Constructs and Drugs," *Journal of Studies on Alcohol and Drugs* 73, no. 5 (2012): 772–782; K. M. Keyes et al., "Understanding the Rural–Urban Differences in Nonmedical Prescription Opioid Use and Abuse in the United States," *American Journal of Public Health* 104, no 2 (2014): e52–e59.

9. R. D. Fallot and J. P. Heckman, "Religious/Spiritual Coping Among Women Trauma Survivors with Mental Health and Substance Use Disorders," *Journal of Behavioral Health Services and Research* 32, no. 2 (2005): 215–226; A. B. Laudet and W. L. White, "Recovery Capital as Prospective Predictor of Sustained Recovery, Life Satisfaction, and Stress Among Former Poly-substance Users," *Substance Use & Misuse* 43, no. 1 (2008): 27–54; B. J. Grim and M. E. Grim, "Belief, Behavior, and Belonging: How Faith Is Indispensable in Preventing and Recovering from Substance Abuse," *Journal of Religion and Health* 58, no. 5 (2019): 1751–1752.

10. T. M. Powledge, "Addiction and the Brain: The Dopamine Pathway Is Helping Researchers Find Their Way Through the Addiction Maze," *BioScience* 49, no. 7 (1999): 513–519.

11. R. D. Ashford, A. M. Brown, and B. Curtis, "Substance Use, Recovery, and Linguistics: The Impact of Word Choice on Explicit and Implicit Bias," *Drug and Alcohol Dependence* 189 (2018): 131–138.

12. Ashford, Brown, and Curtis, "Substance Use, Recovery, and Linguistics."

13. National Institute on Drug Abuse, "Drugs, Brains, and Behavior: The Science of Addiction—Drug Misuse and Addiction," 2020, accessed 2/29/24, available from https://nida.nih.gov/publications/drugs-brains-behavior-science-addiction/drug-misuse-addiction; National Institute on Drug Abuse, "References," 2021, accessed 2/29/24, available from https://nida.nih.gov/publications/drugs-brains-behavior-science-addiction/references.

14. National Institutes of Health, "Alcoholism Isn't What It Used to Be," *NIAAA Spectrum*, September 2009, www.spectrumniaaa.nih.gov/Content/Archives/Sept.2009.pdf.

15. National Institutes of Health, "Alcoholism Isn't What It Used to Be."

16. M. Oshin, "This 45-Year-Old Study on Heroin-Addicted Vietnam War Veterans Reveals Why It's So Hard to Break Addictions," Ladders, 2019, accessed 2/29/24, available from https://www.theladders.com/career-advice/this-45-year-old-study-on-heroin-addicted-vietnam-war-veterans-reveals-why-its-so-hard-to-break-addictions.

17. Wikipedia, "List of syndromes," 2024, accessed 2/29/24, available from https://en.wikipedia.org/wiki/List_of_syndromes.

18. A. B. Laudet, R. Savage, and D. Mahmood, "Pathways to Long-Term Recovery: A Preliminary Investigation," *Journal of Psychoactive Drugs* 34, no. 3 (2002): 305–311; American Addiction Centers, "Alcohol and Drug Abuse Statistics (Facts About Addiction)," 2024, accessed 3/3/24, available from https://americanaddictioncenters.org/addiction-statistics; SAMHSA, Center for Behavioral Health Statistics and Quality, "Key Substance Use and Mental Health Indicators in the United States: Results from the 2020 National Survey on Drug Use and Health (HHS Publication No. PEP21-07-01-003, NSDUH Series H-56, 2021); C. Chapman et al., "Delay to First Treatment Contact for Alcohol Use Disorder," *Drug and Alcohol Dependence* 147 (2015): 116–121.

## Chapter 2: Getting Back to the Hook

1. J. D. Buckner et al., "Social Anxiety and Cannabis Use: An Analysis from Ecological Momentary Assessment," *Journal of Anxiety Disorders* 26, no. 2 (2012): 297–304.

2. J. P. Smith and S. W. Book, "Anxiety and Substance Use Disorders: A Review," *Psychiatric Times* 25, no. 10 (2008): 19; National Institute on Drug Abuse, "Common Comorbidities with Substance Use Disorders Research Report—Part 1: The Connection Between Substance Use Disorders and Mental Illness," 2020, accessed 2/29/24, available from https:// nida.nih.gov/publications/research-reports/common-comorbidities-substance-use-disorders /part-1-connection-between-substance-use-disorders-mental-illness.

3. M. Zhang, Y. Zhang, and Y. Kong, "Interaction Between Social Pain and Physical Pain," *Brain Science Advances* 5, no. 4 (2019): 265–273.

4. Bessel van der Kolk, *The Body Keeps the Score: Brain, Mind, and Body in the Healing of Trauma* (New York: Penguin, 2014), 3.

5. van der Kolk, *The Body Keeps the Score*.

6. van der Kolk, *The Body Keeps the Score*.

7. E. Dworkin et al., "Child Sexual Abuse and Disordered Eating: The Mediating Role of Impulsive and Compulsive Tendencies," *Psychology of Violence* 4, no. 1 (2014): 21; H. A. Smith et al., "Sexual Abuse, Sexual Orientation, and Obesity in Women," *Journal of Women's Health* 19, no. 8 (2010): 1525–1532; T. Gustafson and D. Sarwer, "Childhood Sexual Abuse and Obesity," *Obesity Reviews* 5, no. 3 (2004): 129–135; J. Veldwijk et al., "The Prevalence of Physical, Sexual and Mental Abuse Among Adolescents and the Association with BMI Status," *BMC Public Health* 12, no. 1 (2012): 1–9.

8. N. J. Eisenberger and M. D. Lieberman, "Why Rejection Hurts: A Common Neural Alarm System for Physical and Social Pain," *Trends in Cognitive Sciences* 8, no. 7 (2004): 294–300.

9. C. J. Evans and C. M. Cahill, "Neurobiology of Opioid Dependence in Creating Addiction Vulnerability," F1000 Research, 2016, 5; F. Porreca and E. Navratilova, "Reward, Motivation and Emotion of Pain and Its Relief," *Pain* 158 (suppl. 12017): S43.

10. P. Lally et al., "How Are Habits Formed: Modelling Habit Formation in the Real World," *European Journal of Social Psychology* 40, no. 6 (2010): 998–1009.

11. W. R. Miller, "Researching the Spiritual Dimensions of Alcohol and Other Drug Problems," *Addiction* 93, no. 7 (1998): 979–990; S. Aziz and A. A. Shah, "Home Environment and Peer Relations of Addicted and Nonaddicted University Students," *Journal of Psychology* 129, no. 3 (1995): 277–284.

12. M. De Haan et al., "Brain and Cognitive-Behavioural Development After Asphyxia at Term Birth," *Developmental Science* 9, no. 4 (2006): 350–358.

13. J. S. Eccles, "The Development of Children Ages 6 to 14," *The Future of Children* (1999): 30–44; K. A. Duffy, K. A. McLaughlin, and P. A. Green, "Early Life Adversity and Health-Risk Behaviors: Proposed Psychological and Neural Mechanisms," *Annals of the New York Academy of Sciences* 1428, no. 1 (2018): 151–169.

14. National Institute on Drug Abuse, "Drugs, Brains, and Behavior: The Science of Addiction—Treatment and Recovery," 2020, accessed 2/29/24, available from https://nida .nih.gov/publications/drugs-brains-behavior-science-addiction/treatment-recovery; L. Walker,

"Drug and Alcohol Addiction Relapse: Stages, Prevention, and Treatment," accessed 2/29/24, available from https://drugabuse.com/addiction/relapse/.

15. J. R. McKay, "Making the Hard Work of Recovery More Attractive for Those with Substance Use Disorders," *Addiction* 112, no. 5 (2017): 751–757.

16. M. D. Brubaker et al., "Barriers and Supports to Substance Abuse Service Use Among Homeless Adults," *Journal of Addictions & Offender Counseling* 34, no. 2 (2013): 81–98; R. Hammarlund et al., "Review of the Effects of Self-Stigma and Perceived Social Stigma on the Treatment-Seeking Decisions of Individuals with Drug- and Alcohol-Use Disorders," *Substance Abuse and Rehabilitation* 9 (2018): 115–136.

## Chapter 3: Addiction as a Hook Response

1. S. McLeod, "Operant Conditioning: What It Is, How It Works, and Examples," Simply Psychology, https://www.simplypsychology.org/operant-conditioning.html, 2023; M. Koren, *B. F. Skinner: The Man Who Taught Pigeons to Play Ping-Pong and Rats to Pull Levers* (Washington, DC: Smithsonian, 2013); J. H. Capshew, "Engineering Behavior: Project Pigeon, World War II, and the Conditioning of B. F. Skinner," *Technology and Culture* 34, no. 4 (1993): 835–857.

2. T. B. Baker and D. S. Cannon, "Taste Aversion Therapy with Alcoholics: Techniques and Evidence of a Conditioned Response," *Behaviour Research and Therapy* 17, no. 3 (1979): 229–242; R. L. Elkins, "Aversion Therapy for Alcoholism: Chemical, Electrical, or Verbal Imaginary?," *International Journal of the Addictions* 10, no. 2 (1975): 157–209; C. H. Jørgensen, B. Pedersen, and H. Tønnesen, "The Efficacy of Disulfiram for the Treatment of Alcohol Use Disorder," *Alcoholism: Clinical and Experimental Research* 35, no. 10 (2011): 1749–1758.

3. G. F. Koob, "Drug Addiction: Hyperkatifeia/Negative Reinforcement as a Framework for Medications Development," *Pharmacological Reviews* 73, no. 1 (2021): 163–201; G. F. Koob, "Neurobiology of Opioid Addiction: Opponent Process, Hyperkatifeia, and Negative Reinforcement," *Biological Psychiatry* 87, no. 1 (2020): 44–53.

4. P. Bach et al., "Association of the Alcohol Dehydrogenase Gene Polymorphism rs1789891 with Gray Matter Brain Volume, Alcohol Consumption, Alcohol Craving and Relapse Risk," *Addiction Biology* 24, no. 1 (2019): 110–120; S.-C. Wang et al., "Alcohol Addiction, Gut Microbiota, and Alcoholism Treatment: A Review," *International Journal of Molecular Sciences* 2, no. 17 (2020): 6413; H. Cichoz-Lach et al., "Alcohol Dehydrogenase and Aldehyde Dehydrogenase Gene Polymorphism in Alcohol Liver Cirrhosis and Alcohol Chronic Pancreatitis Among Polish Individuals," *Scandinavian Journal of Gastroenterology* 42, no. 4 (2007): 493–498.

5. N. D. Volkow, "Stigma and the Toll of Addiction," *New England Journal of Medicine* 382, no. 14 (2020): 1289–1290; S. E. Wakeman and J. D. Rich, "Barriers to Medications for Addiction Treatment: How Stigma Kills," *Substance Use & Misuse* 53, no. 2 (2018): 330–333; Johns Hopkins University, "Study: Public Feels More Negative Toward People with Drug Addiction Than Those with Mental Illness," 2014, accessed 2/29/24, available from https://publichealth.jhu.edu/2014/study-public-feels-more-negative-toward-people-with-drug-addiction-than-those-with-mental-illness.

## Chapter 4: Introducing SPARO and EAT

1. Bessel van der Kolk, *The Body Keeps the Score: Brain, Mind, and Body in the Healing of Trauma* (New York: Penguin, 2014).

2. Joseph Campbell, *The Hero with a Thousand Faces*, 3rd ed., Bollingen series XVII (Novato, CA: New World Library, 2008), xiii, 418.

## Chapter 5: Let's Start at the End...The Outcome

1. E. L. Deci, R. Koestner, and R. M. Ryan, "A Meta-analytic Review of Experiments Examining the Effects of Extrinsic Rewards on Intrinsic Motivation," *Psychological Bulletin* 125, no. 6 (1999): 627; M. Gagné and E. L. Deci, "Self-Determination Theory and Work Motivation," *Journal of Organizational Behavior* 26, no. 4 (2005): 331–362; M. R. Lepper, D. Greene, and R. E. Nisbett, "Undermining Children's Intrinsic Interest with Extrinsic Reward: A Test of the 'Overjustification' Hypothesis," *Journal of Personality and Social Psychology* 28, no. 1 (1973): 129; R. M. Ryan and E. L. Deci, "Self-Determination Theory and the Facilitation of Intrinsic Motivation, Social Development, and Well-being," *American Psychologist* 55, no. 1 (2000): 68; R. J. Vallerand, "Toward a Hierarchical Model of Intrinsic and Extrinsic Motivation," in *Advances in Experimental Social Psychology*, vol. 29, ed. M. P. Zanna (New York: Elsevier, 1997), 271–360.

2. G. C. Williams et al., "Motivation for Behavior Change in Patients with Chest Pain," *Health Education* 105, no. 4 (2005): 304–321.

## Chapter 6: Stimulus

1. Daniel Gardner, *The Science of Fear: Why We Fear Things We Should Not—and Put Ourselves in Greater Danger* (New York: Dutton, 2008).

2. K.-A. Kwon et al., "High-Speed Camera Characterization of Voluntary Eye Blinking Kinematics," *Journal of the Royal Society Interface* 10, no. 85 (2013): 20130227.

3. C. I. Bird, N. L. Modlin, and J. J. Rucker, J. J. "Psilocybin and MDMA for the Treatment of Trauma-Related Psychopathology," *International Review of Psychiatry* 33, no. 3 (2021), 229–249; Z. Walsh et al., "Ketamine for the Treatment of Mental Health and Substance Use Disorders: Comprehensive Systematic Review," *British Journal of Psychiatry* 8, no. 1 (2022), e19.

## Chapter 7: Perception

1. D. J. Simons and D. T. Levin, "Change Blindness," *Trends in Cognitive Sciences* 1, no. 7 (1997): 261–267; R. A. Rensink, J. K. O'Regan, and J. J. Clark, "To See or Not to See: The Need for Attention to Perceive Changes in Scenes," *Psychological Science* 8, no. 5 (1997): 368–373.

2. S. Ann-Christin, A. Chaibi, and P. McCarthy, "More Than Meets the Eye: Inattentional Blindness," *International Journal of Radiology and Imaging Technology* 4 (2018): 037.

3. M. S. Jensen et al., "Change Blindness and Inattentional Blindness," *Wiley Interdisciplinary Reviews: Cognitive Science* 2, no. 5 (2011): 529–546.

4. W. A. Johnston and V. J. Dark, "Selective Attention," *Annual Review of Psychology* 37, no. 1 (1986): 43–75; A. M. Treisman, "Selective Attention in Man," *British Medical Bulletin*, 1964.

5. Johnston and Dark, "Selective Attention"; Treisman, "Selective Attention in Man."

6. R. Teper, Z. V. Segal, and M. Inzlicht, "Inside the Mindful Mind: How Mindfulness Enhances Emotion Regulation Through Improvements in Executive Control," *Current Directions in Psychological Science* 22, no. 6 (2013): 449–454; A. Grecucci et al., "Mindful Emotion Regulation: Exploring the Neurocognitive Mechanisms Behind Mindfulness," *BioMed Research International* (2015).

7. T. Kohonen and P. Lehtio, "Storage and Processing of Information in Distributed Associative Memory Systems," *Parallel Models of Associative Memory* (1981): 129–167; H. Eichenbaum and N. J. Cohen, *From Conditioning to Conscious Recollection: Memory Systems of the Brain* (New York: Oxford Psychology, 2004).

8. L. E. Williams and J. A. Bargh, "Experiencing Physical Warmth Promotes Interpersonal Warmth," *Science* 322, no. 5901 (2008): 606–607.

9. S. N. Talamas, K. I. Mavor, and D. I. Perrett, "Blinded by Beauty: Attractiveness Bias and Accurate Perceptions of Academic Performance," *PloS One* 11, no. 2 (2016): e0148284.

10. Wayne W. Dyer, *History and Experience* (Cologne, Germany: Wolfgang Leidhold, 2006).

11. D. Abrams et al., "Knowing What to Think by Knowing Who You Are: Self-Categorization and the Nature of Norm Formation, Conformity and Group Polarization," *British Journal of Social Psychology* 29, no. 2 (1990): 97–119.

12. J. C. Turner, R. J. Brown, and H. Tajfel, "Social Comparison and Group Interest in Ingroup Favouritism," *European Journal of Social Psychology* 9, no. 2 (1979): 187–204.

13. R. S. Nickerson, "Confirmation Bias: A Ubiquitous Phenomenon in Many Guises," *Review of General Psychology* 2, no. 2 (1998): 175–220.

14. A. Furnham and H. C. Boo, "A Literature Review of the Anchoring Effect," *Journal of Socio-economics* 40, no. 1 (2011): 35–42.

15. M. E. Oswald and S. Grosjean, "Confirmation Bias," in Rüdiger F. Pohl, ed., *Cognitive Illusions: A Handbook on Fallacies and Biases in Thinking, Judgement and Memory* (Hove, East Sussex, UK: Psychology Press, 2004).

16. Nickerson, "Confirmation Bias."

17. Brené Brown, *Dare to Lead: Brave Work. Tough Conversations. Whole Hearts* (New York: Random House, 2018).

18. Bruce Lipton, *The Biology of Belief: Unleashing the Power of Consciousness, Matter & Miracles*, 10th ann. ed. (Carlsbad, CA: Hay House, 2016).

## Chapter 8: Activation

1. W. J. Freeman, "The Physiology of Perception," *Scientific American* 264, no. 2 (1991): 78–87; G. Pourtois, A. Schettino, and P. Vuilleumier, "Brain Mechanisms for Emotional Influences on Perception and Attention: What Is Magic and What Is Not," *Biological Psychology* 92, no. 3 (2013): 492–512.

2. R. Yu, "Stress Potentiates Decision Biases: A Stress Induced Deliberation-to-Intuition (SIDI) Model," *Neurobiology of Stress* 3 (2016): 8; P. Morgado, N. Sousa, and J. J. Cerqueira, "The Impact of Stress in Decision Making in the Context of Uncertainty," *Journal of Neuroscience Research* 93, no. 6 (2015): 839–847.

3. S. F. Maier and M. E. Seligman, "Learned Helplessness at Fifty: Insights from Neuroscience," *Psychological Review* 123, no. 4 (2016): 349.

4. C. Liston, B. S. McEwen, and B. Casey, "Psychosocial Stress Reversibly Disrupts Prefrontal Processing and Attentional Control," *Proceedings of the National Academy of Sciences* 106, no. 3 (2009): 912–917; A. F. Arnsten et al., "The Effects of Stress Exposure on Prefrontal Cortex: Translating Basic Research into Successful Treatments for Post-traumatic Stress Disorder," *Neurobiology of Stress* 1 (2015): 89–99; A. F. Arnsten, "Stress Signalling Pathways That Impair Prefrontal Cortex Structure and Function," *Nature Reviews Neuroscience* 10, no. 6 (2009): 410–422.

5. H. Rosenberg, "Relapsed Versus Non-relapsed Alcohol Abusers: Coping Skills, Life Events, and Social Support," *Addictive Behaviors* 8, no 2 (1983): 183–186; R.-P. Juster, B. S. McEwen, and S. J. Lupien, "Allostatic Load Biomarkers of Chronic Stress and Impact on Health and Cognition," *Neuroscience & Biobehavioral Reviews* 35, no. 1 (2010): 2–16; S. C. Segerstrom and G. E. Miller, "Psychological Stress and the Human Immune System: A Meta-analytic Study of 30 Years of Inquiry," *Psychological Bulletin* 130, no. 4 (2004): 601.

6. M. S. Oitzl et al., "Continuous Blockade of Brain Glucocorticoid Receptors Facilitates Spatial Learning and Memory in Rats," *European Journal of Neuroscience* 10, no. 12 (1998): 3759–3766.

7. Joseph Campbell, *The Hero with a Thousand Faces*, 3rd ed., Bollingen series XVII (Novato, CA: New World Library, 2008), xiii, 418.

## Chapter 9: Response

1. D. Harper, "Model," Online Etymology Dictionary, 2024, accessed 2/28/24, available from https://www.etymonline.com/word/model; A. Acher, M. Arcà, and N. Sanmartí, "Modeling as a Teaching Learning Process for Understanding Materials: A Case Study in Primary Education," *Science Education* 91, no. 3 (2007): 398–418; A. Bandura, *Psychological Modeling: Conflicting Theories* (Piscataway, NJ: Transaction Publishers, 2017).

2. Bruce Lipton, *The Biology of Belief: Unleashing the Power of Consciousness, Matter & Miracles*, 10th ann. ed. (Carlsbad, CA: Hay House, 2016).

3. Carol S. Dweck, *Mindset: The New Psychology of Success* (New York: Random House, 2006).

4. Wheatley Institute, Brigham Young University, "National Couples and Pornography Survey 2021," 2021, accessed 2/29/24, available from https://wheatley.byu.edu/national -couples-and-pornography-survey-2021.

5. A. Chernev, U. Böckenholt, and J. Goodman, "Choice Overload: A Conceptual Review and Meta-analysis," *Journal of Consumer Psychology* 25, no. 2 (2015): 333–358; B. Scheibehenne, R. Greifeneder, and P. M. Todd, "Can There Ever Be Too Many Options? A Meta-analytic Review of Choice Overload," *Journal of Consumer Research* 37, no. 3 (2010): 409–425.

6. K. A. Ericsson, "Deliberate Practice and the Acquisition and Maintenance of Expert Performance in Medicine and Related Domains, *Academic Medicine* 79, no. 10 (2004): S70–S81.

## Chapter 10: Revisiting Outcomes

1. Carol S. Dweck, *Mindset: The New Psychology of Success* (New York: Random House, 2006).

## Appendix A: Unhooked for Life: Key Strategies and Practices

1. Carol S. Dweck, *Mindset: The New Psychology of Success* (New York: Random House, 2006).

2. J. L Burnette et al., "Mindsets of Addiction: Implications for Treatment Intentions," *Journal of Social and Clinical Psychology* 38, no. 5 (2019): 367–394.

3. E. B. Raposa, H. B. Laws, and E. B. Ansell, "Prosocial Behavior Mitigates the Negative Effects of Stress in Everyday Life," *Clinical Psychological Science* 4, no. 4 (2016): 691–698.

4. T. K. Inagaki and L. P. Ross, "Neural Correlates of Giving Social Support: Differences Between Giving Targeted Versus Untargeted Support," *Psychosomatic Medicine* 80, no. 8 (2018): 724–732.

5. W. T. Harbaugh, U. Mayr, and D. R. Burghart, "Neural Responses to Taxation and Voluntary Giving Reveal Motives for Charitable Donations," *Science* 316, no. 5831 (2007): 1622–1625.

6. Simon Sinek, *Start with Why: How Great Leaders Inspire Everyone to Take Action* (New York: Portfolio, 2011).

7. S. J. Belouin and J. E. Henningfield, "Psychedelics: Where We Are Now, Why We Got Here, What We Must Do," *Neuropharmacology* 142 (2018): 7–19; P. Plesa and R. Petranker, "Manifest Your Desires: Psychedelics and the Self-Help Industry," *International Journal of Drug Policy* 105 (2022): 103704; D. B. Yaden, M. E. Yaden, and R. R. Griffiths, "Psychedelics in Psychiatry—Keeping the Renaissance from Going off the Rails," *JAMA Psychiatry* 78, no. 5 (2021): 469–470; T. Noorani, "Making Psychedelics into Medicines: The Politics and Paradoxes of Medicalization," *Journal of Psychedelic Studies* 4, no. 1 (2020): 34–39.

8. National Library of Medical Trials, accessed 4/8/24, available from https://clinicaltrials.gov/search?intr=Psychedelic&locStr=United%20States&country=United%20States&distance=50.

# INDEX

261